TRUE TO THE ROOTS

Americana Music Revealed

MONTE DUTTON

UNIVERSITY OF NEBRASKA PRESS | LINCOLN & LONDON

Library of Congress
Cataloging-in-Publication Data

Dutton, Monte.
True to the roots: Americana
music revealed / Monte Dutton.
p. cm.
ISBN-13: 978-0-8032-6661-2
(paperback: alkaline paper)
ISBN-10: 0-8032-6661-8
(paperback: alkaline paper)
1. Country music—History
and criticism. I. Title.
ML3524.D88 2006
781.642—dc22
2006006822

Designed and set in Janson
by A. Shahan.

dictable Walker had changed his mind. Instead, Walker spent about four hours with Pawless, telling stories and reflecting on his career.

"That was more valuable than the guitar," recalls Pawless. "Now, I don't know if Jerry Jeff would even recognize me if I walked up right now, but for whatever reason, he was just in a mood to talk, and I wouldn't give anything for it. I don't know whether, deep down, he felt bad for having me drive all the way down there, but it was quite an experience."

I think to myself about how much Vince Pawless reminds me of the subject of Walker's song "Charlie Dunn," which is about a boot maker, not a guitar maker, but Charlie Dunn, in his idealized Capital Saddlery, where he works "out in the back," is not too far distant in my mind's eye from Pawless, retreating from the rat race to a place he will always call home and plying a valuable trade with guitars crafted, like Dunn made boots, with his own two hands.

If ever I desire another guitar—and that's undoubtedly going to happen—then I conclude, to paraphrase Jerry Jeff, that Vince Pawless, he's the man to see.

To Thine Own Self Be True

Slaid Cleaves lives in a modest wood house not far from downtown Austin. His travels have forced him to become adept at basic automotive repair, and the old van out front matches the image conjured up by some of the stories from the road he has posted on his Web site, slaid.com.

Slaid.com. Perfect. A simple web site name for a songwriter who specializes in simplicity.

Cleaves tells stories about simple people with simple problems into which they descended simply. There's sadness inherent in their plight but also a sense of hope. Cleaves's tormented people still have hope.

"That probably started with me being such a Springsteen fan," he says. "I have an affinity for people who are struggling, and that's kind of stayed with me all this time.

"Oh, it's definitely observations," he adds. "Things someone in my family has gone through, or stories I've heard. I'm inspired by movies and other beautiful stories. Most of my

35

songs are observational. Usually there are one or two songs that are confessional."

His latest compilation, *Wishbones*, includes a song inspired in part by Laura Hillenbrand's book *Seabiscuit*. "Quick as Dreams" is written from the perspective of a young 1930s-era jockey who, many years later, in the twilight of life, composes an ode to a fallen colleague.

Cleaves, like predecessor Jerry Jeff Walker, is a transplanted Texan, although he hasn't reinvented himself as a Texan the way Walker has. Walker *is* a Texan; Cleaves just lives there. But like Walker, he grew up in the Northeast—Walker in New York, Cleaves in Maine and Massachusetts—and like Walker, he found a musical home in Austin after kicking around and living somewhat the gypsy life.

"I never thought of that before," Cleaves says. "I just met [Walker] last week for the first time. He organized a caroling thing and brought a bunch of people over to his house. We all got on a bus and went to the hospice and the children's hospital."

There is an appealing naïveté to Cleaves, so much so that there seems to be a disparity between his quiet personality and his song content rife with tempests and inner conflicts.

This interview seems more notable for Cleaves playing off and complimenting my questions than, well, *complementing* them. He is almost painfully nice, and the answers are thoughtful. There just isn't much to them.

I ask about his views on religion, and he replies: "Churches are political organizations. That's what it comes down to."

Continuing on this theme, I offer my own view that people who suffer from AIDS are kind of the lepers of this age, to which he replies: "Wow, that's perfect, yeah. I agree."

Maybe he plays all his cards in the writing of songs. After all, he makes money off those choice nuggets. He doesn't have to rhyme to stir the soul, though. Cleaves's Web site includes commentaries from the road that are masterful, most notably a tale titled "The Perfect Gig," which almost reads like a short story.

"My folks were really into music," he says, finally elaborating a bit. "I lived in Virginia until I was five. My folks, from high school on, were real music buffs. My mom was into folk and jazz and some country. She was into Pete Seeger, Mahalia Jackson. My dad was more of a rockabilly guy: Chuck Berry, Buddy Holly, and others."

I offer my notion that Elvis was overrated.

"Yeah, songwriting-wise," he says, "but Elvis was such an icon. He was so beautiful."

Cleaves is almost itinerant in wandering across the country from club to club. Well, not always clubs. His schedule lists appearances at Unitarian churches in New England; the venues are as disparate as they are extensive.

"I was on the road almost constantly for a couple of years, yeah, just because I had gathered up all the things I needed to tour, which I had always wanted to do," he says. "I had a band together, I had a record that was getting some airplay, and I had a booking agent, a little bit of history and a little bit of momentum. When my last record [prior to *Wishbones*], *Broke Down*, came out in 2000, I felt everything was in place for me to tour and take advantage of what I had going.

"That was the album I had been trying to make for ten years. Everything just came together perfectly, and I started playing two hundred shows a year. I loved it. It was fun to see all the new places and to find an audience developing out there."

What *Broke Down* gave Cleaves was a niche. It was an album that declared a sound all his own. It was popular in the folk community, although Cleaves doesn't really see himself as a member.

"I just had all this music playing as a kid, and you know

a girlfriend. It's about going back and spending time with someone you wish you could see more often."

Cockrell's distaste for what passes as country these days is considerable. He doesn't particularly care to mold his music to what the establishment demands.

"I'm just trying to balance out the stuff that's on the radio," he says. "The thing is, why can't Willie Nelson get on the radio anymore? Tell me you can't sell him.

"'Is my tractor sexy?' Why in the world would a grown man have anything to do with music like what's on the radio right now? It's such a dumb song. It's soulless music. It all sounds like a business proposal to me. What Nashville doesn't realize is this. Johnny Cash was a bad-ass. He was a rebel. He was a renegade. So was Waylon Jennings. So is Merle Haggard. So was Charlie Rich. The people who have made country music what it is today had unbelievable renegade personalities. The music today is too comfortable, at least the part of it that gets widespread airplay."

Then he echoes what Robbie Fulks called "the integrity scare" of the late 1980s.

"I think what happened is that Nashville made a really bad choice. They had some people who were making amazing, viable country music: Dwight Yoakam, Steve Earle, some really great people who were just making their mark, and then you had, like, McBride and the Ride, people like that. Brooks and Dunn. They decided to go with the wrong group.

"You know what? We spend billions of dollars every year for things we can get for free when we turn on the box, you know. People aren't necessarily as dumb as Nashville considers them. The average Joe who buys the country records now isn't any less literate than the ones who bought the country records twenty-five years ago or thirty-five years ago. Is the music of Hank Williams simple? Yes. But it's honest. Beautifully honest. The shows back then were so much better and meant so much more, but the people weren't any different. They were just getting stuff they could feel empathy for."

Just because Cockrell doesn't care much for the establishment doesn't mean he isn't ambitious, though. Perhaps his evangelical fervor comes from the religion.

"Between you and me, you know who's going to bring this back around? This asshole named Thad Cockrell. You should check him out."

If It's Broken, Don't Fix It

AUSTIN, TEXAS | DECEMBER 2004

Shortly after I show up, James White shows me why the Broken Spoke is the best honky-tonk in Texas or anywhere else. It's not just the leaky roof; it's what he did to fix it.

For years the roof leaked in the room White has filled chock full of memorabilia from all the greats who have played the Spoke since he opened it in 1964. He solved the problem by building a little tin gutter—one that carries the dripping water right out onto the earth out front. White erected himself a little second roof, one not so different from what a rancher might use to fix his barn. And it works.

Country music isn't supposed to be slick. It's not supposed to be conjured up from the results of marketing surveys. It's not supposed to be played by musicians who slap six strings on a banjo to make people think they can play one, and it's not supposed to be played by cowboys who hang guitars around their necks and use them as little more than props. It's supposed to be about life's imperfections and the outrageous, ill-conceived ways that flawed human beings remedy

63

the obstacles that the wind blows into their paths.

As White says, "Don't do it the easy way; do it the cowboy way."

White is a son of Austin. He grew up on West Mary Street, only a mile away from the simple honky-tonk that enabled him to realize his dreams. It's all original, from the ramshackle roof to the bumper sticker that says, "I'd rather be a fencepost in Texas than the king of Tennessee."

"They're all heroes," White says, pointing to all the photos and memorabilia of forty years of honky-tonk nights. "They're all on the top shelf and at the top of the ladder. I've loved country music all my life. I get to live my dream being right here at the Broken Spoke, and people let me do it. When I got out of the army back in 1964, I started thinking, you know, I've been in honky-tonks. I've always had a good time, so why not, when I get out, open up a place of my own.

"I came out under the big old tree out front, right here on South Lamar, and I visualized a place like no other. When I got it built, I named the place the Broken Spoke. People ask me how I thought of that name. I was kind of thinking about something western, something original, something country, something Texas, and, anyway, I was thinking about wagon wheels in my brain, and all of a sudden I thought about this old movie, *Broken Arrow*, and it just kind of clicked in. Kind of like the lightbulb went on, and I thought, well, I'll just call it the Broken Spoke. I'll just buy me a couple of wagon wheels, and I'll knock a spoke out and I'll put them out front where people are walking in. I kind of figured that was all there was to going into business, but I found out over the years there was a lot more to it, but at least I got a good start.

"I love the true country music, like Don Walser said, 'When you cut out the roots of country music, you just cut out the soul, and you're cutting out the country music altogether.' I like the sound of a steel guitar. I love the fiddle. The guitar and everything just blends right in together. Country music tells a story, a lot of them soul-wrenching and about the hardships of life or about drinking beer in a honkytonk. When you get up and you sing those songs, it brings back memories. I've had so many good times, and there are a lot of upbeat old country songs too. It's what I grew up on: Ernest Tubb, Bob Wills, Hank Williams, George Jones, country in its purest form. If Roy Acuff were still alive, he wouldn't be allowing a lot of this stuff you see on TV nowadays. Nashville today, if he was still there, along with people like Ernest Tubb and Hank Snow, they'd frown on some of the stuff that's popular now."

Go to the Spoke any night of the week except Monday, and there will be something compelling to see, whether it's Debra Peters with her accordion or Jerry Jeff Walker celebrating his birthday. White even mounts the stage on most Tuesday nights, along with Alvin Crow, for the weekly "Hard-Core Country Music on Tuesday Nights."

"We do a lot of the old songs. Alvin does a lot of the old Jimmie Rogers songs, and I'll jump in there with some songs that I like," White says. "I've been here forty years, and I figure I can pretty much tell it like it is, and people seem to like to hear it. I don't have to change nothing. I ain't getting no hanging fern baskets on the ceiling. No Grey Poupon—we got the real mustard here. But we do have cold beer, good whiskey, and good-looking girls to dance with, so what else do you need?"

It doesn't take many questions to conduct an interview with James White. Just turn on the tape recorder and let the good times roll.

"It was always good to see Ernest Tubb and the Texas Troubadours come here," recalls White. "He'd flip that guitar over and say thanks."

Tubb, you see, lettered *Thanks* upside down on the back of his guitar.

"Ernest would sit up there on the bandstand, sign everybody's autograph and everybody's picture," says White. "Through his whole break, he'd be up there mingling with the people. The guy was a true Texas troubadour. He traveled all across the country, and he must have done three hundred dates a year or close to it. He loved it, and he always promoted it."

The Broken Spoke is a country music mecca. Big-name acts, even the ones that fill football stadiums, still play there every now and then, but White has a soft spot for what country music used to be. He has his standards. They aren't the same as the ones used by the record companies and the Clear Channel stations, but they're just as restrictive.

"They'll repeat the same words over and over again," he says. "It doesn't have enough soul in it anymore, as far as I'm concerned. It's just, with the bands that play here, I don't really have any what I call 'copy bands' anymore at the Broken Spoke. A lot of them play original music, and even if they do some famous man's songs, they'll do their versions. You don't hear no top forty on the radio, and I think it's a shame that the radio stations have got to the point where people can't hear the music they say they like. Now it's: 'This is your playlist. This is what you'll play.' I loved it back in the Loretta Lynn days, when she'd go to a radio station and pitch 'em a song, give them a 45-RPM record, and do a little guest appearance. Those days were just so good.

"Now the big boys are going to force it down your throat, whether you like it or not. When they pulled Ralph Emery off the air (on the old Nashville Network), it was a crying shame when they did that because there were so many pure-country people who loved 'Nashville Now.' They yanked him off because he wasn't young enough looking. He wasn't playing enough of the young artists. Now the whole darn thing is sold out."

White helped raise money to relieve Willie Nelson's income tax woes. He's seen all manner of behavior and lifestyles that don't necessarily jibe with his own. He never expected the heroes to be perfect, though. Heroes are the performers who rise above their flaws.

"Jerry Jeff Walker is one of my biggest draws," White says. "He plays the Friday night here when his birthday party kicks off [it's called the BDB, for 'Birthday Bash'].

"I've had 'Jerry duty' a few times back in the old days. Jerry duty is when you get to take Jerry Jeff Walker home when he's had too much to drink. We get along just wonderful, him and his wife, Susan, and his kid, Django Walker, his son, who's doing real good writing songs now. We had a good time."

The Spoke has been ranked the best honky-tonk in Texas by at least one publication, and another rated its chicken-fried steak the best in town. The front room is a restaurant that's open for lunch, even though the steel guitars don't crank up generally until after the sun goes down.

"I love the music, and I hate to see it changing like it is, getting too slick, too imitation, too plastic," White says. "It's just not there, but every now and then, some of the stations will throw us a bone and play some good country music. I wrote a song called 'Putting the *C* Back in Country.' I haven't got it on CD yet, but I mention the doghouse bass and the steel guitar. You know where you are when you hear that steel guitar, you know. There's nothing any better than a steel guitar and a fiddle sound when it's played correctly."

But no one could say the world has passed the Spoke by, at least no one present to see Asleep at the Wheel play on a Saturday night. Country radio gears itself to a young demographic—not only young but with limited sensibilities, it seems—but the Spoke reflects the larger population. Every age group is represented on the dance floor, from the gentle shuffles of an elderly couple staring warmly into each other's eyes to the advanced, showy version of the same dance as practiced by college kids. A lot has changed, White concedes.

"Sometimes you kind of reflect back to when you were in high school, and that's what I do sometimes, only I reflect way back to the opening day of the Broken Spoke," he says. "I was still working sixteen hours a day out front, beer was two bits a bottle as fast as we could pop it, and there were some good, hard-core drinkers back in those days.

"I mean, well, there would be a fight. There'd be a knock-down, drag-out. I remember, they'd get to fighting and knocking one another down, and people stood up and went to the side of the wall, and they'd just let 'em fight it out. After a while, the bouncers would drag 'em on out, the best they could. We've weeded out a lot of troublemakers over the years. I think they respect the Broken Spoke so much anymore when they come here that they behave theirselves.

"It's more of a dance hall. When you get the rough places, I call them roadhouses. A roadhouse, maybe that might be a little rougher. We used to have a band years ago, and when they'd play here, they'd get the kids in here, and I think the young, they'd get to fighting with or over their girlfriends. If you let them over the pool table . . . we don't let 'em gamble, but I figure it's mainly over women. You know how that goes. That's true of the honky-tonk. They might get in a fight with their friend, and the next minute they're over there buying each other a beer. If it's a fair fight, OK. But if it gets too rough, the way it is nowadays, you don't want to let anything get started because it's harder to stop. All in all, we're real fortunate not to have any problems out here.

"Back when beer was two bits a bottle, it was a lot hard-

"When I call people 'rednecks,'" Livingston says, "I do it affectionately. 'Redneck mother' [the Ray Wylie Hubbard song that has been a Jerry Jeff Walker standard for thirty years], you know. I don't think Lubbock's full of rednecks, but certainly those really, really, truly conservative people who didn't want any change were there in force when I was."

Other cultures have the same kinds of folk. What Livingston has discovered is that love, in the form of music, can shape a common ground.

One-Chord Song

I've arrived in the Deep Ellum section of Dallas trying to come to grips in some metaphysical sense with the term *red dirt*. It's a movement that grew out of the bars around Stillwater, Oklahoma. I've listened to the music. I've interviewed members of the band Cross Canadian Ragweed. Here, though, is a unique opportunity to see it up close and personal.

What I expect, when I walk through the doors of the Gypsy Tea Room, is an appearance by Stoney LaRue and his Organic Boogie Band. What I get is quite a bit more.

LaRue has completed an album, and in the general party that follows, he brings along four other musicians. The gig at the Gypsy Tea Room ends up being one with no headliner at all. Five stools are placed onstage, and LaRue, Mike McClure, Kevin Webb, Scott Evans, and Jeremy Watkins take turns performing songs. The first four play acoustic guitars. Watkins wields a fiddle.

"If we get drunk," LaRue tells the audience, "we need people who will take care of us."

A pause for both effect and applause.

"Anybody got any weed?"

Although the affair is a bit, uh, drunken, it evolves into a unique opportunity to see one of red dirt music's defining characteristics. It's cohesive, if not coherent. It's one big party. The principals get along. They're in this thing together. Maybe when they're all older and either more successful or out of the business, they'll look back at nights like these as the good old days. Perhaps it's inevitable that times like these will be fleeting, but none of them believes it.

"You can't go up to some person, and I'm not picking apart anyone from Texas or any kind of country music genre, but I've never seen any other genre where you can go up and hug the guy that's singing a song next to you," says LaRue.

The music ranges from the humorous—Webb sings a song in which he spells out the letters in Schaefer Beer ("*E* is for every girl you love . . . *F* is for girls you take home")—to the defiant ("If I'm going down, I'm going down in flames").

"To me it's just a group of people who I grew up with," says McClure. "Well, not really grew up with. When I went to college, when I went to [Oklahoma State University in Stillwater], it was kind of a bohemian atmosphere. I came from a small town in Oklahoma called Tecumseh. When I moved there [Stillwater], it was like going to New York City in a way. I heard Van Morrison, Bob Dylan, Neil Young, stuff that I'd never heard. My dad had *Willie [Nelson] Sings [Kris] Kristofferson*, and I'd already gotten into those lyrics. I remember writing all those lyrics down on a legal pad when I could just barely write."

In the red dirt scene what has evolved is equal parts populist and cosmic. It's not too unlike what developed around Austin in the 1970s, when hippies mingled with cowboys at the Armadillo World Headquarters. The influences once again range from Bob Wills to Bob Dylan, but it's not the same because these guys have sifted through and scooped up what's happened in the interim. They don't seem at all obsessed with commercial success, and while they're grateful for fans in Texas who have embraced them, they don't much care to have their music swept into any categorization that includes the Lone Star State. Hence the term *red dirt music*. They thrive on performing live music and, quite obviously, party like the ship could sink at any moment. Many Texans hedge their bets when talking about the record companies and mainstream radio. They may not care much for what's going on, but they'd like to be embraced by Nashville. In the red dirt scene Nashville might as well be Baghdad.

About popular music McClure dismisses it as "all advertising time." "They've got this little formula that keeps people listening, and it keeps radio stations selling ads. That's why I'm so excited about XM [Satellite] Radio. There's very little talk, and if there is talk, it's talk pertaining to the album. Now, with most radio stations they may give the artist's name, but used to be, they'd tell you what album it's on, playing album cuts and whatnot.

"You can either get mad about it, or you can find an alternative. I got really pissed off about it for a long time, and then I just decided being pissed off isn't going to change anything."

During a break the room backstage is cloudy and raucous. A cell phone rings, and McClure picks up a banana and conducts a conversation with it. Webb lurches over, yanks the banana out of McClure's hand, and spikes it, smashing it on the wood floor.

"If you can't enjoy the music, man, that means you're giving up on humanity," McClure observes, surveying the banana mush.

Here's a surprise. McClure cites Jack Kerouac as an influence. "I started traveling because of the Kerouac influence, a poem—to do that. It was comforting, though. And thought provoking. Two things I needed in my hours of need.

But from the title song through a personal favorite, "In the Wilderness" (which was partly responsible for my abrupt detour to the Kings Mountain National Military Park—wrong war, but the best I could do at the time), and on through other gems like "Blues Too Blue to Mention," "Glad It Ain't Me," and the gospel number "Tidal Wave," Roby's music gave me, well, maybe not serenity but at least a glimpse of it and a few moments of much needed clarity.

A year passes. I decide to write a book about music. I want to include a chapter on Kenny Roby. I notice several of his songs have baseball references, so I decide that it might be useful to get in touch with Roby and use a minor league game as the setting for our interview.

Alas, that strategy doesn't work out. We go to a game, but we watch it. The bulk of the interview takes place in a Raleigh restaurant.

Roby seems world-weary and, compared to what I'd anticipated, contrarian. I have a hard time getting him to step away from what seems like a dogged intent to play devil's advocate to virtually everything I ask. He's friendly enough but seems much more supportive of the musical establishment than I'd anticipated.

The system works, he says. It just hasn't worked for him yet. It's kind of left him depressed, perhaps because at some level he's blamed himself instead of the system.

"I don't think the guy who lives in a trailer park and works in the mill all day is going to listen to Ryan Adams," Roby says. "I just don't think he's going to, and that's the same guy who didn't listen to Townes Van Zandt. That's the same guy who was listening to all the bad country in the seventies. Or the bad rock. In the seventies he was listening to that stuff. He wasn't listening to songwriters."

Great music on the radio? Very rare, Roby tells me. When it happens, it's an accident.

"It's been very rare . . . most of the stuff," he says. "It's like The Band. It was a mistake. It was a mistake they got as big as they did. They fell through the cracks. The Stones had no business breaking through when 'How Much Is That Doggie in the Window?' was going on.

"Producers are businessmen now. In Nashville they're businessmen. That started with people like Billy Sherrill and Chet Atkins, even though those guys made great music. I think they start out with some creative interest, but they reach a point where they know so well what the businessmen want that they [the music industry execs] don't have to come in and look over the producer's shoulder. The suits don't have to come in. He's become one of them. A businessman. The businessmen have not become producers. The producers have become businessmen."

And that's a good thing?

"It's not just music," Roby says. "I think it's movies. I think it's life in general. I don't think we need to make an Oliver Stone movie out of it. It's not a conspiracy. I don't think anyone was trying to frame it this way. It was just something that happened. It's the evolution of society. It's getting more and more boring. More and more bored. They hand us everything. We don't want anyone to make us think. We've become afraid of it."

But the music doesn't cause the problem. The problem causes the music.

"Those people wouldn't be able to foist stuff across on people if it didn't sell," Roby says. "You can't make people literate. You can't do it. It doesn't work."

I refer to several quality songwriters, or at least songwriters whose work I admire. Roby shoots them down. I'm flabbergasted.

"I don't think what they're doing is a hit," he says. "If I was [producer] Billy Sherrill, I'd say, 'Dude, you need to go talk to some songwriters. You need to come and bring them in because I haven't heard you do it. I've heard a lot of that stuff, and I don't hear the hits. I'm sorry. I think Shania Twain—even though I don't like the music—I see why it's popular. I see why 'The Way You Love Me' by Faith Hill is a hit. I've been listening to Steve Miller lately. We'd be better off with him on radio. If they want to compete, they need to jump up and step up to the plate. I don't think it's just the record companies.

"It might serve their purpose better to take up some other people's songs. There's a little more room out there that isn't being filled, but mainly all these guys are just jealous. They wouldn't have a problem with it if they hadn't been turned down. I was in the middle of that stuff. I was in Nashville in the mid- to late 1990s. 'In Search of Alt-Country.' Well, if Nashville was so bad, why is everyone still living there? Why is Rodney Crowell still living outside Nashville? It's where the industry is. It's where the money is.

"A lot of stuff was just bad. It was about, just anything, a small percentage of stuff was good. See, that's another thing. None of these guys can hold a candle to George Jones. They can't hold a candle to a lot of guys—as vocalists, and that's the thing. Nashville's never been a writer-friendly place. Tom T. Hall didn't have as many hits as he wrote."

The only limit on Roby's rant is that he won't discuss individuals. He just sort of excoriates them in bulk.

Finally, I give up. It's obvious that Roby's personal views, or at least the ones he espouses in the interview, are contrary to most of my own views and most of what I've encountered in my conversations with the other musicians. But the reason I asked him was that I wanted to know how he felt.

I take the interview in another direction and ask Roby about the practical matter of how he writes songs.

"There's probably, like, three different sides," he says. "There's the guy sitting on the back porch drinking coffee in the morning, smoking a cigarette and tapping into what he experienced the night before and writing it. Half of it's still in the world; part of it is wondering what the kids are going to have for breakfast. I write a lot when I wake up. Then there's just the fan. I'm a fan, too. This is where an interview gets dangerous because if you say what you think, it could be seen as sour grapes. It could actually *be* sour grapes. You look at me different if you know I'm an artist and I'm talking about another artist's music. If I go, Man, I think that's crap, well, that's completely separate from the Kenny Roby that's a singer-songwriter. That's the Kenny Roby the fan who's heard some good shit, and that ain't nowhere close to it."

So, in fact, Roby has sort of wandered away from the question about songwriting and returned to the topic of everyone I think is good being bad.

"It's different," he continues. "I can sit there. I can be a fan of music, and when I'm in a group of people, and they know I'm a writer or they like my music or whatever, and if I talk about the Old 97's, which I fucking hate, but that's the fan. That's not jealousy. There are people who just sit around and talk shit about other musicians all the time. That's not what I like about it. I like the music. If I don't like it, I don't have to read it or listen to it or talk about it. My job is not to slam other bands.

"Just because I might sell two thousand copies and not fifty thousand, I still think I have kind of an obligation to show some respect for other people and other musicians and not slam them. I don't want people slamming me. I don't mind critics doing it, but for a musician to do it, it just looks bad. It's one of those gentleman things. Maybe I'm deceiving myself to think that anybody cares about what I say. I think a lot of those guys on country radio can sing a lot better than these insurgent guys . . . At least they grew up with a mom and dad cooking grits, and they're a little different from some of the people from Illinois. I've only heard one person not from the South who can pull it off, and that's Gillian Welch.

"In my eyes that's the only one [Welch] who has pulled it off. I just don't think . . . there are too many other influences. Too much information. Too much stress. Too many other things in life to keep making that simple old country music like they used to make. It's hard to sing George Jones when you've got Hilfiger on your waist."

Roby's latest album, *The Mercy Filter*, is a radical departure away from country. It's melodically much more diverse than the two previous CDs, *Rather Not Know* and *Mercury's Blues*, which I adored. *The Mercy Filter* is a pop album with far less country music, which is not to suggest it isn't a fine album but is, rather, to suggest that it isn't as appealing to me as Roby's previous work.

The longer the interview goes, the more I'm struck by just what a walking, talking contradiction Kenny Roby is. Tom T. Hall once described a character who was "about as happy as a thinking man can be," and this is the phrase that keeps coming back to me as we talk. The same man who has just finished cutting a pop album now starts talking about how country is reeling off in a direction that takes it even farther from its roots.

"Now we look back on Garth Brooks, man, and we'd be lucky to get Garth Brooks back," Roby says. "You go back now and listen to 'I've Got Friends in Low Places' right now, and it would sound like Hank Williams Sr.

that is included on Green's latest album, *Lucky Ones*.

Finally, Paisley's concert begins, and it's as slick as Green's is raucous. I think to myself that Paisley isn't near the natural showman that Green is, but it's fascinating to observe just how meticulously rehearsed and practiced Paisley's act is. Every little wisecrack to the audience is carefully chosen, even though it's so well delivered that there is a facade of originality.

Paisley is a guitarist of righteous virtuosity. I've been told this before, but it's something that must be seen in person to appreciate fully. I'm so impressed that later I go on the Internet to review *Rolling Stone*'s list of the hundred greatest guitarists ever and become more than a little pissed off when Paisley isn't listed among them.

All the while I think that, yes, this man, this Brad Paisley, could be the new savior. He's considered a brilliant songwriter by the people who decide such things from Nashville's perspective. The songs are all clever but hardly wise. He's got his heart in the right place, and he genuinely pays homage to the music's history and traditions. Everything about his act is so detached, though, and clichéd.

I can't help but think about when I bought Paisley's most recent album, *Mud on the Tires*, earlier in the year and had the same reaction I'd had to the one by him that I'd bought before. The first song I like, then I listen to the second one, and it leaves another positive impression. But there's this slow, gradual descent that culminates in disgust when I listen to "The Cigar Song," which is derived from a familiar joke that's been circulated by e-mails for years now. It's about a man who tries to claim his Cuban cigars on his fire insurance because, well, they've burned up. I guess the same people who've forwarded this story to me five or six times might love the song, but I get so disgusted at what I consider to be the song's utter and complete silliness that, when I return home, I toss the CD into a box where I'm saving stuff I'm going to trade in at a secondhand store.

I'm happy to report that Paisley doesn't perform this song during his Vegas concert.

For all these reservations of mine that might be considered nitpicky, the Paisley concert leaves me with a positive overall impression. I've been snared and perhaps hoodwinked by the videos that accompany virtually every song, and I feel only mildly annoyed when the image of Alison Krauss shows up on the gigantic screens to sing an electronic duet, "Whiskey Lullaby," cowritten by Bill Anderson and Jon Randall, with Paisley. Live and Memorex, in one swell package.

Accompanying the title song of his CD, Paisley says: "I love it because we're those kinds of people. This if for all you rednecks who can't keep your trucks clean."

I just can't help but look at those carefully creased pants and hat and the starched collar without doubting the sincerity of his supposed ad-libs. Here is a man who stretches the bounds of his guitar without stretching the bounds of his music.

But then the band leaves the stage. Paisley trades his electric guitar for an acoustic, sits on the edge of the stage, and performs a touching rendition of "How Great Thou Art," and I'm captivated again.

When the show is over, I feel confident about the anticipated interview. I've taken good notes, and I prepared my questions in advance. But then I find myself in a line with about a hundred other people, and the ones closest to me are jabbering on about how great it is to drink a shot of Jägermeister. They're convivial drunks, all loaded down with cameras so that they can have their photos taken with Paisley. There are also eight-by-ten glossies, CDs, and all other manner of autographable goodies in abundance.

Ah, that sinking feeling again. I'm struck by how odd it

must look to everyone else that I'm standing there in this interminable line with only a digital recorder and a notepad in my hands. A laughing man behind me—and there aren't many people behind me—starts to look a little nervous and is undoubtedly wondering why I'm scribbling furiously in the notepad. Then I realize that many of these people represent radio stations. I realize this because I can't help but overhear a conversation that I can't begin to understand:

"Lee is, like, ohmigod, have you been out with Mike?"

"Dude, you just don't get it!"

"He, like, said, 'Every time you see a skunk, you hit it!'"

Everyone laughs but me. I'm sure my expressions betray me.

Finally, I arrive at the front of the line, where there to greet me is genuine, heartfelt, wholesome Brad Paisley and, just to the right and behind, genuinely nervous Brent Long.

I make a little joke about not having anything for him to sign and tell Paisley I'm in Vegas to do an interview, and then I briefly explain what my book is about and why I think it's important to have him in it. Long intercedes and says something like, "Yeah, Brad, you remember, I was telling you about it."

Paisley looks me right in the eye and says, "Yeah, I think I've heard people talking about that book. We'll certainly take care of it."

That's it. I move along. I play my final card by noting to Long that Paisley is scheduled to appear at the next night's session of the rodeo. Could we talk then?

"Yeah, I think that might work," says Long, and I think to myself that this is at least the third time he's said this to me. "Come see me at the rodeo."

The next night Paisley and Long appear on press row after Paisley's song opens the show. I walk a few steps toward them, raise my hand to draw Long's attention, and he returns the favor by making that signal that generally denotes A-OK. I monitor Paisley's presence, but that's difficult because on press row at the rodeo there's a need to make sure one doesn't get conked in the head by a flying cow turd or something just as unpleasant. I do notice, however, when Paisley rises and walks along with a small entourage into the bowels of the arena. I try to walk, not run, after them, but it's all done so swiftly. By the time I get out of the glare of the lights and into a short hallway where TV announcers interview rodeo cowboys, the star has been whisked away into the night.

At that moment I make a decision that I will make no more calls to Brent Long. Paisley has told me, "We'll take care of it," and now I wonder about the sincerity of that remark. Is he despicably nice? Has he avoided me by having his road manager put up smokescreen after smokescreen? Has there been a marketing survey of journalists that has revealed that telling them no causes too much irritation and that a more prudent course is just to avoid them endlessly? Or is this all just a consequence of having a road manager with much too much to do?

I wait a month before hearing again from Brent Long. In the interim I talk to Pat Green about Paisley. The two are friends. When I describe my frustrations, Green is vividly amused.

When I offer the opinion that Green is as spontaneous as Paisley is calculating, Green pokes fun at himself by saying, "There's a difference between spontaneity and cluelessness.

"Brad and I met because we were up for a Grammy two years in a row. Different categories, but we both lost both years, so that's kind of how we got to be friends. You can walk around in your life—I've seen a lot of guys walk around in their lives pointing the finger at people and saying stuff about them when they don't know anything about them.

"I was one of those guys. I used to throw my rocks at people that I didn't know. I found out that ain't a good way to do things. Hey, look, I didn't know Brad from a hole in the wall, but he had one song that I didn't think was that great, but then he had a couple of songs that I thought were number one, out of this world. I thought 'the fishing song' ['I'm Gonna Miss Her'] was funny as hell. So, when I had an opportunity to meet him and talk to him, I took it, and it turns out not only is he a great guy; he's a funny guy. He's really funny.

"I'm the self-professed, number-one drunk in town. You know, I can be a flat-out, roaring idiot, and he hasn't ever had a drink. We're complete opposites. He doesn't cuss a lot; I cuss like a sailor. We're two opposite people that came together, and, you know, when we got together to do a duet, we didn't even record the better song. The better song was 'Before December,' but it's not what the record needed. I tend not to think about myself personally when we're putting out a record. I think of the record as its own entity. That song 'College' needed to be in there. Our record, I felt, was a little bit overwhelmingly serious. I needed just a little levity to break things up so that people would go, 'Ah, OK, we still got that in there.'"

Amazingly, I eventually get my interview with Brad Paisley. It occurs in that soulless modern way—an exchange of e-mails—but I get the chance to ask the questions I had prepared two months earlier by scribbling them on a notepad, and Paisley's replies reflect a thoughtful, frank mind-set. He is, it seems, truly the nice guy I had hoped he was and not the good-natured marketing whiz whom in darker moments I had conjured up.

Paisley's studied approach to his career is apparent in his live shows and in the composition of his albums. My first question is about how carefully he prepared himself to be exactly where is today.

"My education about the music industry came in two different ways," he replies. "The first was when I became a regular member of Jamboree USA in Wheeling [West Virginia, his home state]. The Jamboree is a long-running radio show much like the [Grand Ole] Opry, where different headliners pass through there on Saturday nights. Over the years I opened for almost all the greats. I got to perform before George Jones, Jimmy Dickens, Steve Wariner, Charley Pride, Lee Greenwood, The Judds, Charlie Daniels—you name them, they came through there. I learned by osmosis, by just being around that.

"Secondly, by transferring to Belmont University as a junior, I got into the Nashville business by being around that as well. By interning for three very different organizations [ASCAP, Atlantic Records, and Fitzgerald/Hartley Management], I got an overview of the three parts of an artist's business: songwriting and publishing, record labels, and management.

"I didn't anticipate that the music business would be constantly changing as much as it does now. There was a time when just having a hit or two meant a long career was probable. Not anymore. It takes reinvention and constant creativity to remain competitive in the modern country music world."

The trouble with such a clinical approach is that it can stifle creativity in the same manner as what is practiced by the recording and radio industry and decried throughout this book. The paradox embodied in Paisley's career is that he must balance his own fondness for the music's roots with the very trends that take it away from them. To his credit he is mindful of the dangerous waters into which he is wading.

"The critics of new country are very quick to cite the differences between today's music and the past," Paisley writes. "On one hand, they have a point in that it *is* different, but, on the other, there is more validity here than [what] they are willing to recognize. Nostalgia is a wonderful thing, but just because something is old or antique doesn't mean it's better, necessarily. On the radio I just had a hit with a very dark account of a couple who let alcohol destroy there lives ['Whiskey Lullaby'], at the same time that Sara Evans had a huge hit with a Cajun-flavored tune about soap bubbles and a clothesline, and Josh Turner had a huge hit about sin and temptation and trains, which also was on the chart simultaneously with pop-sounding stuff. It's a very big umbrella, and fans are not really complaining much. I admit that there have been times, throughout our history, when there were very, very strong songs on the charts simultaneously. Look at the early sixties, or the outlaw seventies, or the early nineties. However, in every one of those eras there were also pieces of crap that did well too. The thing is, some of those turds are considered classics just because they are old songs now. That's the beauty of hindsight.

"At the time 'Achy Breaky Heart' came out, people were calling it a low point. In retrospect it was very catchy, and it sold a lot of records and really made people happy to hear it. In my mind that is a classic due to the effect it had, regardless of the intricacy of its song structure. I think, looking back at today, there will be plenty of high points to discuss.

"The one thing I would like to see return are more songs about personal experience and less that seem merely an attempt to be clever. Ironically, the biggest hits are usually honest. As I listen to songs for my next album, I can't tell you how many songs sound like recalculated equations. I wish more people were pitching stuff that was autobiographical."

By sheer coincidence, since Paisley and I are neither talk-

Two-Night Stand

On a NASCAR off-weekend I travel to the Neighborhood Theatre, about an hour and a half away, for consecutive concerts.
The theater is located in what's known locally as the NoDa
[North Davidson Street] Arts District. It's a formerly rundown area now brimming with art galleries, coffeehouses,
and other shops. Over the years I've attended dozens of concerts at the renovated movie house to see artists like Jerry
Jeff Walker, Robert Earl Keen, Billy Joe Shaver, and some
who don't even have three names.

Buddy Miller is a favorite of mine. He's the most unas-
suming of artists, not to mention one of the more talented.
For many years Miller has played lead guitar for his close
friend Emmylou Harris, who is at least indirectly responsible for the title of his latest CD, *Universal United House of
Prayer*. The cover is a black-and-white photograph of an actual house of worship, shown beneath a cloudy sky, located
in a rundown neighborhood of Nashville next to an automobile repair shop. After completing work on the album, Miller

sent a copy to Emmylou, accompanied by a Xerox copy of the cover photo.

"The label [New West] liked the record, but they weren't sold on the title or the cover photo," Miller says. "I figured I'd just let it go. You know, I figured they were the experts, and it wasn't something to quibble about."

In a conversation with Harris, however, he let slip in passing the news that the title was apparently about to be changed. This did not sit well with her, so she made a call to the label, after which the original title and evocative photograph were restored.

"I went back to the church and found it boarded up," says Miller. "I guess in Nashville, you don't have the opportunity to go worship while your car is being fixed anymore."

Miller, often accompanied by his wife and songwriting collaborator, Julie, goes it alone this time, with a three-piece band backing him. He arrives onstage wearing a faded cap, his gray, shoulder-length hair cascading out of the back like a mountain waterfall. Almost every song is previewed by a low-key, rambling dialogue that is charming for its very lack of direction. He nonetheless apologizes repeatedly for his streams of consciousness.

The band works well together despite the fact that the bassist, Denny Bixby, is on loan from Rodney Crowell. A recent birth in the family of Byron House created the gap that Bixby adroitly fills. The friendship between Miller and his jack-of-all-trades, Phil Madeira (on organ, accordion, lap steel, and guitar), and drummer Bryan Owings is obvious as they exchange private quips during the entire concert.

"My voice is trashed," says Miller, "so I'll call it character."

Worn or not, Miller's voice is nothing if not strong and distinctive. In terms of plaintiveness he's kind of a male alternative to Lucinda Williams. I haven't heard a voice as distinctive since the relatively brief prime of Vern Gosdin's career. It's a take-no-prisoners voice, and since Miller doesn't sound like a thousand other singers, it's probably an acquired taste for some listeners. There's a lot of blues and soul there, but most of the songs are hard-core traditional country. Many of the songs are the creative work of Miller and his wife, but the concert also includes samplings of Mark Heard, the Louvin Brothers, Bob Dylan, Tom T. Hall, Jim Lauderdale, and, near the end, Hank Williams, who never sang "You Win Again" any better.

Twice nominated for a Grammy Award, Miller seems blissfully unaware—and if not, then ambivalent—about his own considerable talents. Although he won a Grammy neither time, he takes pleasure in telling the audience that one of the losses was to Bob Dylan. The most memorable aspect of the Grammy ceremonies just completed, he says, was the fact that the food "was so beyond anything you can imagine."

"I'm one of those guys who can't tune and talk at the same time," he says during one of the between-songs monologues. "Actually, I can't tune . . . and I can't talk."

The lead-in act, by the way, is a pleasant surprise. Miller produced Bill Mallonee's CD *Audible Sigh*, and Mallonee, who lives in Athens, Georgia, performs for about an hour, accompanying himself with guitar and harmonica, before Miller's band joins him for a couple of songs at the end.

When I walk out into the cold night air, I get sidetracked on the way to my truck by the sound of music being played nearby. I head in the direction of the sound and find a couple of young men set up in the grass, one with an electric guitar and the other on drums, in front of a small specialty shop. After listening to a couple of Hank Williams Jr. standards, I put a couple of bills in the guitar case. They outnumber the audience two to one at this point since several people leave as I arrive in the yard. For a few moments I pick up a spare guitar and strum it, although an electric guitar is alien to me, not to mention trying to play it with a stiff pick (*plectrum*, I believe, is the formal term).

It's hard to embarrass oneself in a group of three people, but I'm doing it, so I put the guitar up, chat for a while, and then they indulge me by letting me sing a few verses of Hall's "The Year That Clayton Delaney Died." I fumble the lyrics several times, so they let me acquit myself with another simple standard, Harlan Howard's "Pick Me Up on Your Way Down." That's enough to send me on my late-night way with enough adrenaline flowing to make it home safely.

I get my nephew to accompany me the following night after he discovers that Charlie Robison's song "El Cerrito Place" is currently being featured on Country Music Television. Once we arrive in NoDa, we queue up until the doors open, at which time we walk into the arena to mark our seats, then, with a plastic band safely fastened around our right wrists, we walk back outside to window-shop at the various galleries and antique shops. The first sign that something is slightly amiss occurs when two women in line with us inform me that they have never heard of Robison, that they are "huge fans" of Paul Thorn (the opening act), and that they have come all the way from Virginia to see Thorn.

My nephew, Ray Phillips, does not share my political views, and he smells liberals almost immediately when we start walking around. He seems as confused and mystified by the existence of affluent liberals as I am by working-class conservatives.

I've heard of the Paul Thorn Band, but I've never heard a single one of his songs. All I know about him is that some members of an online message group are really big fans. Based on these recommendations, I await his concert with some enthusiasm. I'm not disappointed. Thorn is about as far from country as anyone in these pages, but he's the kind of artist who springs, powerful and unrepentant, from charismatic religion. It comes as no surprise when Thorn tells the audience that he has a father who is a Church of God preacher and an uncle who is a pimp. He says his father taught him about God and his Uncle Merle taught him about women, and off we go on that tantalizing Jimmy Swaggart/Jerry Lee Lewis slippery slope.

Some of Thorn's songs could've been sung by Marvin Gaye or Al Green. Some are rock. Some are rhythm and blues. Some are just blues. Precious little could be categorized as country. The music is satisfying, though, and full of humor and occasionally even wide-eyed innocence. The between-song monologues are priceless. Thorn tells about how he and his honey used to sit around the trailer, eat bacon and Miracle Whip sandwiches, and procreate while watching Jerry Springer. He misses watching her prance around in her purple thong, he says, but the breakup was his fault.

"I cheated on her," Thorn says, "and she cheated on me, and pretty soon we was having us a cheat-a-thon."

One of his songs is about "Joanie the Jehovah's Witness Stripper." There's a little something that's demeaning about watching this throng of Thorn fans rollicking at one zany song after another. Thorn sings about his life—of that I have little doubt—but to those around me who have taken up most of the seats in the front rows, it's almost like slumming. Most of these people arrived in BMWs and Lexus SUVs. It's easy for them to look at Thorn as being some kind of musical version of *The Beverly* Hillbillies' Jethro Bodine, and that's selling him and his background fairly short. But I guess it's a living.

After a break, most of which is dominated by Thorn fans streaming to the exits, Charlie Robison arrives onstage to a crowd grown sparse and quiet. A couple of drunks seem to exist to block my view. One carries a sixteen-ounce can of

Budweiser that he repeatedly hoists with one hand while sig-naling the stage with the two-fingered "Hook 'em Horns" gesture familiar to University of Texas fans.

Bud Man does everything but climb up on the stage. Ro-bison, who has experienced limited mainstream success with three stellar studio albums in a row, mentions with a some-what sheepish tone that the video is number seven on the CMT charts and encourages fans to vote for it online. He's uncomfortable with self-promotion, though, and he acquits himself a bit by saying, "Besides, I'm tired of watching Ken-ny Chesney frolicking on the beach all goddamned day."

The Robisons of Bandera, Texas, represent quite a con-trast in styles. It's hard to believe that Charlie and Bruce Ro-bison are brothers. One similarity is that both married well. Charlie's wife, Emily Robison, is one of the Dixie Chicks. Bruce's wife, Kelly Willis, is a phenomenal vocal talent who is inexplicably underappreciated outside the borders of the Lone Star State.

Charlie Robison calls brother Bruce "the greatest song-writer on earth," and while there might be a bit of familial bias in that, Bruce concedes, "The main thing that I make money from is songwriting." He wrote "Lonely Too" (Lee Ann Womack), "Travelin' Soldier" (Dixie Chicks), and "An-gry All the Time" (Tim McGraw). Bruce Robison's most fa-miliar tune, at least among those heard on radio, is "What Would Willie Do?" a whimsical ode to Willie Nelson. An-other notable song is "Wrapped," which was the title song of his own album and was covered by his wife on her critically acclaimed 1999 CD *What I Deserve*.

Bruce is laid-back, with a vocal style that somehow re-minds me of Don Williams. Charlie is out there on the rock edge of country. Charlie's show is full of crowd-pleasers like "Barlight" (a nursery rhyme for grownups), "Sunset Bou-levard," "My Hometown," "Desperate Times," and "The

Wedding Song." The last was released on his *Step Right Up* CD as a duet with the Chicks' Natalie Maines. In concert Charlie sometimes recruits audience members to sing the female part.

Irony defines Charlie Robison. Why else would there be a song called "Life of the Party" on his 2001 album *Step Right Up* but no such song on his album called *Life of the Party*, which came out three years earlier?

It's a great show but a strange one. I've seen Robison play to raucous, beer-chugging Texas crowds, and it's no inconvenience to me that this audience has only two obvious drunks in it, although I would prefer that those two were not blocking my view of the stage. One, by the way, eventually gets escorted out. Robison watches with good humor and notes that he's played to rowdy audiences and he's played to sedate ones, but rarely has he played to such a polarized one as this.

The whole atmosphere is kind of weird. For one thing, the throng of Robison fans is situated mostly in a low balcony, or really more of a platform, to the left of the stage. That's because the prime seats have now been vacated by departing Paul Thorn fans and, presumably, the Robison fans are either too comfortable or too drunk to move. The beer stand is in easy access to the fans watching from the platform. It could be that there are dozens of rowdy fans over there. I can't see because of a barrier at the front. The only drunk I can see is Bud Man, sloshing beer around and dancing like a goose on Quaaludes.

Despite all this, Robison and his really tight band carry on for an hour and a half, performing brilliantly on a night when they could be excused if they cut out early.

Ray, my nephew, is convinced that everyone in Charlotte is a lunatic, but he'll be in college soon and will learn that it's really true of everyone, uh, everywhere.

The American Crisis and the American Dream

'These are the times that try men's souls.'

With this lament, Thomas Paine began the series of revolutionary tracts known as *The American Crisis*. There is something in the cadence and phrasing of his first article that is reminiscent of Shakespeare's *Henry V*, when young King Hal rallies his troops before Agincourt. It is fitting, then, that George Washington had Paine's words read out to his dispirited troops before they embarked on a dangerous mission across the Delaware River in December 1776.

It is fitting, too, that Barack Obama drew on this text in January 2009 when he was inaugurated as the forty-fourth President of the United States. His address was sombre and portentous. The nation was at war and the economy was weakened. Homes were lost. Jobs were shed. There had been, he said, a sapping of confidence in the country. Obama then referred to the darkest days of the American Revolution by quoting directly from a passage in *The American Crisis*: 'Let it be told to the future world, that in the depth of winter, when nothing but hope and virtue could survive, that the city and the country, alarmed at one common danger, came forth to meet and to repulse it.'

Truly these have been times to try men's souls. Obama took office at the end of a tormented decade for the United States.

First and foremost, there was the terrorist atrocity of '9/11': the death and destruction caused by eighteen men (armed with nothing more than box-cutters) crashing jet-liners into those iconic buildings was grim enough, but the magnitude of the attack was amplified by the damage done to America's sense of invulnerability. Smaller terrorist incidents, including the anthrax attack against Congress and the scourge of the Washington sniper, seemed to provide evidence of malign intent directed against the representatives of the republic.

Then there were the natural disasters – tornadoes, wild-fires, hurricanes and the first flu pandemic in forty years. In 2009, H1N1 – or 'Mexican Swine Flu' – briefly fuelled a bout of xenophobic angst about the northward flow of Hispanic immigrants. However, Hurricane Katrina had already revealed deeper flaws in the country's social fabric. The physical devastation wreaked on New Orleans and its environs was dwarfed by the psychological fall-out: the whole country experienced a sense of ignominy both at its inability to act expeditiously and at the desperate suffering of the have-nots in the richest country on the planet.

A third blow to the United States' self-esteem came in 2008, when the nation experienced a financial super-crisis arising from excessive levels of personal and public debt. Credit markets seized up, liquidity froze, banks crashed and, with a recession threatening to turn into a depression, the world's greatest champion of Free Market Capitalism saw major financial institutions become effectively nationalized.

It is not surprising, then, that the raw and penetrating glare from these thunderbolts has revealed fractures and stress-lines in the social fabric of the nation. This has led one writer, Juan Enriquez, to describe his country as the 'Untied States of America', and Barack Obama himself has expressed concern about the conflicted nature of society: '. . . if we don't change course soon, we may be the first generation in a very long time that leaves behind a weaker and more fractured America than the one we inherited'.

This book – *The Cracked Bell* – is essentially a survey of the gap between the American Crisis and the American Dream. It began as a dispassionate attempt to review the state of America at the advent of the twenty-first century, employing the tools and techniques of social anthropology. It has found a country suffering from an array of conflicted conditions, where questions about the essence of the American Way – profound questions about identity, security, power and opportunity – reveal rich and confusing patterns of paradox.

In one sense, this revelation does little more than confirm Kant's memorable dictum that 'out of the crooked timber of humanity no straight thing was ever made'. However, American culture appears to offer the anthropologist exceptional levels of contrast. Michael Kammen has produced a history of this phenomenon in *People of Paradox* – a book that teems with terms like 'dualism', 'biformity', 'contradictory tendencies', 'the perplexity of unstable pluralism' and 'syzygy' (a word beloved of *Scrabble* players, meaning a paradoxical coupling of opposites).

There are many different explanations for this cultural dissonance, but as I encountered and explored the varieties of American paradox in greater detail I discovered a common denominator: the ideal of freedom. The US seems to be suffering from the afflictions of liberty – a condition emblemized for me by the fractured Liberty Bell in Philadelphia's Independence National Historical Park.

'The old cracked Bell still proclaims Liberty,' the US Park Service asserts in its visitors' guide. Legend has it that the bronze behemoth – weighing in at over a ton – was rung when the Declaration of Independence was read out in 'Liberty Hall'; and it bears an inscription, from the Book of Leviticus, that seems to offer both a mission and a promise for the citizens of the United States: 'Proclaim liberty throughout all the land unto all the inhabitants thereof.'

The bell was commissioned from London's Whitechapel Bell Foundry by the Pennsylvania Provincial Assembly and it first fractured soon after its delivery in 1752. Local artisans melted it down and cast a new bell that gave sound service for almost a century. However, as Philadelphia's *Public Ledger* reported, it was damaged beyond repair on 23 February 1846, when rung in honour of George Washington's birthday:

> This venerable relic of the Revolution rang its last clear note on Monday last and now hangs in the great city steeple irreparably cracked and forever dumb . . . It gave out clear notes and loud, and appeared to be in excellent condition until noon when it received a sort of compound fracture in a zigzag direction through one of its sides.

The crack is as renowned as the bell itself and it is commonplace for images of the 'relic' to be reproduced with the fracture prominently displayed (like a signature on its side, running from lip to crown). It has been a favourite emblem for the US Postal Service over the years, appearing most recently on the 'Forever Stamp' (issued in 2007) that is valid for first-class delivery indefinitely. It also featured on over 500 million 'Franklin Halfs' that circulated as common currency for many years, until a new 50 cent coin was minted in memory of John F. Kennedy in 1963.

I keep a Franklin Half nearby as I write these words. The image of the Liberty Bell – with that deep fault in its side – acts as a Rosetta Stone for me, making sense of those riddles and conundrums encountered in the course of my research. It reminds me that America, early in its prehistory, imported an English ideal of freedom that was tempered and contained by the moral sensibility of the Scottish Enlightenment (aptly symbolized by the fact that the ship that lifted the bell across the Atlantic was called *Hibernia*). However, in the pressured atmosphere of America's 'Liberty Hall', this ideal has been inflated and distorted by a radical form of individualism: it is cracked, like the Liberty Bell, and is now undermining and afflicting the very society that it was intended to underpin.

This conclusion has taken me by surprise. Like most Britons, I have developed a Pavlovian response to the word 'freedom' and spring unthinkingly to its defence. But in *The Cracked Bell* I find myself challenging the place of freedom in a society that attaches the highest premium to this ideal. I argue that there is something almost pathological about a national narrative that is intoxicated by the spirit of freedom while failing to pay sufficient attention to its meaning. And so this attempt at a measured, objective survey has ended with the butchery of a 'sacred cow'.

A corrective is needed at this point, lest I leave the impression that *The Cracked Bell* is a lamentation, or jeremiad, for the twenty-first century. (The jeremiad is little-known today, but some claim that the art-form represents America's greatest contribution to English letters. This product of Colonial New England was characterized by beefy prophecies of social collapse, filled with bitter regret about the moral state of the nation and further seasoned with the hot mustard of puritanical vituperation.) I am no Jeremiah, and a very different vision instigated *The Cracked Bell*. Inspiration, in fact, came from reading *The Americans* by Geoffrey Gorer, first published in 1948. This ethnographic monograph belongs to a genre of European literature that has mapped the cultural topography of North America over the centuries. A feature of the genus – represented by the work of such different writers as Jacques Maritain, Alexis de Tocqueville, J. Hector St John de Crèvecoeur, Captain John Smith of Jamestown and Thomas Harriot – is a focus on the present (not the past), with the author immersing himself into his subject-matter.

Gorer's endeavour appealed to me as a graduate of the Cambridge School of Social Anthropology, but, in truth, the inspiration was more personal than purely academic. There were several elements in Gorer's life-story that appeared to be linked to my own. Here was a Briton who had preceded his assignment in the United States with anthropological research among the Tantric Buddhist Lepchas of Sikkim and whose study of American character was made possible by a wartime posting to the British Embassy in Washington, DC. I, too, had worked as an anthropologist in the Himalayas, studying the Tantric Buddhist Newars of Nepal, and, in 2002, I took up a post in the

British Embassy in Washington, DC, at a time of heightened tension and conflict, when the capital city felt and behaved as if it was on a wartime footing.

As these links in the chain were revealed, I felt inspired and compelled to follow Gorer's example in applying the lens of the anthropologist to reveal contemporary American culture. My path would inevitably deviate from his: I did not, for instance, adhere to the socio-psychological approach that he had learned from Margaret Mead, the American cultural anthropologist. Nor did I share his unbending belief that the future peace and prosperity of the world depended upon the mutual understanding and fruitful collaboration of the English and American peoples and governments.

Nevertheless, I sympathize with Gorer's commitment to helping the world comprehend the United States. He wrote: 'Mutual understanding cannot endure if it is founded on delusions and falsifications; it must be based on the acceptance of our widely differing characters and ways of looking at and interpreting the world.' There may be something impertinent about trying to encompass a society of over 300 million people occupying 3.5 million square miles within the covers of a single volume, but it remains my aspiration that the panoramic, synoptic scan presented in *The Cracked Bell* provides the sort of opportunity for insight, reflection and understanding that Gorer achieved in his own work.

I would go further. With Obama's election to the presidency, this is an appropriate time for the citizens of the republic themselves to take stock. The president has described his mission as the promotion of the unity of hope over conflict and discord, in an effort to reclaim and reconstitute the American Dream. The appointment of this impassioned advocate for change coincides with a growing realization that the age of American hyper-power is drawing to a close. Little by little, the United States' global dominance of the world (economic, cultural and military) will wane through the course of the twenty-first century as China and India grow in strength. The US needs to consider not only how it makes the transition with dignity, but also what this means for 'the American Promise' (including the fragile relationship between freedom, justice and equality).

Each one of the seven chapters that follow is sufficiently self-standing that a reader wishing to contemplate the 'Cult of the New', say, or questions of war and peace could choose to go directly to 'The Lattice Constant' or 'The Cicada's Wing'. Only the eighth chapter, with its comparative analysis of the United States and the United Kingdom based on what has gone before, needs to be taken on a full stomach – once the seven American paradoxes have been reviewed. There is no great science to the order in which these paradoxes appear, but the question of identity – the riddle of 'e pluribus unum' – is so fundamental to the life of every American that this seems the obvious place to begin.

CHAPTER ONE

The Many and the One – On Identity

'We Are All Americans Now,' proclaimed the French newspaper, *Le Monde*, after the world watched terrorists fly jet-liners into the twin towers of New York's World Trade Center and into the Pentagon. A fourth attack was almost certainly destined for the Capitol (the heart of America's democracy).

That phrase captured the sentiment of millions around the world who – for a few weeks, at least – were overtaken by an overwhelming sense of solidarity with the American people. It also reflected the fact that, within Al-Qaeda's makeshift incinerators, the flesh, blood and bones of people originating from around the world, from every race and creed, were reduced to ashes.

Three arcane words, embossed into the alloy of America's one cent coin, took on a fresh significance that day: '*e pluribus unum*'. This Latin phrase, meaning 'Out of the Many, One', forms the motto of the US and its appearance on the humble penny suggests a truth as universal as the smallest denomination in the nation's mint.

It is uncertain, however, how many Americans understand the words. Some will recall that *The Wizard of Oz* refers to the United States as the 'The Land of *E Pluribus Unum*'. It is unlikely, though, that many stop to scrutinize these thirteen letters as they go about the rush of business – and Americans are almost always in a rush. It is telling that the National Endowment for the Humanities has funded an '*E Pluribus*

Unum Project' that aims to support students and teachers 'who wish to examine the attempt to make "one from many" in three critical decades of American life'. The project explains how John Adams, Thomas Jefferson and Benjamin Franklin devised this linguistic formula in response to tasking by the Continental Congress, the first national government of the United States; and they did so, if history is to be believed, on that most auspicious of days, 4 July 1776.

It may be a coincidence, but their composition chimes with a line from a Latin poem written almost 2,000 years earlier. In 'Moretum' ('The Salad'), the Roman poet Virgil records the humdrum life of a ploughman called Symilus and describes him preparing his morning meal – a compôte of garlic root, coriander seed, parsley, cheese and salt:

> Then everything he equally doth rub
> I' th' mingled juice. His hand in circles moves:
> Till by degrees they one by one lose
> Their proper powers,
> And out of many comes
> A single colour, not entirely green
> Because the milky fragments this forbid,
> Nor showing white as from the milk because
> That colour's altered by so many herbs.

The intent of Adams, Jefferson and Franklin was to form an epigram of thirteen letters that signified the unifying power of thirteen independent states operating together in a federal republic. However, over time their words have come to express a perceived blending of the peoples of the Old World into the citizens of the New, making a unified nation from a host of different countries and cultures. The *E Pluribus Unum* Project argues that, 'The challenge of seeking unity while respecting diversity has played a critical role in shaping our history, our literature, and our national character.'

This is a challenge indeed. Is it really possible to form a single American identity, and if so, is the USA succeeding in this task?

Arthur Schlesinger expressed his doubts in *The Disuniting of America*, where he sees a 'multiethnic dogma' that glorifies *pluribus* at the expense of *unum*, replacing assimilation with fragmentation and swapping integration for separatism.

It is true – even in a period that has seen Barack Obama elected president – that ethnic intolerance is endemic in the land. While the atrocities of 9/11 were clearly the manifestation of an external threat, it is far more common for Americans to wake to news of attacks motivated by racial hatred from within its borders. In January 2009, for instance, the FBI charged three young Staten Island men with Federal Hate Crime, looking for African-Americans to assault in retaliation for Obama's victory. This phenomenon is not confined to the hot blood of youth: in June 2009, an eighty-five-year-old white supremacist attacked two of his hate objects simultaneously, shooting dead a black guard at the Holocaust Museum in Washington, DC. The following examples, selected at random from the beginning and the end of our decade, illustrate the variety – if not the scale – of the phenomenon.

In April 2000, readers of the *Pittsburgh Post-Gazette* read about the arrest of Richard Scott Baumhammers, after a 'shooting rampage' that left five dead. The victims were Jewish, Vietnamese, Chinese, Indian and Korean. Baumhammers also set fire to the home of his Jewish neighbour and fired on two synagogues, painting swastikas and 'Jew' on the buildings. His parents – Latvian immigrants and successful dentists – were described as 'pillars of the community'. Baumhammers himself held a law degree and had practised law in Atlanta. However, when police searched his home they found a manifesto for the 'Free Market Party': this draft championed the rights of European Americans, complaining that they were outnumbered by minorities and immigrants. The Pittsburgh press lamented the fact that these killings followed another shooting rampage in nearby Wilkinsburg that had left three dead: the gunman (Ronald Taylor) was black, his victims were white, and police found handwritten references to 'white trash' that denounced Asians and Italians.

Ten years later, an attack in Binghamton, some 200 miles north of New York City, seemed to strike at the heart of the American Dream. Jiverly Voong was a Sino-Vietnamese who had migrated to the United States fourteen years earlier and become a citizen in 1995. He shot dead thirteen immigrants sitting a citizenship test in the local American Civic Center before turning the gun on himself. He had taken English classes at the Center but was reputedly teased at work for his poor grasp of the language. Binghamton (population 47,000) has a racial mix that is 83 per cent white, 8.5 per cent African-American, 4 per cent Latino, 3 per cent Asian and 0.25 per cent Native American. It is telling that a short list of 'Binghamton in Books' opens with *A History of the Binghamton Slovaks* (described as 'a chronicle of one of the city's largest ethnic populations'). The list of Voong's victims, in turn, shows the cross-section of people seeking to build a new life for themselves in the United States. In addition to two staff at the Center – Roberta King (a substitute teacher) and Maria Zobniw (a part-time caseworker, originally from Ukraine), they were: Almir Olimpio Alves (43) from Brazil; Layla Khalil (53) from Iraq; Parveen Ali (26) from northern Pakistan; Dolores Yigal (53) from the Philippines; Lan Ho (39) a migrant from Vietnam; Marc Henry and Maria Sonia Bernard (44 and 46) from Haiti; Jiang Ling (22), Hong Xiu 'Amy' Mao Marsland (35), Li Guo (47) and Hai Hong Zhong (54) from China.

Voong posted a letter (with a stamp bearing the image of the Liberty Bell) to a television station before embarking on his murderous mission. His words exhibit symptoms of paranoia and delusion as he rants against undercover policemen who are harassing him with messages left on his voicemail telling him to go back to his own country; and the letter concludes with one of the few fluent phrases he had mastered: 'And you have a nice day.'

American history is, of course, littered with examples of mob violence directed against racial minorities: Indians, blacks, Germans, Japanese, Jews and Hispanics have all suffered to a greater or lesser extent over the decades, but there are countless other symptoms of the racism inherent in America. There is, for example, something deeply emblematic about the nation's first television broadcast. In New York, in April 1927, viewers watched 'live' pictures of a popular vaudeville comic – A. Dolan (whose given name has disappeared in the mists of time) – who stood before the camera in a studio in Whippany, New Jersey, and told some Irish jokes before blacking himself up and entertaining his audience with 'darkie' gags.

There is also something significant about those plentiful examples of espionage against the state, enacted by individuals who feel a closer allegiance to a foreign government than to their own. There is a distinction to be drawn, here, with the ideological motivation that drew British spies – sickened by a hide-bound class system – to betray their country to the Soviet Union. In the United States, hyphenated-espionage has been perpetrated over the years by German-, Japanese-, Chinese-, Jewish- and Hispanic-Americans who have passed on secrets to Germany, Japan, China, Taiwan, Israel and Cuba.

What, then, are the realities of *e pluribus unum*? How do Americans perceive themselves – as Many or One? Can they claim to be, metaphorically, the Children of Symilus, or is the country like the array of tribes and barbarians that ultimately overthrew the empire that Symilus served?

From a distance there appears to be substantial uniformity to American society. Through the lens of TV and cinema screens, or through encounters with those few Americans who venture abroad, a common identity transcends any differences in ethnic, cultural or economic makeup. A universal American style is projected: an easy confidence; a positive can-do attitude; self-belief and tolerance; energy and humour. This has been defined by Samuel Huntington as an Anglo-Protestant identity, whose distinctive qualities include a shared sense of community, a strong work ethic, individualism, belief in the gospel of success and – often – a crusading moralism. It is remarkable that 80 per cent of US nationals say they are 'very proud' to be Americans, compared with similar sentiments expressed by only 45 per cent of Britons, 38 per cent of French and 18 per cent of Germans. This strong attachment to the nation seems to be affirmed by Organization for Economic Co-Operation and Development (OECD) statistics that show a tiny proportion of Americans living permanently abroad: 1,200,000 – less than 0.5 per cent of the national population. (This compares with over 9 per cent of British nationals.)

Marriage across the ethnic divide is one of the most prominent ways in which a common American identity is forged. Geoffrey Gorer paid homage to this distinctive sense of identity in the dedication placed at the front of *The Americans*. It is to 'Erling C. Olsen, Jr., half-Norwegian, half-Czech, good American, killed in Normandy, July 1944'. Americans have given mythical status to their first inter-racial union, between John Rolfe and Pocahontas in seventeenth-century Virginia, and it is commonplace to hear Americans describe the ethnic cocktail flowing through their veins. The old strictures that forced marriage to 'your own kind' – the world of Puerto Ricans and Italians in *West Side Story* (1957 stage musical; 1961 film) – have given way, at least in modern, middle-class America, to marriage across ethnic and religious boundaries. At weddings like that between Mike (three-quarters German, one-quarter Welsh, Lutheran) and Julia (English mother, Lithuanian father, Catholic) beside a wooded lake in Minnesota you can hear people rehearse their ancestry: Tony has a Swedish mother and a Ukrainian father; Keenan's mum is Russian, her dad a mix of Portuguese, Irish and French. Valerie, counting the countries of origin off on her fingers, says: 'Poland, Nova Scotia, British, then it gets complicated: France on one side; Colombia, Spain, and Mexico on the other.'

There is no better example, at the moment, of this racial integration than the story of the United States' forty-fourth President. Barack Obama has described family get-togethers over Christmas taking on the appearance of a United Nations (UN) General Assembly meeting:

> As the child of a black man and a white woman, someone who was born in the racial melting pot of Hawaii, with a sister who's half Indonesian but who's usually mistaken for Mexican or Puerto Rican and a brother-in-law and niece of Chinese descent, with some blood relatives who resemble Margaret Thatcher and others who could pass for Bernie Mac, I've never had the option of restricting my loyalties on the basis of race, or measuring my worth on the basis of tribe.

He believes that part of America's genius lies in its ability to absorb newcomers, to forge a national identity out of the disparate lot that arrived on its shores.

There are, of course, other factors that contribute to a shared American identity. Some are deep and subtle, others more superficial. All seem to act, like the hand of Symilus in the mixing bowl, to merge diverse ingredients together.

Firstly – language. 'People have a duty to America to speak the language,' says Frank, born in Nazi Germany to a Jewish father and German mother who migrated to America to escape Hitler's regime. 'That is the price you pay, the coin you should pay, for moving here.' He worries about poor migrants from El Salvador who live in communities where no English is spoken or heard. He remembers how hard the German and Hungarian migrants of his childhood home – Brunswick, New Jersey – worked to conform to American standards of speech, behaviour and dress. He chuckles at the memory of his German-speaking cousins as they started producing Americanisms – parroting slang was a way of belonging.

Education is another mainspring. The principles were expressed – albeit in a blatant act of internal colonialism – by Thomas Jefferson Morgan, Commissioner for Indian Affairs, in 1888 when he rehearsed the fictional pleas of Indians begging to gain American identity through schooling:

> Our only hope is in your civilization, which we cannot adopt unless you give us your Bible, your spelling book,

your plow and your ax. Grant us these and teach us how to use them, and then we shall be like you.

That reference to the spelling book rings true, even today. There is a Cult of Spelling in the country, dating back to Benjamin Franklin's proposal for a public spelling contest in 1750. Spelling matches promote a standard pronunciation of words and, hence, a linguistic hegemony. They feature in Myla Goldberg's novel *Bee Season* (2001), about a Jewish girl from Pennsylvania with an extraordinary gift for spelling. The tradition is also celebrated in one of the most successful documentaries of all time: *Spellbound* (2003) follows the progress of eight children out of the 9,000,000 who participate each year in the National Spelling Bee Championship. Here we witness the principle of *e pluribus unum* harnessed and set to work: competitors include the daughter of a Mexican cow-hand who speaks no English (in fact, he is only ever seen lowing and hallooing at cattle); two children of middle-class migrants from India, now living in California and Florida; a black girl from the ghettoes of Washington, DC; a poor white girl from Pennsylvania; a farmer's son from Missouri; and a rich Jewish girl from Connecticut. This may be a far cry from the stories of Gold Rush pioneers resorting to knives over the spelling of *gneiss*, but the sentiment – and the social imperative – is the same.

For many first-generation Americans, progress through the educational system has provided a springboard for success as US citizens. Viet Dinh is an exemplar: in 1978, he was a ten-year-old refugee from Vietnam, washed up on a Malaysian beach. By 2002, he was assistant attorney general of the US, drafting the Patriot Act – the Justice Department's response to the terrorist attacks of 9/11. In between, he migrated to California, attended high school, became a leading law student at Harvard and worked as a clerk in the Supreme Court, before becoming professor of law at Georgetown University. Through the bamboo curtain of a strong Vietnamese accent you can hear him speak with pride at the honour of being an American.

Another formative American experience is the summer camp. This is an important rite of passage and many recall their initiation into the summer camp cabin with its own songs; ghost stories told around the fire; ordeals set by camp counsellors who imbue their young charges with American values; and the first kiss between young campers.

There are also the 'egg-white' festivals that bind the nation together. Giuseppe, an Italian barber who migrated to Washington, DC, from Abruzzo forty-four years ago, says that he still celebrates the old saints' days that meant so much to him in Italy. Yet he became an American, he said, by celebrating the Fourth of July and Thanksgiving. He prides himself on cutting the locks of Robert Mueller, director of the FBI; and now his sons have abandoned the sacred days of his forefathers and it is these American festivals that matter to them. Thanksgiving is of special significance, celebrating collaboration and commensality between the Pilgrim Fathers and the Native Americans. There is extraordinary power to the shared ritual of the nation's families consuming turkey together, regardless of whether the bird is free-range and oven-roasted or – as is the case of migrant communities throughout the country – the white meat comes pre-sliced and shrink-wrapped from the Wal-Mart sandwich counter, to be eaten by American-Chinese with stir-fried bamboo shoots, or by Mexican-Americans with black beans.

Then there is music and sport. Madeleine Albright, a Czech immigrant who became secretary of state in the Clinton administration, has described jazz as an embodiment of American diversity and freedom, becoming the symbol of democratic hope and opposition to communist tyranny during the Cold War. Different cities vie for bragging rights to be known as the nursery of jazz: the truth is less important here than the serial myth-making, since it sheds light on something that matters to Americans. New Orleans speaks of slaves gathering in Congo Square to dance to drumbeats from West African rites (where each spirit had his own, personalized, syncopated rhythm); of the brass bands accompanying Mardi Gras parades and funeral marches; of West African 'hollers'

J.K. Galbraith (the leading liberal economist who died in 2006, aged 97) was in no doubt that selling had become a formidable force in the United States by the mid-twentieth century. He wrote in *The Affluent Society* that 'many of the desires of the individual become so only as they are synthesized, elaborated and nurtured by advertising and salesmanship'. Advertising and sales were now some of the nation's most important and talented professions, boosted – in keeping with the pseudo-religious language associated with commerce – by President Woodrow Wilson when he addressed a salesmen's convention in Detroit in 1918:

Lift your eyes to the horizon of business with the inspiration of the thought that you are Americans and are meant to carry liberty and justice and the principles of humanity wherever you go, go out and sell goods that will make the world more comfortable and more happy and convert them to the principles of America.

There is a view that inherent value sells itself. This is encapsulated in the dictum, attributed to Ralph Waldo Emerson, that if you build a better mousetrap the world will beat a path to your door. In the doctrine of the free market, the salesman performs an ethical job ensuring that the consumer is equipped with information to make rational, efficient decisions.

However, boosting had been a prominent feature of life in the US for many years. A young English pioneer, Evelyn Hertslet, encountered the phenomenon shortly after she arrived in the Napa Valley in the 1850s. The record of her adventures in America can be scrutinized in the Reading Room of the Library of Congress (beneath the approving gaze of pale, powdered Commerce) where one discovers her surprise at the town's undertaker putting an advertisement in the local news-sheet: 'cholera is coming, so buy your coffins now, while stocks are plentiful and prices low!'

This anonymous undertaker unwittingly demonstrated the 'AIDA Rule' decades before it was expounded by E. St Elmo

Lewis – one of the founding fathers of the advertising industry. Lewis, who is memorialized in the 'Advertising Hall of Fame', cut his teeth as head of marketing for National Cash Register Company and Burroughs Adding Machine Company in the early years of the twentieth century. In 1900 he devised his rule: 'attract Attention, maintain Interest, create Desire, get Action'.

Another revered ancestor for the 'ad-men' is Helen Lansdowne Resor – renowned for her work as a copywriter with J. Walter Thompson, the agency that came to dominate the advertising industry in the twentieth century. Her style, which aped the look and layout of popular magazines, has been described as 'aesthetic and intuitive'. A typical Resor page would combine a picture with persuasive copy that contains arguments for buying the product and an offer of a free or cheap sample by mail. Her most famous advertisement – for Woodbury's Facial Soap in October 1921 – shows a handsome couple in evening dress, with the man pressing his chin to her cheek, and the headline 'A skin you love to touch'. It is credited as the first commercial to use sex appeal, with seven paragraphs of copy that told the reader:

> Your skin is changing every day! As the old skin dies, new skin forms in its place. *This is your opportunity.* By using the proper treatment you can keep this new skin so active that it cannot help taking on the greater loveliness you have longed for.

Fewer than 300,000 people are employed in the American advertising industry, but their work imposes itself on every individual in the land and they generate substantial revenue – $220 billion in 2005 (close to the revenue of America's powerful defence sector). Posters and billboards create a grand canyon of hype through which any journey takes us: our attention is drawn to the merits of this product and that service by messages plastered across once redundant surfaces or inserted into once open spaces. Billboards separate the traveller on the freeway from the natural world, as if the insurance policies, white goods or beauty products that they sell deserve our attention more than the prospect of forests and hills that lie behind them. The messages are repeated on the flanks of trailers, trucks and buses, and projected via posters, banners and multimedia fibre-optic screens at subway stops, airports, escalators, street corners and crossroads. The traveller will find no sanctuary in newspapers or magazines and, when they open their front door, they are bound to find a catalogue or similar mail-shot waiting for them. (Direct mail accounts for the biggest earner of all for the advertising industry, at some $55 billion per annum.)

The very commodities that people crave to own in their homes – radios, televisions and computers – act as channels for more advertisements. Upbeat voices urge us to eat cheesy snacks, rebundle our debts and sleep soundly on new mattresses. Cures are offered for flatulence, impotence, coronary disease and low energy levels (before the voice descends into monotonous overdrive to deliver the obligatory small print about unpalatable side-effects that all too often seem to induce low energy levels, coronary complications, impotence or flatulence).

Wealthier households pay to exclude the worst of the ads by procuring TV channels like Home Box Office. (They are like the elite in Orwell's *Nineteen Eighty-four* who number among their privileges the ability to turn off the machines that spout forth propaganda.) The majority must sit through banal, repetitive promos that play half-hour after half-hour, month in, month out, as if the mind was a stone on which the drip-drip-drip of marketing will ultimately make an impression. Ads for cars, trucks and fast food predominate. Offers of 'cash-back', together with promises of extended '0 per cent finance', must leave the buyer believing this truly is the American Dream – come home from the shops with a Honda Civic *and* more money in your pocket! Healthy hikers are seen driving their SUVs across deserts and up mountains suggesting that ownership of these 4x4 gas-guzzlers will unleash the elusive freedom that every American craves – to roam a wilderness that is, in fact, fenced in and picketed with 'No trespassers' signs. Fast-food ads emphasize the quantity and economy of the meals on offer, with nuclear families excited and fulfilled at the chance to consume super-size chicken nuggets at less than $1. A commercial on the cartoon channel has a child's voice declaring what might be a clause from the Manifesto of American Consumerism: 'It's every girl's right to change her shoes and her skirt again and again and again!' The ad – echoing the high-minded tone of Burger King, quoted above – promotes Happy Meals at McDonald's (whose 'golden arches' are branded on the built environment of every town in the country), where girls are tempted by a give-away plastic doll called Betty Spaghetti with different costumes to clip on.

The advertising industry is now turning to the internet, as the proportion of Americans with regular access to the world wide web has climbed to 72.5 per cent by the end of 2008. 'History shows that advertising ultimately follows the audience,' says Tom Hyland of Price Waterhouse's New Media Group. 'We believe advertising budgets will continue to shift more online.' Revenue from commercials on this new medium confirms this: it grew from $6 billion in 2002 to $23.4 billion in 2008.

Sport has become another pack-horse for advertisers. A commercial net enfolds the major events in American football, baseball, NASCAR races, tennis and golf. By 2009, advertising companies were paying $3 million to broadcast a thirty-second commercial during the Super Bowl Final on *Super Sunday* – the summit of the American Football season with almost 100 million domestic viewers. An hour's play is stretched to over three and a half hours, partly to accommodate all the commercial breaks. There are plenty of college kids who admit they are drawn to watch the tournament not for the sport, but for the spectacular new ads made especially for the occasion.

Companies also raise awareness through sponsorship of both sporting events and teams. They do so, for instance, in the stock car racing that is immensely popular with both TV audiences (coming second to American Football) and spectators. NASCAR races – named after the National Association for Stock Car Auto Racing that manages the sport – draw some of the biggest crowds, typically on a Sunday: more than 13 million people went to over a hundred races in 2004. Nextel Communications, the mobile phone company, is spending $75 million a year over ten years to get 'naming rights' for the flagship championship. The main sponsor for each of the forty-three teams will pay $10–15 million a year and altogether 1,100 companies – including 102 from the Fortune 500 – are backing the NASCAR phenomenon, inspired by the adage: 'Win on Sunday: Sell on Monday.'

One reason for building the link between product and sport is to develop a brand image – a novel concept developed by the advertising industry at the turn of the twentieth century. Early in America's history, a brand was the mark of ownership burned on to the hide of an animal with a hot iron (with darker connotations, beyond the realm of cowboys and ranches, of the branding of slaves and criminals). However, in the Temple of Trade a brand has become the symbolic embodiment of all information connected to a company, product or service, evoking in the consumer's mind the notion that a product has unique and appealing qualities. This phenomenon emerged in the burgeoning age of industrialization, when the producer was far removed from the consumer: the brand provided some compensation for the loss of trust that followed the disappearance of local production networks. Campbell's Soup, Coca-Cola, Juicy Fruit Gum, Aunt Jemima and Quaker Oats were some of the first products to be 'branded', carrying the reassurance of quality and helping to build 'brand loyalty'.

In the 1940s, manufacturers realized that consumers were developing psychological relationships with their brands (rather than the product), associating them with values such as youthfulness, fun or luxury. Furthermore, the association of an individual or lifestyle with a particular product could affect its brand image, although the first recorded instance of a film star having this effect had a negative impact on the marketplace: in 1934 the sight of a vest-less Clark Gable in *It Happened One Night* sent sales of vests plummeting – manufacturers of this undergarment had to await Marlon Brando's appearance in *On the Waterfront* (1954) to restore the balance. Today, there are marketing companies dedicated to product placement in films, television dramas and even computer games. The urban slang phrase 'Brand Slave' has been developed – seemingly oblivious to the sinister association between those two words – to describe someone who will only buy or wear clothes because of their brand (the Tommy Hilfiger flag, the Lacoste crocodile) regardless of value, taste or style.

Today, it is estimated that almost a fifth of Coca-Cola's market value is based on the 'familiarity and favourability' deriving from its brand. As with other major companies (such as General Electric, Microsoft and Wal-Mart), this value – a symbol of trust and faith that in pre-industrial societies might be invested in a deity or saint – is measured in tens of billions of dollars.

'Our life is brands,' Michael Shvo has asserted. This Israeli immigrant owned taxis before becoming reputedly one of New York City's biggest estate agents by incorporating brand into the mix. In 2006 he was promoting his transformation of the Chase Manhattan building in Pine St into the Armani/Casa whose apartments were equipped with products designed by the Italian fashion icon, Giorgio Armani. The launch of the sales campaign was timed to coincide with the payment of Wall Street's January bonuses and it was reported that one-third of the flats were snapped up within days for prices between $800,000 and $10 million. For some, Shvo came to personify Manhattan's real-estate bubble in the mid-2000s. However, he was still riding high in May 2009, combining bubbles and brands as he was reported to have sprayed $90,000 of Dom Perignon champagne over brunchers at Bagatelle's in the Meatpacking District of New York City.

Recently, the US's largest house-builder, KB Homes, has joined forces with Martha Stewart, the 'Queen of Homemaking' who has achieved celebrity through TV programmes and journals such as *Martha Stewart Living*. (Her star status barely wobbled when, in 2003, she was indicted on charges of securities fraud and obstruction of justice. She eventually served five months in Alderson Federal Prison Camp in West Virginia.) The houses are based on three of Stewart's New England homes, complete with Stewart's choice of interior decor and furniture and with concrete driveways stamped to resemble cobblestones. In early 2006, KB Homes completed the first of 650 houses, each costing $250,000–$500,000, on a site called Twin Lakes in the suburban community of Cary, North Carolina. Hundreds of buildings based on design-patterns associated with the 'domestic goddess' – 'Lily Pond', 'Dunemere', 'Skylands' and 'Katonah' – are now being sold by KB in Greater Los Angeles, Houston, Denver and Orlando Florida.

Bigger names – bigger even than Giorgio Armani and Martha Stewart – have lent their images to the branding industry. One might be forgiven for thinking that Saint Valentine and Saint Patrick have been enrolled into the American Advertising Federation. On St Patrick's Day we are expected to sprinkle powdered blarney stone on our corn flakes, if the salespeople are to be believed. One internet service provider tells its clients, 'You don't have to be Irish to get into the spirit of St Patrick's Day. Your eyes will be smiling after trying some touch o' green recipes or learning about shamrocks, leprechauns and Irish customs.' We are urged to enjoy the 'Luck o' the Irish' by clicking on links that lead to the 'all new St-Patricks-Day.com website dedicated to the Irish diaspora around the world', with the pages fringed with more commercials.

The festivals of Christmas, Thanksgiving and Halloween also provide emotional buoyancy to advertising campaigns: the themed commercials begin weeks before these special days, in a bid to inspire sales. Rites that were once heavily imbued with spiritual, patriotic or religious significance are now vehicles for promoting commodities. It was Marx who wrote of the revolutionary nature of capitalism: 'all fixed, fast-frozen relations, with their train of ancient and venerable prejudices and opinions, are swept away, all new-found ones become antiquated before they can ossify. All that is solid melts into air, all that is holy profaned.'

Any reflection on the state of marketing in the United States encounters a 'chicken and egg' conundrum. What came first: the purchase or the sale? There is more than enough evidence to suggest that Americans go out of their way to look for goods, rather as their forebears went out to hunt and gather. Those who doubt this should listen to the deafening footfall in the mall.

Consumer spending accounts for two-thirds of America's economic activity. The 2000 census revealed that 20 million people were employed in supporting this consumption through their work in the wholesale and retail trade (making it the largest industry in the country) and there are 20 feet of shelf-space per head in the United States (ten times the amount in Britain). The United States has led the world in the innovation of the shopping experience. The nation has invented new kinds of credit and currency (postal money orders, travellers' cheques, credit cards and instalment plans) and new forms of marketing (the department store, mail-order catalogues, the supermarket, the mall, outlet parks and internet trading).

Malls come in different shapes and sizes. Downtown, they range from an enclosed arcade to a multistorey complex with cinema, food outlets and underground car-park. In the suburbs, there are discreet crescents of terraced shops with dedicated car-parking. Out of town, they form an encircling eczema of 'outlet stores' and 'retail parks' – cavernous, insulated ware-houses with extravagant signs surrounded by acres of parking connected to four- or six-lane highways. When Mall of America of Minneapolis (the country's biggest mall with 4.2 million square feet of space) opened it was predicted to attract more people in the first year of business than the Grand Canyon.

It comes as no surprise, then, that contemporary artists have been inspired by this phenomenon: David Opdyke's sculpture USS Mall appears to be an aircraft carrier, until closer inspection reveals the hull of the ship to be rock and stone (as if sliced out of the earth); the deck is a car-park with tiny automobiles; and the superstructure is made up of outlet stores. Meanwhile, Barbara Kruger has explored in her work the slogan 'I shop therefore I am', and it is true that Americans spend an average of twelve hours a month in these emporia – more time than they devote to any activity other than sleeping, eating, working and watching television (where, of course, they ingest hours of commercials).

The day after Thanksgiving carries a particular weight: 'Black Friday' is so named because retailers believe this is when their accounts move out of 'the red'. Its dimensions are frequently measured out as if to demonstrate the nation's economic potency. Rumours will circulate of crowd-sizes in the malls which – in the Orient – would be associated with religious festivals in Mecca or on the Ganges: in 2002, for instance, it was said that over 600,000 people visited Potomac Mills, Virginia, in the first hour of trading. News channels report official sales figures collected by specialist companies like ShopperTrak (monitoring thousands of outlets) and special attention is paid to one emblematic company – Wal-Mart. The media reported Black Friday turnover for this chain amounting to $1.46 billion in 2002, rising to $1.52 billion in 2003. Sadly, in 2008 news channels reported a grimmer story, when a worker – Jdimytai Damour – was trampled to death by shoppers chanting 'push the doors down' as they stampeded across the threshold of a Wal-Mart store on Long Island. One witness described the crowd acting like savages: 'When they were saying they had to leave, that an employee got killed, people were yelling "I've been on line since yesterday morning!" They kept shopping.'

Wal-Mart is the biggest name in retail and in 2007–08 was competing with Microsoft and Exxon for the title of Biggest Company in the World (each with a market capitalization of between $250–300 billion). Sam Walton established his first shop in Rogers, Arkansas, in 1962; by 2008, his company had 4,100 stores across the US and the estate was growing at a rate of 10 per cent a year. Facts are frequently presented by the media to illustrate Wal-Mart's status:

- It is like a country in a country, with turnover comparable to the GDP of many sovereign nations (ranking ahead of Pakistan, for instance); group sales for 2007–08 were $374.5 billion, when profits rose to $12.73 billion.
- About 112 million shoppers pass through a Wal-Mart every week, spending, on average, $35 each; 80 per cent of all households visit Wal-Mart at least once a year.

- 8 per cent of all expenditure in US retail outlets (excluding spending on cars and car parts) goes through its cash registers, and it sells more than one in four of all shampoo bottles and nappies bought in the US.
- Wal-Mart's trade with China exceeds that of Russia or Australia, and its imports account for 10 per cent of the US trade deficit with China.
- It employs 1.4 million staff (out of a national workforce of 138 million): there as many Wal-Mart employees as there are US military personnel, or Estonians, or residents of Washington, DC, and Boston combined.

If Wal-Mart stores are truly temples of trade, their icon is the lemon-yellow smiley face that signifies salvation through price 'rollbacks' and 'every day low prices'. Sam Walton's philosophy was to compete aggressively on price in the sale of basic goods: 'Always Low Prices – Always' is its motto. Price and turnover dominate this mass retail industry and business schools make much of the techniques developed by Wal-Mart to optimize these. The company's obsessive drive to cut prices is said to save American consumers $80–100 billion a year.

However, the nation's shopper is not entirely in thrall to the cut-price store. Travelling through the country one encounters victories for the little retailer. In Taos, New Mexico, in 2003, for instance, citizens voted to turn down the chance for a Wal-Mart and cities like Annapolis, Maryland, and Santa Barbara, California, feature small shops opening on to the street in the European tradition. In a society as rich and variegated as the United States, there are outlets to suit all tastes and persuasions. For lovers of literature, there are havens like Square Books in Oxford, Mississippi, where visitors can take a volume, a coffee and a homemade cookie out on to the veranda to while away the hours, watched over by photographs of local authors William Faulkner and Eudora Welty. For collectors of ethnographic curiosities, there are the Indian crafts of Eagle Plume in the Colorado Rockies. Eastern Market, close to the Capitol in Washington, DC, provides shoppers with a traditional covered market where game (pheasant, duck, partridge, turtle-dove) is sold as well as farm-reared birds such as turkey and chicken. At a stall specializing in salamis and sausage, the mustachioed vendor speaks German to his clients and – around Christmas time – an old lady who might have stepped from the pages of a Charles Dickens novel sits by a brazier selling vegetables.

Boutiques range from traditional clothes shops to specialists in niche markets to purveyors of the twee and bizarre. In the gay enclave of Provincetown, the laws of gravity have been overturned by the dizzying levity of the *double entendre*: confectionary shops sell 'sexy sweets to pucker up to'; soap and perfume is for sale at Good Scents; Binky's Ice-Cream offers 'the Best Licks in Town'; and Board Stiff has clothes for men promoted by images of handsome models with well-filled boxers asleep on the shore. (In case we don't get the allusion, the pants are trimmed with the words 'B Stiff'.)

Pet-owners are lavish shoppers and there are emporia throughout the country dedicated to their needs and whims. They can buy costumes (clip-on devil's horns and mortar boards are particularly popular) and beauty products for their beloved creatures. Chains like Petco charge $50 to wash, trim and comb a dog, squeeze its glands and clip its nails; and a shop in Santa Barbara has sweetmeats arranged on the counter which dogs select by pointing their nose through the glass. Laney exemplifies the fusion of dog-love and commerce. She is the proprietor of a dog-walking service in Eastham, Cape Cod, and drives a car with 'The Pampered Paw' on its door. Her goal, she says, is to 'saturate Cape Cod'. Her pamphlet – blue card with black paw-prints dotted over it – contains a number of references from satisfied customers such as that of R. Ryan from Brewster: 'I went away for 10 days and Laney took care of both my toy poodles. It was a good feeling to know my little boys were well taken care of.'

Testimonials like this touch on what Americans themselves regard as an essential feature of their consumer society – customer service. Complaint is an essential element in an ethos which emphasizes the primacy of the customer (and appears to be another outcome – like the brand – of the loss of personal enduring relationships that are such a feature of the traditional marketplace). People regularly return goods they are dissatisfied with, expecting to be compensated. Liz, who managed the shop in National Geographic's headquarters, described the man who walked in with an atlas he had bought there, asking for a replacement because the spine was damaged. The problem, she pointed out, was that this was 2001 (two days after 9/11) and he had bought the book in 1957. She could not countenance a replacement since it was reasonable to expect some wear and tear after forty-four years! Her customer disagreed and threatened to write to the president of National Geographic unless he got satisfaction. Liz was delighted that she could give some service at last: 'Let me spell his name for you,' she said.

This disgruntled shopper might have been more at home in the network of second-hand shops that exist – like a shadowy underworld – to serve the penny-wise wealthy as well as the deserving poor. Washington, DC, has been described as a 'city of closet thrift-seekers', where socialites, judges, ambassadors and politicians hunt for bargains in consignment shops such as Secondi in Connecticut Avenue, Secondhand Rose in Wisconsin Avenue, and Once Is Not Enough in Macarthur Boulevard. Somewhere out there, you can probably buy pieces from the wardrobe of Nan Kempner, the New York socialite and dedicated *haute couture* shopper, who said memorably (in a line that deserves to be the motto of God & Mammon Partners Inc.): 'I want to be buried naked! I know there'll be a store where I'm going!'

With all this shopping, all that engorgement, something has to give. There are certain events that play an almost ritualistic part in the purging process, when consumers relieve themselves of acquisitions. In suburbs across the country, the weekend after Labor Day is a popular time for garage or yard sales (suitably aligned with Black Friday, so that the gorging can begin again a few weeks later). These sales are typically advertised in the immediate vicinity of the home, with a few handwritten fliers distributed by the children. But the news spreads far and wide – as if transmitted by the telegraph poles that carry the posters.

All manner of goods are available at knock-down prices, attracting bargain-hunters who crowd streets that are normally serene and orderly. There are 45 rpm records, a bread-maker without the instruction manual, diaper-bins, a long-shaft engine for a motor-boat, the glass lining to a vacuum flask, a cooker, books, toys and so on.

Then, at the end of a life well spent, there is the estate sale. This is, in essence, a super-sized yard sale. The same handwritten posters appear on street corners, though now the event may be organized by professionals (such as Diener Jewelers in Washington, DC). Buyers will walk through the door to hear how an old widow has passed on: 'She accumulated a huge amount of stuff,' the sales staff will say. 'She must have been a shopaholic. The house is crammed with stuff she never used. Her husband was a doctor. He earned a packet!'

Everything is for sale. Everything has a price. The estate sale, like the yard sale, is indeed one of those rare occasions when Washington, DC's social boundaries become porous: professionals from the immediate neighbourhood – white and middle-class – mix with African-Americans from the ghetto and car-loads of Chinese diplomats. An elderly gentleman addressed as a 'General' manhandles his acquisitions out of the house and loads them into a car. Other buyers wander through rooms full of furniture, clothes, knick-knacks, old golf clubs, rugs, crockery. 'If something hasn't got a label with a price on, you ask!' an assistant says. But most items are marked up, usually in the simplest terms: 'Tallboy', one label states bluntly. A frosted glass vase has a tag of $2,500: 'That's an art-glass work. Very popular. Look on the internet.' There is even a dressing-table with vanity mirror, carrying a message scrawled in capital letters with a felt-tip pen that seems to snub the pedantic prose of a Sotheby's catalogue: 'ME LOVE YOU LONG TIME IF YOU BUY ME.'

The consignment shop, the yard and estate sales, and now – in these days of the world wide web – eBay, represent links in a chain of exchange that runs through society and punctuates human existence – the American answer to the gnostic's 'Circle of Life'.

We have touched on the breadth of commerce in America in our review of the dominant position held by buying and selling in society. Now it is time to feel the quality.

In the middle of the twentieth century, J.K. Galbraith – in *The Affluent Society* – felt compelled to call on America to free itself from an idea that he regarded as the 'central problem of our lives': production. From the beginning, America has been a source, not a sink, for raw materials and commodities. The intention of the adventurer companies who set sail across the Atlantic was to produce. They were to harvest the New World for all the natural and mineral riches that it had to offer. As early as 1602, Bartholomew Gosnold, the Suffolk sea-captain credited with naming Cape Cod, had undertaken a voyage to 'Northern Virginia' and returned with a profitable cargo of fur, cedar and sassafras (a popular cure for syphilis at the time). In Jamestown, John Rolfe began to cultivate a ceremonial plant procured from the Indians. The first substantial cargo of tobacco amounted to 105 lbs, and exports rocketed, with 2,300 lbs in 1616 rising to 3,000,000 lbs by 1638. Tobacco became the only commodity not regulated or controlled by the English government, and the weed dominated the economy of tidewater Virginia and Maryland for centuries.

Further south, exports of indigo, rice, wheat, tobacco and cotton brought immense wealth to the plantation owners, although this was only made possible by that most egregious of imported goods – the slave. Further north, New England traded with markets as far afield as Arabia, China and Japan, creating the nation's first millionaires in the early nineteenth century in Salem; many of them resided in Chestnut Street – one of the finest manmade vistas in America, with handsome houses built with the fortunes accrued by sea-captains and their widows.

By the twentieth century, the United States was a manufacturing powerhouse and production was, indeed, the key indicator of national prowess. This was the era when branded 'consumer durables', 'convenience items' and 'comfort goods' spearheaded an American invasion of overseas markets. Galbraith blamed producers for generating synthetic demand. He likened American society to a squirrel in a cage racing to keep up with a wheel propelled by its own efforts. He argued that, 'If production creates the wants it seeks to satisfy, then the urgency of the wants can no longer be used to defend the urgency of this production.' There were more pressing needs that society was failing to address because of the way in which priorities were set: social housing, for instance, or the health and education of the poor.

In one sense, the United States of the twenty-first century has heeded Galbraith's advice. It has relinquished its dominant role as a producer, with the mantle passing to the tiger economies of Asia. However, the consumption continues and Americans seem to be proud of their capacity for acquisition. This is nothing new. When Tocqueville visited the country in 1831, he found that 'the desire of acquiring the good things of this world is the prevailing passion of the American people'. In 2003, President George W. Bush praised those attending a dinner to raise funds for his re-election by suggesting he was among 'the haves and the have mores'! A telling statistic was published in the *Financial Times* that same year: 19 per cent of the US population believe they are in the richest 1 per cent bracket of the country; a further 20 per cent believe they will eventually get there. This reveals the optimism and aspiration of the American people and how well off so many people feel.

It is no accident that American economists have developed a model called 'hedonic pricing' for better assessing the value of goods and services by accounting for all the benefit and value that accrues from a possession. We shall examine later the extent to which the pleasure principle at work here is establishing a culture of immediate gratification. It seems that the acquisition of goods and services does seem to serve a deeper, symbolic function: it helps to construct 'self' and provide 'security' in a society where there is confusion about identity and where the liberated citizen has to navigate through unpredictable waters. Brands have become 'personal philosophies', allowing the consumer to express and affirm their values, viewpoint and standing in the world. A comment by Michael Shvo is instructive here: he has said of the Wall Street traders who pay premium prices for an Armani/Casa apartment: 'It's the new money that really feels they want to be a part of something. It's the assurance of feeling like they belong.'

This insecurity about identity extends to self-conservation. Americans show excessive interest in restoring the body when it ails, but also in preserving and improving it. This may seem at odds with what Americans do with all other goods – use, dispose, replace. However, the body is the one thing they cannot easily dispense with, so they treat it the way that Europeans care for their chattels. Teeth, breasts, blood, heart and faces are all conserved. The importance of the smile is a case in point. Americans take no little pleasure in baring their whitened fangs at the state of European – and especially British – mouths (a running gag, for instance, in the Austin Powers films). It is no accident that the world's first dental school began in Baltimore in 1839, but dentistry really took off in the States after the Second World War. Dentists rank as some of the country's highest-paid professionals, with orthodontists ensuring that teeth are straight and that white enamel is used so that no unsightly fillings show.

A distinctive aspect of the American way of health is the practice of going directly to specialists. The doctor who is a 'general practitioner' continues to play a prominent part in the life of the Old World, providing continuity and cohesion in the most broken of communities – a source of ritual healing in societies bereft of magicians and ministers. In the US, it is far more common for the customer to self-diagnose and then call upon the services of a cardiac, skin or liver specialist. This reveals something about how Americans regard the body – as a collection of disparate parts or goods rather than a holistic whole. The mind represents one such product that might merit a workout or more remedial treatment: hence the prominent role that the 'shrink' has to play in the lives of many.

The luxury of cosmetic surgery is gaining popularity in the United States. A familiar sight at the smarter cosmopolitan parties is the line-free sheen on the faces of older women who direct their taut grins towards the bee-sting lips and silicone breasts of their ex-husbands' new 'trophy wives'. The men, more likely, will be members of the 'zipper club', having had open heart surgery to replace a valve or bypass some veins; they may have had a stent inserted to open a blocked artery, or they may simply be on statins to reduce the 'bad' cholesterol and increase the 'good'.

A procedure involving botox, implants and a chin-tuck is one thing, but a procedure that relies on the lucrative but illegal trade in body parts is something else. In his 1979 film, *Clonus*, Robert S. Fiveson painted a macabre picture of the future where clones (thinking, feeling human beings) are created and matured for the sole purpose of being harvested to replenish and revitalize their 'sponsors': they live in a colony and a select few win a lottery to go to a promised land called 'America'. (Incidentally, the director was reported to be considering a lawsuit against the makers of *The Island*, a 2005 blockbuster with a similar theme. One film about the horrors of cloning would appear to have been, itself, cloned!)

As yet, the dystopian vision of *Clonus* may be a fantasy, but the United States is already becoming the world's trade centre for human 'egg donation'. The Government's Center for Disease Control and Prevention has tracked a 60 per cent surge in the use of donor eggs, from 10,389 in 2000 to 16,976 in 2006. (Stem-cell research, still in its infancy, is expected to add to demand for donor eggs.) Donors undergo three weeks of hormone injections followed by a surgical procedure to remove some fifteen eggs from their ovaries. The standard fee – described as compensation for the donor's time, effort and discomfort – ranges from $3,000 in the countryside to $8,000 in New York. However, prices skyrocket for special requests: it has been reported that an advert posted in campus newspapers at Ivy League universities in 1999 offered $50,000 for the egg of a woman with top test scores who was at least 5ft 10in. tall; more recently, a full-page spread in Stanford University's student newspaper promised $100,000 to a Caucasian woman under thirty 'with proven college-level athletic ability'. There are now 'egg brokers' who will add to the base fee by $500 if a previous donation has resulted in a pregnancy or $250 if the donor gets good grades at university.

There is also a macabre and illegal trade in organs of the dead. Commerce has made a commodity out of our mortal remains. In December 2005, British sensibilities were bruised when news broke of the theft of the journalist and broadcaster Alistair Cooke's cancerous bones, hours before his cremation. There is a grim irony to this treatment of Cooke, whose weekly *Letter from America* on the BBC gained iconic status for British listeners over many decades. He suffered a surprisingly common American crime – one of hundreds of corpses illegally plundered for profit in the United States' organ transplant and body tissue industry. The ensuing investigation by the Brooklyn District Attorney centred on a New York undertaker and the manager of a body-tissue processing company, amid allegations that they harvested bones, veins, skin, heart valves and other body parts from corpses before selling them on to unwitting and reputable surgical transplant companies. The body of one woman, exhumed in the investigation, had plastic plumbing tubes put under her shroud instead of legs.

There is even a market for virtual bodies. The internet hosts a number of American-created make-believe worlds within which users can operate through the medium of a computer-generated avatar. These avatars gain in value as their skills develop over time, and they can be traded in online markets. An avatar's rank (based on overall competence) is by far the most marketable attribute, but other characteristics that affect price include gender and class (e.g. being a wizard rather than warrior).

This is a society that celebrates immediate, rather than deferred, gratification. However, there are unintended consequences as technology and market forces enable desires to be satisfied ever more quickly and cheaply. The drive to bring down the price of Levi-Strauss jeans has led to the closure of factories in the United States, but clothes that cost half what they used to deteriorate faster, lasting no more than five years compared with the fifteen-year life of the originals. Commerce has adapted to the changing needs of a society that no longer values long-lasting goods – the fashion will pass on well before those flared trousers do. In the same way, there is little point in building houses, or creating their interior décor, to endure since Americans value what is new: it would be rare to find a kitchen in middle-class America whose units outlived a pair of old-fashioned Levis!

There are claims that intellectual activity is affected by the pursuit of easy gratification. In the corridors of power, serious decisions are as likely to be taken on the basis of a PowerPoint presentation (the 'fast-food' medium of the hard-pressed bureaucrat) than an extensive policy paper; and Camille Paglia, professor of humanities and media studies at Pennsylvania's University of the Arts, has noted that interest in and patience with long, complex books and poems has diminished among college students in the US. The use of narcotics and other illegal stimulants fits with this model of the rise of easy gratification. Statistics published by the Drug Enforcement Agency show that adults aged 18–25 are particularly prone to using proscribed narcotics: in 2005, 28 per cent admitted using marijuana in the previous year, and 6.9 per cent admitted taking cocaine.

Meanwhile, appetite for some legal substances – salt, animal fats and, above all, sugar – is taking its toll on the nation's health. In 2006, for instance, the Institute of Medicine estimated that 33 per cent of US children are at risk of obesity and in 2007 the Federal Trade Commission released a report that was not unrelated: half of the ads for junk food, sugary cereals and soft drinks are on children's programmes.

American consumerism is also anathema to conservation. Sixty years ago, Geoffrey Gorer wrote of the disastrous consequences of the American attitude to land and its products: 'the vegetable world is spoken of and treated as though it were a mineral world'. Crops were extracted, land was mined and wood was extricated until the vein was exhausted. Gorer's concern was with a particular phenomenon of his era – the dust-bowl. At the dawn of the twenty-first century, ours must be with the globe, with the carbon emissions generated through the production and transportation of goods.

This danger was powerfully and awfully illustrated in the events that unfolded around New Orleans on 1 September 2005. It is of passing interest that 62 per cent – by value – of all consumer goods sold in the United States flow through the port of New Orleans; the thirteen 'South Louisiana Ports' on the Mississippi River alone handle 290 million tons of cargo a year. The links between this activity and global warming are attenuated and complex: those who sow the wind will not necessarily reap the whirlwind. Nevertheless, as Labor Day 2005 approached, the sea-temperature off the Gulf Coast reached 30°C (86°F), and this was the engine that drove Hurricane Katrina into Mississippi and Louisiana, leaving more than 2.3 million homes without electricity, and towns like Biloxi and Gulfport, to the east of New Orleans, wiped from the map.

Those who could do so had evacuated the area before the storm struck, leaving behind an impoverished, mainly black, underclass numbering tens of thousands. People sought shelter, paradoxically, in the city's two centres of entertainment and commerce – the Superdome and Convention Center. Here, it was said, they were dying of hunger and dehydration, but armed gangs were spotted when helicopters tried to bring aid and pilots refused to touch down. These gangs, it seemed, were intent on living the American Dream, only this retail therapy was enacted in a Theatre of the Absurd against a backdrop designed by Hieronymus Bosch. Rioters with automatic weapons chased fire-fighters away from a burning shopping mall in Gretna. Gangs waded through flooded streets emptying shops of televisions, jewellery and guns. They emerged pushing the shop furniture itself – massive metal display cases that run on roller-ball wheels, packed with goods spoilt by the oily, polluted waters of the Mississippi (itself contaminated with the spill-off of much of America). Few of the looters had homes in which to install these commodities and there was no electricity to power them. This was postmodern shopping, deconstructed to the point where it became a form of performance art – an end in itself.

A vengeful anarchic mob had taken over the Big Easy within hours of the thin veneer of law and order being removed. Penny, an officer with NOPD who remained on duty throughout, says she knows to the minute when the moral fabric of the city fell apart. She spent the next week with a team of colleagues protecting hundreds of refugees who were holed up in a multistorey car-park, with police communications out and armed vandals trying to break in: 'By Day 7, we were almost out of food, drink and ammunition.'

The anger and appetite of the hurricane's wrath may have been engendered by the radiation of a consumer society, but in turn it exposed the anger and appetite of an underclass that knew no other values than those preached in the Temple of Trade. But Americans did not have to wait for Katrina to find this underclass. In 2000, 11.3 per cent of the population of the United States was living in poverty; by 2007, this had risen to 12.5 per cent, or 37 million people. In a society that lacks a free health service comparable to Britain's NHS, 47 million Americans are without health insurance coverage; and in May 2008, over 28 million people were registered with the Food Stamp Program (an indicator of hunger in the nation). There is no Wal-Mart or five-and-dime store to serve the needs of the underclass. They must rely on charity.

In a society where government is largely removed from the provision of social services, the philanthropist has a major contribution to make. Universities flourish as a result of donations from alumni, and billionaires like Bill Gates and Larry Ellison have created medical foundations that challenge the more conservative approach represented by the National Institutes of Health, and promote high-risk research.

Charitable giving is found at almost every level of society. According to *Giving USA*, the yearbook of philanthropy, contributions in 2005 amounted to over $260 billion (2.1 per cent of GDP – more, it should be acknowledged, than revenues from advertising). This included contributions of over $7 billion to three major natural disasters at home and abroad. Most households claim to have contributed to a charity, with the donors giving to churches and religious organizations (50 per cent), disaster relief organizations (47 per cent), community groups (35 per cent) and human service organizations (34 per cent). Despite the absence of major natural disasters in 2006, a record $295 billion was given in that year and 65 per cent of households with income less than $100,000 gave to charity.

There are tens of thousands of benevolent women and (to a lesser degree) men who have created their own charities. Given the dominance of commerce in this society, it is interesting to see how many of the great public art collections around the country were assembled not by aristocrats or manufacturers, but by shopkeepers or tradesmen or – tellingly – by their daughters. This is the case, for instance, in Salem (the Peabody Essex Museum), Boston (where Isabella Stewart Gardner's father made his fortune in the Irish linen trade), Baltimore (with its collection by the Cone sisters, whose fortune came from grocery and textiles) and Richmond, Virginia (the Lewis family). The Bartlett family acquired their wealth through a hardware store that flourished in Chicago in the nineteenth century: Frederic Clay Bartlett endowed the city's Institute of Art with glorious Impressionist works. His sister, Maie Bartlett Heard, founded the Heard Museum in Phoenix, Arizona, in 1926, and Florence Dibell Bartlett founded the Museum of International Folk Art in Santa Fe, New Mexico, in 1953. The trend continues today with Alice Walton (whose personal Wal-Mart fortune is valued at $18 billion) supporting the new Crystal Bridges Museum in Bentonville, Arkansas; the museum, designed by Moshe Safdie, will focus on American painting and Native American art when it opens in 2010–11.

Philanthropy has given the United States so much more. The

Yellowstone and Acadia National Parks, the world-class exhibits of the Smithsonian Institution and the high-quality broadcasts of National Public Radio have all been 'made possible' through private donations. Yet, to the jaundiced eye of the anthropologist tutored in rites of conspicuous consumption (like the *potlatch* of the Haida Indians in the Pacific Northwest), charity can all too easily appear as another form of image-building, especially when public display is a prominent feature. Philanthropy will, for instance, procure for the more extravagant donor – who allows his or her name to be associated with acts of tax-efficient generosity – a place on the 'Washington Social List', gaining privileged access to the rich and powerful in countless events through the year (private parties, fundraisers, balls, galas, art openings, book launches and movie premieres).

In a society that claims to be classless, it is also instructive to observe how often a public 'pecking order' is used to rank benefactors. Take, for instance, the annual rodeo organized by the Snowmass Western Heritage Association in Colorado which badges its benefactors according to size of donation: Rancher – $15,000; Marshal – $10,000; Buckaroo – $5,000; Cowboy – $2,500; Wrangler – $1,000; and Posse – $500. The Aspen Festival, nearby, operates with rather more gravitas but applies a similar scheme: Premier Associates – $25,000; Associates – $10,000; Benefactors – $6,000; Patrons – $3,000; Sustainers – $1,500; Affiliates – $500; Friends – $250; Contributors – $100; and Subscribers – $50.

A powerful driver behind the compulsion to consume is the need for identity and status in a society that offers little of either. However, there may be other factors to be taken into account. Poet Cole Swensen attributes consumerism to a need that is, she believes, peculiar to Americans – the need to act: 'It is the act of buying that matters, not the acquisition.' Bill Bryson, in *Made in America*, analyses the demographics of the mid-twentieth century (1946–60) when the US population rose by 40 per cent and the number of teenagers grew by 100 per cent. In the mid-1950s, 16.5 million teenagers had $10 billion to spend, buying 9 per cent of all new cars, 40 per cent of all radios, records and cameras, and over 50 per cent of movie tickets. Many features of contemporary American culture and mores, then, seem to have formed in this hormonal crucible of adolescent extravagance and exuberance.

There is also the collective memory of periods of privation. Each year, at Thanksgiving, schoolchildren re-enact the story of hungry Pilgrims rescued by Indians. The 'Starving Time' of 1609–10 is especially emblematic, with a population of 500 Virginia colonists reduced to sixty survivors, many of whom were described as 'crazed for want of food', digging up graves to consume corpses and eating human excrement. Things were not much better in 1623, when Richard Frethorne wrote, in a pitiful letter home to his parents from Jamestown, Virginia: 'And when we are sick there is nothing to comfort us; for since I came out of the ship I never ate anything but peas, and loblollie (that is, water gruel).'

As late as 1739, George Whitefield was collecting supplies in London to take to a thousand needy souls who represented the population of a fledgling colony called Georgia. His cargo contained necessities to survive in the sandy scrubland of Savannah. This catalogue of aid to America is worth setting out, to understand the level of privation in the land at that time:

> Stockings, shoes, caps & hats; canvas breeches, striped flannel waistcoats, handkerchiefs, tapes, laces, buttons; paper, quills, sealing wax, copybooks, pencils, tin pots, tinder boxes, ink-pots & ink-horns, corks & corkscrews, knives, gunflints & gunpowder, shot, scissors, buckles, combs, spoons, porringers, claw hammers, nails, gouges, gimblets, axes, files, chisels, planes, hatchets, saws, shovels, spades, locks, hinges, fishing tackle; butter, cheese, lemons, barrels of raisins, hogsheads of white wine, cinnamon, sugar, brimstone, cloves, mustard, pepper, oatmeal, oranges, potatoes, sage & onions.

To the present day, of course, some migrants come to the United States seeking refuge from famine, pogroms and poverty in the Old World. Meanwhile, Americans have not forgotten the profound impact that the Great Depression – lasting for at least a decade from 1929 – made on the lives of their parents and grandparents, when 25 per cent of the workforce (15 million) became unemployed and pandemonium broke out on the trading floor of the New York Stock Exchange on 'Black Tuesday', 29 October 1929.

The United States has travelled a bumpy, uneven road from famine to feast – from the ordeal of the 'Starving Time' to an era when starvation diets are pushed as a way of managing weight and reducing obesity. In the process, commerce – the selling and buying of goods and services – has come to dominate American culture. It is deeply engrained, today, into the habits, practice and fabric of American life. Commerce is the defining American cultural construct, providing imagery that saturates everyday dialogue. Commerce is commonplace, a feature of the quotidian world, where money – as the media mogul Ted Turner has said – 'is how we keep score'.

Yet there is something about the scale, the all-encompassing presence, the dominance of that invisible market force, that adds another dimension to the way people think and feel about it. It is a spiritual force: it is a calling and evokes devotion. Consumerism in America is not just business – it is belief, and it is hard-wired into the nation's value system. For most Americans, this is one of the ways in which they define themselves. If pressed to explain, they will typically refer to the line that Thomas Jefferson inserted in the Constitution. Everyone knows about 'the pursuit of happiness' since who could be happier than those who can gratify their wishes, desires and appetites? There are, of course, citizens who eschew materialism, advocating a self-denying lifestyle where enlightenment is achieved through literature, music, or the call of the wild. However, American fulfilment rarely flows from the sort of purification that comes with an ascetic religious tradition; fulfilment comes literally through filling up.

The anthropologists Mary Douglas and Baron Isherwood remind us that 'Overconsumption is more serious and more complicated than personal obesity, and moral indignation is not enough for understanding it.' People buy goods for material and psychic welfare, and for display; but goods also act as a form of metaphorical reasoning: 'Goods are neutral, their uses are social; they can be used as fences or bridges.' Consumption makes categories of culture both visible and stable.

However, the beliefs and practices pursued within America's Temple of Trade are not without consequences. Those looking to benefit from what Émile Zola termed the 'democratization of luxury' submit to a demanding work ethic that puts pressure on family values: those in work are employed 395 more hours a year than the British (a fact cited by apologists for each nation to demonstrate superiority over the other). The consumerist creed of an ownership society engenders a candy-floss culture, dominated by the drive for instant, but insubstantial, gratification. The fall-out from this includes obesity, debt, poverty and pollution.

The spirit of consumerism – aerated by the Jeffersonian mandate to pursue 'happiness' – falls like kerosene on the torch of liberty. While the ensuing conflagration will warm and enlighten many, it must scorch and blind countless others.

CHAPTER THREE

Trick or Treat – On Belief

America is self-consciously modernistic in its outlook, with its face set firmly towards an infinite future. However, on the last night of October each year, one ceremony in the nation's festal calendar recalls the timeless rites of pre-modern societies.

There is an early premonition weeks before, with homes across the country undergoing a ritual make-over. This may be quite simple, with the threshold decked out with little more than a bale of straw, a sheaf of corn and the ubiquitous pumpkin carved into a grinning jack-o'-lantern – its tangerine hue reflecting the changing colours of fall. Mock gravestones appear on lawns, carrying gloomy inscriptions ('Here Lies Jack', 'Dying to Meet You', 'I Told You I Was Sick'). Skeletons hang from windows, witches appear to fly through trees and richer households may install elaborate displays of deep blue or purple lights that flicker mysteriously.

Halloween is one of those egg-white occasions that unite the country: it covers the cracks between ethnic and class divisions, and binds together the generations. Mardi Gras may hold a special place in New Orleans, but this is the closest the whole nation comes to carnival, or the Saturnalia of Ancient Rome. On the night, as darkness falls, the roads of the nation fill with small children dressed as witches and demons (led in crocodile-file by attentive parents) or packs of teenagers, boisterous in their disguises. Colleges put on costume parties; hotels and clubs arrange balls; downtown bars and restaurants run themed events; and Manhattan is one of many cities and boroughs to organize a Halloween Parade.

The festival has come to be associated – first and foremost – with the secular age of American consumerism. 'Halloween is all about scaring grown-ups so they give you sweets,' kids hear on a festive episode of *Rugrats*, and this is a version of the lesson their parents learnt from Disney's *Trick or Treat* (1952) when Huey, Dewey and Louie tried to shame Donald Duck into giving them candy with the help of Witch Hazel.

Not only does Halloween facilitate the ingestion of vast quantities of candy, but it also involves extensive expenditure on costumes and decorations. Halloween ranks as the second festival of the nation's calendar in terms of consumer spending. Polling data show that in this first decade of the twenty-first century, 80 per cent of adults hand out sweets and 93 per cent of children go out to deliver the doorstep challenge 'Trick or treat!' In 2008, the National Retail Federation found that the average American planned to spend $66.54 on the holiday and total Halloween spending was estimated to reach $5.77 billion.

However, this event is more than a children's sugar-fest and another chance to party. It is linked to two old Christian festivals: All Saints is still a Holy Day of Obligation in the Roman Catholic calendar and All Souls (or 'All Hallows' – hence All Hallows Eve or *Halloween*) was traditionally the occasion when the faithful prayed for the dead. In Washington, DC, a United Methodist Minister tells his congregation that sweets should be collected to commemorate the lives of the departed and especially the souls of dead relatives. The Hispanic communities of the southwestern states can be found celebrating the 'Day of the Dead' and in southern California, for instance, Roman Catholic priests ceremonially bless the Halloween costumes to be worn in that pageant.

There is another layer to Halloween, connected to a darker heritage. Many churchmen reject or condemn the festival for saluting – even celebrating – the presence of evil in the world. They point to its roots in the pre-Christian fire festival of *Samhain*. The Celts believed that on this night the dead revisited the mortal world, so they lit bonfires to ward off evil spirits. This image of Halloween feeds the fear that evil lurks around the corner: the manicured lawns and white picket-fences of suburbia could mask a minatory, Gothic underworld. One evangelical pastor told his flock in Washington, DC, in 2003, 'The festival of Halloween is beyond redemption.' He described the Druid feast, where householders waited in trepidation for a knock on the door from priests requesting food: one of those who answered the door would be selected for ritual sacrifice by disembowelling on the capstone of the Neolithic tombs.

This remains a special night for the Church of Satan and the Wicca (or witchcraft) cult. They call it 'Devil's Night' in Detroit – a city that has suffered decades of economic deprivation and racial tensions – where a favoured activity is the torching of abandoned buildings. Up to 800 buildings would burn each Halloween in the 1980s; by 2007, the figure stood at around 150 (thanks to a 'youth curfew' imposed by the city authorities, who also deploy tens of thousands of volunteers to patrol the neighbourhoods). At the other end of the social spectrum, the Stanley Hotel in the Rockies became notorious for its Halloween Ball, inspiring Stephen King's novel, *The Shining* (1977); the season closes with this ball, and when a psychic was recently employed to report for the local radio station on the big night, she left before the end, saying, 'I've never known so many spirits in one place! I am never going back there again.'

Many ministers rail against the demons, devils, witches, zombies and tormented ghosts who parade – in the company of Frankenstein's monster, Fester, Morticia, and Cruella de Vil – through the city blocks, suburbs, main streets and prairie trails of the nation. The American Tract Society, publisher of religious pamphlets since 1825, sells almost 3 million 'Halloween outreach' items a year, for handing out to unsuspecting trick-or-treaters when they knock at a Christian's door – a righteous equivalent to those chocolate-coated sprouts that tricksters hand out to fool their callers! Wayne Braudrick, senior pastor of Frisco Bible Church near Dallas, Texas, urges his congregation to 'stay home on Halloween and wait by the door! I believe we are recapturing the holiday for the Lord.'

This militant language suggests that Halloween has become a theatre of operations in the 'culture war' – that metaphorical crack that has appeared on the surface of America's Liberty Bell in recent years. Although the term is used to describe the polarized views of entrenched Republicans and Democrats, it is more commonly perceived as a division between the religious faithful and liberal sceptics. This theme gained traction in the closing years of George W. Bush's presidency, when Dan Gilgoff published *The Jesus Machine* (2007), arguing that evangelical America was 'winning the Culture War'. In 2008, Paul Auster published a novel – *Man in the Dark* – that depicted a parallel universe where the Twin Towers still stood, but where cultural divisions had led the nation into a second civil war.

Despite the election of an emollient Barack Obama, attention is still paid to these divisions and they were emblemized at the end of the first decade of the twenty-first century by emotive arguments about abortion laws and the legalization of same-sex marriage. However, we have to avoid the temptation to descend into caricature here, contrasting the born-again evangelical from the rural Midwest with the East Coast urbanite watching *Sex in the City*. America's metaphysical life is more complicated, more nuanced and more profound than this. The numinous and the sacred are given expression in the mundane fabric of everyday life. We can observe, for instance, the spiritual depth and life-enhancing energy of African-American gospel music or the enlightened relationship between the faith of American Jews and their patronage of fine art and music. We can stand in awe at the humbling display of loving-kindness shown by the Amish of Nickel Mines, Pennsylvania, publicly forgiving the homicidal maniac who slaughtered their daughters before ending his own life in the classroom that he had transformed into an abattoir. We can witness, across the nation, thousands of voluntary associations pursuing benevolent, charitable and spiritual goals: groups like the Greater Pittsburgh Community Food Bank whose 11,000 volunteers distribute 1,000 tons of food through food pantries and soup kitchens to 120,000 people in south-western Pennsylvania.

are subject to non-competitive appointments. It is the norm for the political affiliation of each appointment – especially at state and federal level – to be declared, and although there is an occasional 'independent', the majority will belong to either the 39 million membership of the Democratic Party or the 30 million membership of the Republican Party.

Americans are familiar with periodic revelations about the corruption of local politicians at town, municipal and state level. The nation was shaken, for instance, in December 2008 by news that the governor of Illinois, Rod Blagojevich, had been arrested by the FBI for trying to sell the Senate seat vacated by Barack Obama. Over 1,000 officials and businessmen have been convicted of corruption in Illinois since the 1970s, including three former governors. Illinoisans will point out that surveys show other states – notably Louisiana – are even more corrupt, but they also recognize that the state operates unusual rules for managing the bankrolling of political campaigns, which allow unlimited direct corporate contributions to politicians' campaign funds.

The phenomenon of 'earmarks' – condemned so vociferously by President Bush in his speech at the semiconductor factory – is seen as the ultimate manifestation of political power-broking. At its crudest, a legislator intervenes in the process of distributing federal funds by shoe-horning money into projects that will promote either favoured interest-groups or their own personal standing within their constituency. There is no doubt that earmarks can be used for corrupt purposes: the case of Randall Harold Cunningham, known as Randy 'Duke', represents the most blatant example of this in the first decade of the twenty-first century. He represented California's 50th District (in San Diego) as a Republican member of the House of Representatives from 1991 to 2005. In March 2006, this heroic 'flying ace' from the Vietnam War was sentenced to over eight years in prison after he pleaded guilty to accepting at least $2.4 million in bribes and to federal charges of conspiracy to commit bribery, mail fraud, wire fraud and tax evasion. This is the longest prison sentence ever given to a congressman for bribery.

A notable piece of evidence was the so-called 'bribery menu' where Cunningham had set out – on a sheet of congressional stationery – how much he expected in kickbacks from his co-conspirators in the defence sector for earmarks pushed through Congress: he wanted a yacht worth $140,000 for the first $16 million in government contracts and $50,000 for each additional million thereafter. Cunningham was well placed to influence federal expenditure as a member of the House Appropriations and Intelligence Committees.

The Office of Management and Budget now tries to keep track of earmarks, maintaining a website that allows the 'pork-barrel' element of Bills to be scrutinized. In 2005, for instance, 13,492 earmarks were registered in appropriations bills, totalling almost $19 billion; in 2008, this fell to 11,524 earmarks totalling $16.5 billion. A further 6,335 multi-year earmarks were linked to Authorization Bills at that time, amounting to over $23 billion. Conservatively, the annual 'pork-barrel' expenditure between 2000 and 2009 amounted to $20 billion; the equivalent to the annual Gross Domestic Product of two countries too often associated with wholesale brigandry and corruption – Albania and Georgia.

Public debate in the US focuses on the more absurd or egregious examples of earmarks, such as the 'Iowa Rainforest' (sponsored by Senator Charles Grassley) or Alaska's 'Bridges to Nowhere' (promoted by Senator Ted Stevens and Representative Don Young). However, to the neutral observer, most earmarks appear worthy, even innocuous, with municipal authorities or academic research institutes receiving funds to take forward work that can benefit local communities or society at large. The following list – drawn from the 2005 crop – illustrates the range:

- $400,000 to improve University Drive, Macomb, Illinois;
- $10 million for the reconstruction and rehabilitation of the intersection of K-18 and 12th Street interchange in Riley County, Kansas;
- $200,000 for Streetscape-Cordele, Georgia;
- $15 million for New York Department of Transportation to

purchase three ferries and establish system for ferry service
from Rockaway Peninsula to Manhattan;

- Spin Electronics Consortia led by Arizona State University to
  receive $16.2 million to develop a means to significantly
  increase the density of solid state magnetic storage using novel
  packaging, spin momentum transfer and novel spin transport
  effects;
- Minot Air-Force Base, North Dakota, to receive $8.9 million
  to add/alter Dock 1 to multi-purpose hangar;
- Southern Methodist University in Texas to receive $990,000 to
  develop a multi-fabrication manufacturing technology for
  NASA;
- Balcones Canyonlands National Wildlife Refuge in Texas to
  receive $487,000 for acquiring land;
- $800,000 for the acquisition of land along CA 86 at the Desert
  Cahuilla Prehistoric Site, Imperial County, 'for environmental
  mitigation related to reducing wildlife mortality while
  maintaining habitat connectivity'.

Only occasionally, an entry might encourage those of a
suspicious mien to raise a sceptical eyebrow. However, these are
also acts of conspicuous consumption that demonstrate and
reinforce the political prowess of their sponsors: they become a
source of civic pride and inject funds into the local economy. It is
often argued that this is democracy in action, with effective
politicians bringing material benefits to their constituency.
Nevertheless, interest groups distort local, national and global
markets, undermining the image of an efficient, innovative
American private sector. Rice production is a good example. The
US domestic rice market was saturated long ago, so US rice farmers
export around half their output. However, a paper presented to a
UN conference in 2004 showed that American rice cost $331 per
ton to produce, compared to $70 for Thailand and $79 for
Vietnam. In 2002–06, government subsidies made up a remarkable
39 per cent of US rice farmers' total income, thanks – in no small
part – to the efforts of the American Farm Bureau that has spent
approximately $8 million a year on lobbying in this period.

The 'lobbyist' plays a key role in the process of bargaining between interest-groups and power-blocs – they call it 'pulling and hauling'. There is thought to be a revolving door between Capitol Hill, the Federal Triangle and K Street (where many lobbyists are located): those who have worked as staffers for congressmen, senators and senior figures in the administration take their network and experience to serve new masters in K Street. More than 13,000 lobbyists work in Washington, DC, outnumbering law-makers by 24 to 1; prominent interest-groups involved in hiring their services include the National Rifle Association, the Petroleum Institute, the Aerospace Industries Association, the Association of Realtors, Health Insurance Plans, the Alliance of Automobile Manufacturers and even the Edison Electric Institute. These organizations, and hundreds of others, have substantial resources at their disposal. In July 2005, for instance, the Center for Public Integrity reported that the pharmaceutical industry had spent almost $800 million promoting its interests over the previous seven years ($675 million on lobbying; $87 million on campaign donations to federal candidates and political parties; and $10 million given to advocacy groups). During this same period, congress and government agencies are said to have weakened federal oversight of the industry, strengthening patent protections, granting tax credits and generally protecting the industry's interests at home and abroad.

Many of the country's established companies have their own corporate lobbyists – they are regarded as a forceful source of influence in the capital, working to ensure corporate interests are taken into account by law-makers. League tables of leading lobbyists emerge periodically: on 27 April 2005, for instance, names listed by the congressional newspaper *The Hill* included the representatives of Citigroup, General Motors, Boeing, Microsoft and Ford. Brian Dailey of Lockheed Martin was – in an example of the 'revolving door' – formerly employed on the White House's National Space Council and the Senate Armed Services Committee. During the 2008 presidential election, Barack Obama vowed that 'lobbyists won't find a job in my

White House', but it has been impossible to make good on this promise: by May 2009, 30 out of 267 senior officials in the Obama administration had lobbied in the previous five years, including a Treasury chief of staff who represented Goldman Sachs and a deputy secretary of defense who worked for Raytheon.

Public distaste for lobbyists is a manifestation of a broader disquiet about the potentially corrupting influence of 'big business'. There is a surprising antipathy to the establishment of business dynasties and the incorporation of wealth – as if this in itself represents an echo of the British monarchy that America rejected at the time of the Revolution. As early as the 1840s, Governor Francis R. Shunk of Pennsylvania attacked 'Corporations' for generating wealth by circumventing what he called 'the American law of distributions'. To avoid the creation of an aristocracy, Shunk argued, the founders of the republic had abolished laws of primogeniture and entail, with all descendants receiving an equal portion of any inheritance. Under American intestacy laws, he told his state legislature in 1848, 'all the property of the commonwealth is . . . from time to time divided and put into circulation, the largest accumulations, by the most fortunate men, yield to the resistless influence of our system of distribution'. Corporations, much to his chagrin, had taken on the guise of artificial persons who never died, holding and accumulating property perpetually.

This antipathy to dynastic wealth is aired by contemporary opinion-formers such as Irwin Stelzer (founder and president of National Economic Research Associates) who advocates a 100 per cent inheritance tax: if you believe in affirmative action, he says, you should level the playing field by ensuring that everyone starts from the same line. And Warren Buffett, chairman of Berkshire Hathaway and the second richest man in the world, has memorably argued that the elimination of estate tax leads to the command of the country's resources passing to people who did not earn anything: 'It's like choosing the 2020 Olympic team by picking the children of all the winners at the 2000 Games.'

According to Bernard Gover – an Anglo-American business-man who specializes in acquiring small companies – 'every owner of a mom-and-pop business wants to sell up and retire in Florida'. Unlike their British counterparts, they rarely have an interest in heritage – leaving a business to the next generation. This can reinforce the paradox: while entrepreneurs take their profits in pursuit of happiness in their twilight years, their businesses are acquired by large corporations run by 'company men' who are regarded as the antithesis to entrepreneurialism. The field is dominated – in a society which places immense trust in accreditation – by 'Masters of Business Administration' (MBAs). The MBA has become a rite of passage that initiates the successful graduate into a sort of mandarinate within the US's corporate universe, with 100,000 MBAs graduating each year. This confers grounding in the basics of business – accounting, quantitative analysis, economics, marketing and organizational behaviour. Inevitably, a number of 'Greek' societies exist for students in business, management and administration, including Beta Gamma Sigma (dating back to 1907) and Sigma Beta Delta (1986).

Another generic interest-group – and one dedicated to locking horns with 'management' – is the labour union. Membership has never exceeded 35 per cent of the labour force in the US and it has fallen from the high-tide mark of the 1930s to less than 15 per cent today. There continue to be sectors of the US economy – manufacturing, mining, construction, transportation and government – where organized worker-power is as entrenched as in the most unreconstructed of socialist republics, with tens of millions belonging to one or more unions.

The power of unions is still felt in the country. In the weeks after Labor Day 2007, for instance, there was a strike by 73,000 United Automobile Workers (UAW) union members at General Motors (GM) plants across the country after union leaders and company officials failed to reach an agreement on a new contract. This was the first national strike by the union against GM since 1970. 'It's about time the union stood up against the company and stood for the people,' said Sylvia Hill, who has worked for the company for thirty years and was manning a picket in Detroit. Soon after, the Teamsters – one of the largest unions in the land, with a membership of almost 1.5 million – voiced its support for the UAW strike: its 10,000 members would not cross the picket lines at GM factories. The Teamsters' president, James P. Hoffa, announced, 'Workers should not solely bear the brunt of decades of bad business decisions by GM management. By outsourcing good jobs and creating a growing environment of economic and job insecurity, GM has failed its workers and its customers.' A month later, in November 2007, the country learnt of the first strike in twenty years by the American Screenwriters' Guild, representing 12,000 script-writers. The immediate impact was felt on shows like NBC's *The Tonight Show with Jay Leno*, where comic one-liners are produced by a team of writers.

Neither the financial crisis nor Obama's election has muted the unions' *cris de coeur*. In May 2009, for instance, Los Angeles was facing a strike by teachers, while the American Guild of Musicians was threatening to close down the New York City Opera.

Benefits of union membership are simply summarized by Gina (not her real name), a young Italian-American woman working in a longshoreman's shed on Baltimore Docks. 'It's good money,' she says, 'thanks to unionized labor.' She belongs to Local 333 of the International Longshoremen's Association (ILA). The branch was formed in 1974 when a court ordered the (largely) all-white Local 829 to merge with Local 858 (represen-ting African-American cargo-handlers). She is twenty-two, born in Little Italy and has been working on the docks for three years: she got the job with the help of her father – as common a practice in the first decade of the twenty-first century as it was a century ago. (But Gina's gender and the fact that her foreman, Louis, is an African-American show that some things have changed.) The door over the office where Gina works carries a sign declaring 'Support your union' and once visitors have passed the threshold – looking for help in collecting freight, for instance – it is as if a Dickensian atavism or Kafkaesque dystopia has taken over the Land of the Free. The 'Local' manages the movement of goods on these wharfs and it wields its authority with the aloof indifference of inherited privilege. Louis scrutinizes every page of the sheaf of documents presented by the 'customer' before calling to Gina to take the visitor to fetch his goods. She sits by an electric fire with her feet on the desk pretending to be asleep. When he speaks, she asserts her independence by snoring loudly and melodramatically in the hope that the job will move elsewhere. When the boss persists, Gina stirs and rises slowly, as if out of a deep slumber.

There again, many in the ILA have been in a deep slumber. They have – according to the Department of Justice – allowed organized criminals to dominate the union's activities. Recent scandals have included embezzlement from the union, racketeering, extortion and payoffs, and a $400,000 contract fraud scheme from the ILA healthcare plan. In 2003, *The Wire* (the HBO series about the Baltimore police) gave a fictional account of this world, focusing on Frank Sobotka, secretary of the 'International Brotherhood of Stevedores: Local 1514', who is smuggling contraband to finance his political campaign to rejuvenate the docks.

In the public imagination, corruption is an entrenched feature of American unions. Harry – a financier who has run pension funds for labour unions – says, 'If the workers knew what their executives were up to, they would sack the lot of them!' Union corruption regularly features in the news: in August 2005 and June 2006, for instance, former officials working for the Washington Teachers' Union were found guilty of embezzling millions of dollars for their personal gain. James B. Dworkin, associate dean of Purdue University's Krannert Graduate School of Management and an expert on labour relations, defends the role of the union in US society. It provides a system of checks and balances, he argues, forcing management to act in a more enlightened manner towards employees: 'Without unions, management would enjoy the power to make all decisions on a unilateral basis. In a free society, that type of system won't work very long.'

However, Dworkin accepts that the public has a poor opinion of unions. The cause is not only the disruption caused by walk-outs and the periodic stories of corruption. It is also their restrictive practices that seem the antithesis of America's 'can-do' culture. Dan voices a commonly held opinion. He was raised in a small farming community in Nebraska. He did not go to college, working instead as a carpenter on different building-sites around the country – Colorado, Texas and Tennessee – but the lack of camaraderie among his fellow labourers drove him to leave for New Zealand: 'In the US, union rules kept strict demarcation lines between the trades.' For the aforementioned financier, Harry, the organizations are egoistical:

> My fund was obliged to employ unionized labor in any of its projects. But when developing a property in Chicago, we had two unions – the Carpenters and Painter/ Decorators – down tools because they couldn't agree as to which trade had the right to spackle and finish off the interior walls.

Time and time again, we see Americans bridling at the perceived inequity of interest-groups distorting the level surface of the playing field. 'Greek' and secret societies, politicians and lobbyists, big business and unions all come in for criticism. Ultimately, this web of competing interests is judged to corrupt and undermine the competence of government itself – a complaint that is frequently reflected in news headlines: 'Study shows public feels government is inefficient'; 'US health care expensive, inefficient'; 'Critics: US food-aid programs inefficient'; 'GAO criticizes Homeland Security's efforts to fulfill its mission'.

In recent years, a school of political science has emerged to explain why government decisions are so often unsatisfactory. The New Institutionalists argue that public bureaucracy is not designed to be effective given the American democratic process. Terry Moe, professor of political science at the University of

Minnesota, writes, 'Because interest-groups are out for themselves, and because legislators have electoral incentives to do their bidding, bureaucracy is built in a piecemeal fashion.'

In *Flawed by Design* (1999), Amy B. Zegart extended this analysis to the evolution of the Central Intelligence Agency, the Joint Chiefs of Staff, and the National Security Council: 'Anyone who has ever filed a tax return or stood in line at the Department of Motor Vehicles will tell you that government agencies are far from perfect.' She suggests Americans expect more when it comes to foreign affairs, where the stakes are higher, but this is not the case. Domestic and foreign policy agencies differ in fundamental ways, but they all arise from an American political system that hinders effective design.

Zegart argues that the rational desires of interest-groups, legislators and presidents lead to irrational agency structures. Frequent elections focused on districts provide a bias towards local rather than national interests. The separation of powers may limit the risk of a despotic president, but effective unilateral action by the executive is stifled. The president is the only elected official with an incentive to consider national concerns, but even the bureaucrats who serve him are likely to resist any executive order that threatens their own power-base. 'Like their domestic policy counterparts, American national security agencies are irrationally designed for rational reasons,' Zegart writes.

Anyone who pays close attention to the nation at dialogue with itself will discern a tension between the two value systems of innovation and vested interests. The lionization of the entrepreneur and inventor fits with the philosophy of individualism. Liberty has got legs and is exploring new frontiers. The current of opinion favours the innovator and innovation, judging the 'new' to be a distinctive part of the American character. Novelty is valued.

However, the positive, life-enhancing energy of innovation is contrasted with the enervating machinations of vested interests that channel power away from the many to the benefit of the few. Americans appear shocked to discover that resources and influence are transmitted along power-lines in the United States, no less than they were in the city-states of medieval Italy, the mud palaces of Yemen and the commissariats of the Soviet Union. There is something un-modern and un-American about the rites of Phi Beta Kappa, the pork-barrel antics of Congress, political patronage or the restrictive practices of unions. All of this leaves a sense of disappointment – of utopia deferred – that shows through the heat-haze of optimism that pervades the American Way. There is, in the words of the technicians working the production-line in Manassas, VA, a mismatch in the Lattice Constant.

Those who allow their ideals to be bruised by hard realities overlook the fact that a revolutionary feature of the American political process has been the democratization of power-blocs. Americans are a nation of joiners who have developed the largest collection of associations and corporations in the world. These voluntary groups give the many a chance to enjoy the benefits of a privileged minority. The levers of power are not restricted to the princes, bishops, landed gentry or burghers of the Old World. There are scores of established interest-groups: the farming lobby, labour unions and business corporations, not to mention women's groups, eco-warriors, gay-rights activists, hunting enthusiasts, etc. Each of these can cajole, lobby or pay those in local, state or federal authority in the hope that decisions and resources move in their favour. These opportunities are sustained by the rational, democratic principles of the American Revolution: separation of powers; regular elections; majority rule.

In *The Audacity of Hope* (2006), Barack Obama is clearsighted about the realities of having – as a politician – to make accommodation with interest-groups who can be a source not only of funds but also of the organization that is needed to win votes and achieve office. He also acknowledges the rich variety of 'special interests' occupying niches in the US's political ecosystem:

to my mind, there's a difference between a corporate lobby whose clout is based on money alone, and a group of like-minded individuals – whether they be textile workers, gun aficionados, veterans, or family farmers – coming together to promote their interests; between those who use their economic power to magnify their political influence far beyond what their numbers might justify, and those who are simply seeking to pool their votes to sway their representatives. The former subvert the very idea of democracy. The latter are its essence.

The strong emphasis on that idealized image of the innovator in the American narrative overlooks certain inconvenient truths: the significant variation of performance between states; a foreign-born bias, where there is greater likelihood that the American Dream is realized by an immigrant than a home-grown citizen; evidence that institutionalized innovation can become a power-play in its own right, with corporate conservatism eclipsing the creative impulse; and the crucial role that government plays in laying down both ground-rules and infrastructure to facilitate the free market and to ease the flow of new techniques and technology.

However, it is a contention of *The Cracked Bell* that myth and symbolism carry greater substance and gravity than inconvenient facts and 'realities'. The popular text of virtuous innovator and the vilified power-bloc reveals something profound about America's self-image and aspirations. It expresses that irreconcilable gap between the free individual and the wired community.

This theme continues as we stalk the frontier – that mythical preserve not only of the inventor and entrepreneur, but of every pioneering American – to survey the boundaries between wilderness and civilization.

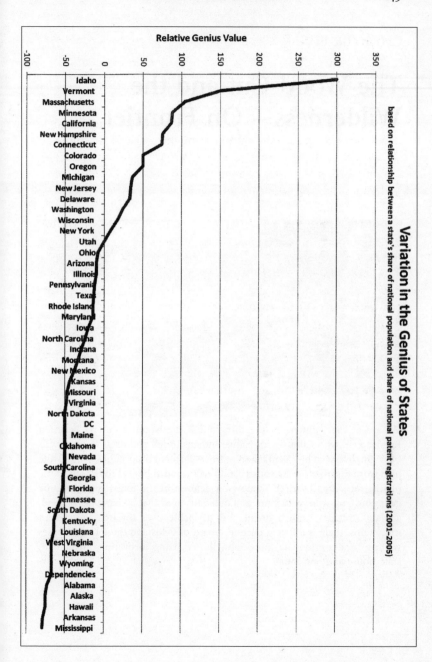

Variation in the Genius of States

based on relationship between a state's share of national population and share of national patent registrations (2001–2005)

CHAPTER FIVE

The Wood-Cut and the Wilderness – On Frontier

We are at the frontier. In the foreground, the wood is cut by behatted Englishmen, who labour with Native Indians to fell and dress the trees. To the right, overseen by a gentleman in frock-coat and tricorn, black and white men work together on the construction of a wooden house. To the left of the picture, obscured by deep shadows, a denizen of the forest appears to be gathering fruit from wild vines as if oblivious to all that is changing. Beyond, a plain stretches from a broad and navigable river towards the distant mountains: there is a fort, a chequer-board of fields and three larger spaces waiting to accommodate, no doubt, the civilizing institutions of church, state-house and law court.

This tiny print appears as a decorative motif above a warrant that advertised, in 1773, a little-known colony called Georgia. It may be almost 250 years old, but it remains powerfully evocative, providing a suitable emblem for another great American paradox: the juxtaposition of Nature and Civilization, the Feral and the Tamed, Freedom and Exploitation.

It is an inconvenient truth that in 1890 the Census Bureau declared the frontier closed. Today, much of the coast and almost all the land-mass of the US is privately owned and commercially exploited. Nature has been packaged into reserves, the open ranges are patrolled by rangers, the birds of the wild forest warble Nokia ring-tones and the frontier spirit has been commoditized into 'Outward Bound'. The hunter and the hiker seek to emulate the nation's progenitors – the trapper and pioneer – overlooking the fact that the pioneers turned the prairies into parcelled conurbations and the trappers decimated their prey. The dream, the ideas and the images of an untarnished frontier persist and Americans still live the myth, regarding engagement with the 'great outdoors' as a process of purification and re-creation.

Walt Whitman argued that the axe was preferable to the American Eagle as the proper emblem of the United States. In his 'Song of the Broad-Axe' (1856) this tool comes to symbolize the clearance of forest, the production of timber for shelter and fuel, and – as an abstraction of American spirit – 'actions that rely on themselves'. His verse grows hypnotic with such simple repetitive tasks as those performed by carpenters who literally domesticate the natural world (and we surely do not need to be a Freudian analyst to recognize an allusive sub-text depicting acts of procreation):

> The house-builder at work in cities or anywhere,
> The preparatory jointing, squaring, sawing, mortising,
> The hoist-up of beams, the push of them in their places, laying them regular,

Setting the studs by their tenons in the mortises according
as they were prepared,
The blows of mallets and hammers, the attitudes of men,
their curv'd limbs,
Bending, standing, astride the beams, driving in pins,
holding on by posts and braces,
The hook'd arm over the plate, the other arm wielding
the axe,
The floor-men forcing the planks close to be nail'd,
Their postures bringing their weapons downward on the
bearers . . .

This wood-cutting, wood-working trope appears again and
again in American culture. In Benjamin Harding's *Tour through
the Western Country* (1819) – an early guidebook for migrants –
the author expresses surprise not only at the beauty of the
country but also at its rapid growth and improvements,
considering 'how few years have elapsed since was first heard the
axe resound, laying low the sturdy trees, where nothing before
was heard but the yell and whoop of the savage'. George
Washington was memorably reprimanded for using his axe to
chop down a domesticated cherry-tree (the wrong sort of
nature); but this is nothing compared with the damage caused
in L. Frank Baum's book *The Wonderful Wizard of Oz* (1900) –
the source-book for the film – when the Wicked Witch of the
East causes an enchanted axe to cut off the limbs of its owner,
Nick Chopper. (He was to become the Tin Woodman without
a heart.)

The broad-axe truly was essential to the country in its infancy.
It was needed not only to exploit the opportunity of all that
virgin land, but also to repel the threat of the 'heathen wilderness'
– a threat powerfully evoked by Nathaniel Hawthorne when he
wrote of his eponymous anti-hero, 'Young Goodman Brown'
(1835), venturing from a New England village to meet the Devil:

The road grew wilder and drearier, and more faintly traced,
and vanished at length leaving him in the heart of the dark

wilderness . . . The whole forest was peopled with frightful sounds: the creaking of trees, the howling of wild beasts, and the yell of Indians; while sometimes the wind tolled like a distant church-bell, and sometimes gave a broad roar around the traveller, as if all Nature were laughing him to scorn.

The wooden houses that emerged from forest like this are celebrated today in the preservation of log-cabins (e.g. Robert Patterson's late-eighteenth-century cabin in the grounds of Transylvania College, Lexington) and salt-box houses (like those restored in Lewes Beach, Delaware); in the exaltation of the 'balloon-frame' (a technique pioneered in early Chicago to construct strong and efficient structures on the prairies); and in the continuing popularity of clapboard as an exterior detail in modern houses of the East Coast. In Peter Weir's film, *Witness* (1985), the community strength and virtue of Amish society is expressed in a barn-building scene, where thirty to forty men come together in an exercise that recaptures Whitman's imagery.

However, the theodolite was no less important than the broad-axe, transforming chaotic wilderness into rational squares of property, as in the print of colonial Georgia. The vision was that of Sir Robert Montgomery, whose 1717 scheme for the colony specified geometric districts of one square mile. It prefigures the Land Ordinance of 1785 that branded the territory west of the Appalachians with a grid pattern that today covers almost 70 per cent of continental America (excluding Alaska). In an exercise that seems to turn the country into that most homely of American folk-objects – a gigantic quilt – this 'Ordinance for Ascertaining the Mode of Disposing of Lands in the Western Territory' divided the land into square-mile sections (following the lines of longitude and latitude) and then parcelled thirty-six such sections into a 'township' of six square miles, in the New England tradition. A twenty-first-century flight across the Midwest reveals the extent of this fretwork applied to the plains and prairies, where the nap of the land has been rubbed away by human activity. This webbing stretches away in every direction, the squares relieved only by circles created by centre-pivot spray irrigation.

The squaring principle applied to urban development as well, and continues to this day in city 'blocks'. When towns were built out West, they followed the lines and the logic of the Ordinance: at the centre, usually, stood the courthouse – expressing the predominance of the law. Some eight blocks would surround it, with churches at the corners of the central blocks. Section 16 in every township was reserved for the maintenance of public schools and it is said that to this day many schools are to be found located there. The underlying principle was the same throughout, but there would be differences to the template.

There is no better place to see the power of this principle at work than Circleville, Ohio – the exception that ultimately proved the rule. Circleville was established as the administrative seat of Pickaway County in 1810 and the commissioners who founded the city chose to build it on the ritual earthworks of Indians who had lived 1,500 years ago. The courthouse was placed in the middle of a flattened mound and, although the outlying blocks followed the standard rectangular format, a group of buildings at the centre followed the lines of that sacred circle. However, in 1837, an act was passed that authorized the Circleville Squaring Company to 'replatt' the curvilinear portions of the town. There was some resistance, but the squaring of Circleville was completed by 1856 and is said to be the first example of urban redevelopment in the country.

American cities, then, do not match the haphazard, evolutionary jumble of their European counterparts. Rationality dominates, with an established protocol that runs streets along a grid, identified numerically in one direction and alphabetically in the other. It may be as simple as A Street and First, but the human need for expression will out and the alphabetical sequence often carries the names of national heroes or local worthies.

The enduring character of the code – as well as American partiality for order – is nicely illustrated by Kansas City's

Voluntary Addressing Guidelines that feature as part of its 'Regional 9-1-1 System':

1. East–West Street Names Streets that run primarily east and west should use the numeric street name grid that is commonly used throughout most of the region. The spacing should be based on the current pattern of 8 numeric names per mile.

2. North–South Street Names Whenever possible, streets that run primarily north and south should use a unique acceptable name. The spacing should be based on the current pattern of 16 names per mile.

Since there are 16 named streets and 8 numbered street names per mile, 'hundred block' designations should normally change every 330 feet on an east–west street and every 660 feet on a north–south street.

The introduction of Zoning Improvement Plan (ZIP) Codes in 1963 applied a new layer of regimentation by placing every address in the land within a coded domain. It was instigated by the US Postal Service as a rising tide of business mail flooded their network, with 80 per cent of the post containing such items as utility bills, bank deposits, advertisements, insurance premiums, dividends and department store catalogues. A five-digit code was assigned to every address in the land: the first number designates a broad geographical area ranging from '0' for the northeast to '9' for the far west (the scale tracking the progress of that mythical frontier); subsequent digits pinpoint areas of concentrated population and zoom in on small post offices or postal zones in larger cities. In 1983, a further four numbers were added to the zip code: the sixth and seventh denoting a delivery sector (e.g. a group of streets or a single high-rise office building); the last two denoting a segment, such as a single floor of an office building or a clutch of Post Office boxes.

The nation is inured to the zip code and can be anatomized and analysed by reference to it. The word 'zip' has become common currency in commercial, political and public-sector discourse. The US Census Bureau provides information on 'Zip Code Business Patterns', detailing the number of establishments, the size of the workforce and the weight of the payroll in more than 40,000 zip code areas. Citizens can find their congressman by zip code search; learn about the consumer lifestyle of their neighbourhood through PRIZM ('The new Evolution in Market Segment Analysis'); or be entertained by memory-artist David Rosdeitcher, who has absolute recall of all the codes in the country and can recommend – for every one of them – the best restaurants in town! The Los Angeles poet, Peter J. Harris, evokes – and kicks against – the grip of the zip in his poem 'The Ocean Is Ours', which starts its three stanzas with the lines: 'don't be foiled or fooled by the zip code', 'don't be tempted or trapped by the zip code' and 'don't be stamped or seduced by the zip code'.

Despite Harris' efforts to 'dis' the system, this ordered, rational topography must inevitably influence the manner in which Americans comprehend their universe. In *Wilderness and the American Mind* (1967), Roderick Nash quotes Henry David Thoreau's lamentation at his inability to buy a blank notebook for recording thoughts: the only ones the merchants in Concord offered were ledgers ruled for dollars and cents! So we should not be surprised that when the US Census Bureau reported the top twenty street names in the country (based on the 1993 Census) the results were:

1. Second (10,866)
2. Third (10,131)
3. First (9,898)
4. Fourth (9,190)
5. Park (8,926)
6. Fifth (8,186)
7. Main (7,644)
8. Sixth (7,283)
9. Oak (6,946)
10. Seventh (6,377)
11. Pine (6,170)
12. Maple (6,103)

13. Cedar (5,644)
14. Eighth (5,524)
15. Elm (5,233)
16. View (5,202)
17. Washington (4,974)
18. Ninth (4,908)
19. Lake (4,901)
20. Hill (4,877)

The omission of 'First' from pole position, incidentally, is explained by the incidence of so many 'Center', 'State' and 'Main' streets. It is significant that (with the exception of Washington himself) all alphabetical street names in this list refer to nature (especially trees – Oak, Pine, Maple, Cedar, Elm – in this arboreal society), although the high score achieved by 'Park' is also noteworthy, given the word's allusion to domesticated wilderness.

For those involved in pursuing the commercial rewards promised by the American Dream, there is nothing sentimental or enlightening about confronting nature in its raw and savage state. Alaska represents the closest thing to frontier territory within the United States today. Indeed, its car licence plates carry the tagline 'The last frontier' and its erstwhile governor, Sarah Palin – who had once been a reporter with the *Mat-Su Valley Frontiersman* – made much of her ability to kill, field-dress and cook a moose when she was campaigning as running-mate to John McCain in the 2008 presidential election. When statehood was granted in 1959, more than 95 per cent of the land could be called wilderness; the total white population of an area twice the size of Texas was under 150,000 (it stands at 700,000 today). However, there is some antipathy from the residents to those who regard Alaska as an endangered wilderness. Joe Vogler, founder of the Alaskan Independence Party, argued:

Anybody who says the ecology is fragile is an ignoramus or a goddam liar. Our climate protects the ecology; our

geography protects it. It's a struggle up here, all the way!
... Anybody who tells me this land was not put here to use
is a socialist enemy of mine! Anybody who tells me trees
shouldn't be cut, I'd use the axe on him.

Ironically, Vogler himself was cut down prematurely. He
disappeared on Memorial Day 1993. A year later, a vagrant
called Manfried 'Cartoon Freddy' West led police to where he
had buried the politician's bullet-riddled body.

In this Temple of Trade, it should come as no surprise that
private property is an important feature in the process of taming
the wild. When the vast territories of the frontier were opened
up, almost 1.5 billion acres of public land were disposed of
through the Land Ordinance, with 50 per cent of the new
townships sold by auction to companies formed to develop the
land and the rest sold directly to white men over twenty-one
years old. The Homestead Act of 1862 continued the process,
granting title to a quarter-section (160 acres) of public domain
to any settler for as little as $30, provided a house was
constructed and land was cultivated. This engendered the
overwhelming sense of ownership that permeates the American
landscape today. Outside the relatively small swathes of public
land, the traveller cannot escape signs – installed at frequent
intervals – that stipulate: 'Posted'; 'Private property'; 'No
trespassing'; 'No hunting. No fishing'; 'Violators will be
prosecuted'.

This phenomenon recurs again and again, even in places
seeking to draw in the public. For instance, visitors approaching
Storm King Arts Center, in Mountainville, New York – a
sculpture park in 500 acres of lush, gently rolling meadows –
encounter notices nailed to trees every fifty yards, warning them:
'Town Road ends here. Private. Do not enter.' Adventurers
rafting the Arkansas River in Colorado are warned to avoid
touching the ground while fishing, in case this invokes
litigation from an incensed landowner: so river-guide Dan
sings (to the tune of the Woody Guthrie classic, 'This Land is
Your Land'):

This land is my land,
It isn't your land,
If you don't clear off,
I'll blow your head off.

The signs even appear in Marquette County, Wisconsin, where America's greatest champion of wilderness conservation – the Scottish-born John Muir (1838–1914) – spent his formative years. Now commuter homes, hobby farms and vacation cottages are starting to change the traditional landscape of the county, as interstate highways make the area accessible to the inhabitants of Madison, Milwaukee and Chicago. New log homes are being built, but the prefabricated 'mobile' home is also prevalent. There is little sign of land-use regulation: people are free, it seems, to develop their property as they see fit.

Enter the suburb. Today, 80 per cent of the US population resides in metropolitan areas that occupy less than 20 per cent of the nation's land-mass – the majority in suburbs where they find some respite from the four-square universe that dominates so much of their realm. The suburb is a form of self-delusion: trees, streams and lawns lull the inhabitants into the false sense of solitude. Traditionally, the boundaries between homes are unmarked and there is an absence of fences. Many generations of Americans recall a childhood where kids would run wild, gathering from different households to play a game of baseball on the open grass. In the suburbs, the grid pattern is eroded by 'eyebrows', as town planners call these curved streets. The Kansas City authorities acknowledge this threat to their gridiron universe when they write – with tight-lipped tolerance – in their standards: 'the curvilinear streets and cul-de-sacs found in newer subdivisions create situations which are far harder to address than the traditional rectangular grid pattern of streets'. Such streets tend to be assigned 'secondary' names, such as 'Way' or 'Close', as if this demotion in the ranks maintains order and accommodates the anomalous.

The suburbs represent a refuge for a growing number of Americans who long for quieter, less hectic lives away from the children of all of the above. Projections indicate, at the current rate, that the cemetery will run out of space in sixty years. Small ceremonies of remembrance and despatch are being performed at Arlington throughout the year, but the greatest begins on the Thursday before Memorial Day, when 1,200 soldiers of the Third US Infantry place small American flags by each of the 260,000 gravestones and guard these with patrols throughout the weekend.

War memorials have also become a major feature in Washington, DC. In addition to the Korean and Vietnam War Memorials, there is now the World War II Memorial, dedicated on Memorial Weekend, 2004. After a service in the National Cathedral, a huge crowd – including many veterans in uniform – gathered in the National Mall to participate in what was termed a 'Salute to Heroes'. President Bush received the monument on behalf of the American people. He spoke of the 'modest sons of a peaceful country' who went to war, making special reference to 462 men who received Medals of Honor. He then described one soldier in the 58th Armored Field Artillery who had the best-kept rifle in the unit but who wanted to cover it with salt when the war ended, hang it on the wall and watch it rust.

A cynic might argue that any gesture that leads to the disposal of old stocks of weapons will be welcomed by the 'military-industrial complex' – that colossus that shadows the Defense Department and the armed services. President Dwight D. Eisenhower initiated the term, in his 'Farewell Address' in January 1961, at a time when 3.5 million people were directly engaged in defence-related work:

> We have been compelled to create a permanent armaments industry of vast proportions. This conjunction of an immense military establishment and a large arms industry is new in the American experience. The total influence – economic, political, even spiritual – is felt in every city,

every State House, every office of the Federal Government.
Our toil, resources and livelihood are all involved; so is the
very structure of our society.

His great fear was that the US's defence industry could gain
unwarranted influence in government, bringing about what he
termed the disastrous rise of misplaced power.

The military-industrial complex remains substantial, despite
presumptions – through the 1990s – of a peace dividend
following the end of the Cold War. *Defense News* publishes its
league table of the 'Top 100' defence companies in the world,
and US companies consistently dominate this: forty-three
companies feature in the latest table (published in 2008),
earning $226.3 billion. The top five US companies are Lockheed
Martin, Boeing, Northrop Grumman, General Dynamics and
Raytheon; between them, defence-related revenues in 2007
amounted to $136.4 billion and they employ almost 600,000
people around the world.

Let us provide some context. The annual revenue of these top
five companies is a close approximation – after inflation – to the
ten-year budget to put a man on the Moon and it is 450 times
the cost (again after inflation) of the Louisiana Purchase that
doubled the size of the American land-mass. This illustrates the
extraordinary traction enjoyed by companies dedicated to
equipping the American war-fighter. It comes as no surprise,
therefore, that these companies contribute hundreds of thousands of dollars to the Democratic and Republican parties or
that they employ an army of lobbyists, publicists and lawyers to
represent their interests on 'The Hill'.

Of course, in the free-market atmosphere of the US, these
companies are susceptible to the shifting currents of opinion
within the Pentagon: one gains a sense of this from a speech
given by Secretary of Defense Robert Gates, on 6 April 2009,
when he set out his recommendations for his 2010 budget. He
identified plans to trim or even abandon some equipment
programmes (e.g. the 'Multiple Kill Vehicle' and the 'Airborne
Laser' aircraft), but his shopping list included: fifty Predator-

class unmanned aerial vehicle orbits by FY11 (a 62 per cent increase); spending $500 million more on helicopters – a capability that is in urgent demand in Afghanistan; buying more Littoral Combat Ships (LCS), increasing the order from two to three ships in FY 2010, but with the goal of eventually acquiring fifty-five LCS; increasing the procurement of F-35 Joint Strike Fighters from fourteen in 2009 to thirty in FY10, with the aim to buy 513 F-35s over the five-year defence plan, and, ultimately, 2,443.

As we saw in 'The Lattice Constant', the merchant, the manufacturer and the entrepreneur have benefited from the warrior state for centuries: profit motive, can-do, and know-how make a potent mixture. It is said that Eli Whitney invented the American system of mass production when supplying 10,000 muskets to the young American army. Whitney is lauded in the American Precision Museum at Windsor, Vermont – suitably housed in the original Robbins and Lawrence Armory – alongside Simeon North, the scythe-maker who signed a contract with the War Department in 1800 for 500 horse pistols to be delivered within one year.

The connection between scientific research, technology and war reached a milestone with the Manhattan Project – the development of the atom bomb in the Second World War. In 1939, the government's total budget for research and development was $1 billion (much of it dedicated to agriculture); but the Manhattan Project cost $2 billion (the equivalent to $25 billion today – still a fraction of what the defence sector now earns) and it was delivered through an unprecedented melding of science, industry and engineering. Just as the first nuclear blast created a new mineral – trinitite – at the White Sands test site, so it is that three extraordinary research institutions emerged from the Manhattan Project: Los Alamos, Sandia and Lawrence Livermore National Laboratories. The US military continues to pride itself on being research-minded and hundreds of thousands of men and women are involved in this work.

Los Alamos is the largest employer in New Mexico, with 10,000 personnel and 1,600 PhDs, located among the isolated canyons and mountain ridges where J. Robert Oppenheimer developed the nuclear bomb under conditions of utmost secrecy. The staff claim, with the braggadocio that Americans cannot resist, that their computers are so powerful that they work out a calculation in one second which it would take a man 10 million years to complete. Sandia designs all the non-nuclear parts of nuclear weapons, but its portfolio extends to such wonders as the Synthetic Aperture Radar that enables US warplanes to see through cloud cover. Gerry Yonas typifies the sort of scientist-entrepreneur who flourishes in the US's defence realm. This expert in particle beam fusion weapons would fit in an Oxbridge seminar-room: a rather conservative, bearded and grizzled gentleman in his late fifties, shooting out ideas like a Catherine wheel spouting sparks.

Yonas will happily enunciate Sandia's vision statement, which opens with the words, 'Securing a peaceful and free world through technology'. This chimes with the language used repeatedly by the American administration and the military establishment. But does this talk of 'peace' and 'freedom' provide cover for an American programme of external predation designed to further US influence and interests? As American troops deploy themselves and their high-tech equipment around the world, are they spearheading – as some fear – the creation of an American Empire?

The question of American imperialism has come to preoccupy a host of intellectuals and political scientists in the country's universities and think-tanks. A survey of recent publications on the subject reveals a long list of books (see Bibliography) bearing the word 'empire' in their title. Interest in this issue was exemplified by the debate held at the American Enterprise Institute in Washington, DC, in 2003: 'The United States Is, and Should Be, an Empire'. At this event, Niall Ferguson (at the time, professor of financial history at New York University) argued that 'empire' had less to do with territory – the US possesses only fourteen dependencies – and more to do with power.

America is a military, economic and cultural 'colossus' in the world, making it an empire despite so many of its citizens refusing to acknowledge the fact.

Robert Kagan (of the Carnegie Endowment for International Peace) disagreed. The US is, indeed, powerful – in fact, it is the most successful global power in history – but this does not make it an empire because it fails to exhibit predatory, territorial ambitions. The American tendency, when intervening in any place around the world, is to commit to an early departure. It is, Kagan argued, precisely because everyone knows that the US will not exercise imperial control that its rising hegemony has been so widely accepted and so little feared.

The nature of this debate rightly reflected the fact that there is little consensus about whether or not an American Empire exists. The battle between opposing camps is usually conducted with decorum – the high-brow equivalent to aerial manoeuvres – but sometimes descends to hand-to-hand combat. Weapons can be interchangeable and references to the 'Monroe Doctrine', the 'Roosevelt Corollary' (see below), the American occupation of the Philippines, or the US military bases around the globe float back and forth between combatants like frisbees on a campus lawn. The arguments – if word-play is appropriate here – are as much non-empirical (based on value judgments and interpretation) as empirical (verified by means of observation or experiment).

Debate over empire is not focused exclusively on the exercise of military muscle. For instance, in *Irresistible Empire* (2005) Victoria de Grazia has charted the infectious spread of America's consumer culture through Europe, spearheaded by such brands as Coca-Cola, Kellogg's Corn Flakes and Wrigley's Chewing Gum. The powerful Bureau of Foreign and Domestic Commerce supported the process, tasking consular attachés to produce detailed intelligence reports on foreign markets. American values, products and technology can be seen to embody a 'soft' power that achieves a cultural hegemony: in this vision of a Mickey Mouse Empire, the US holds a predominant position of influence in the world through the promised delivery of gratification rather than through the threatened delivery of shock and awe. The coke has trumped the nuke.

Nor is the debate confined to the overseas dimension. Historian Charles Maier reminds us that a nation does not need to have an empire: it can simply be one (Tsarist Russia is one example; eighteenth-century Britain might be another). With the odd exception – Hawaii, Alaska – the blocks of real estate that have gone into forming the US have been adjacent to, or lie within, the country's borders. The US has most frequently exercised military authority not in some distant province but in and around its own borders, or to strengthen the wider security blanket. It subjugated the Native Americans. It annexed the Hispanic southwest through military force. Some enthusiasts wanted to add Canada to the bag in the war of 1812, and subsequently to take over Cuba. It acquired a Polynesian kingdom called Hawaii – bearing neither geographic nor cultural links to the North American continent – as a valuable base for its navy in the mid-Pacific.

Today, Puerto Rico and the US Virgin Islands are colonies in all but name. The former, which fell into American hands after the war with Spain in 1898, receives $17 billion in aid each year and is said to supply a greater ratio of fighting men and women than any full-grown state of the Union. The US Virgin Islands were bought in 1917 from the Danish as a defence against the Kaiser's navy, which was thought to threaten US shipping in the Panama Canal. There are those in Puerto Rico and the Virgin Islands who are clamouring to become the 51st State, but Puerto Rico had its own, violent, independence movement, and in many cases (such as the southwestern states, the Indian territories), the populace was pressed into union by an unwelcome, iron embrace. Is this empire- or nation-building?

One can throw into the mix that extraordinary culture war that erupted between North and South in 1861. The different names for the American Civil War are themselves indicative of different narratives: – 'War of Southern Independence', 'War Between the States', 'War of the Rebellion' and 'War of Northern Aggression'. The origins of the American Civil War lie in a complex set of competing issues around concepts of slavery, federalism, identity, innovation and morality, fuelled by party politics, expansionism, sectionalism and economics. Ultimately, a Northern hegemony bore down on the South, imposing its preferred value-system and banishing slavery. There is, in this context, something familiar about these lines from Maier's *Among Empires*:

> Empires are about civilizing missions, the diffusion of cultural styles . . . The suppression of practices perceived as barbaric – such as human sacrifice and suttee. Occasionally they are about bringing peace and the rule of law or defending what we have defined as freedom. But they are also about violence and bloodshed.

Notwithstanding these questions of commercial empires abroad and an internal empire at home, the focus of debate returns to military ascendancy overseas. Robert Kagan may believe the US to be 'a behemoth with a conscience', whose intentions are entirely worthy, but he has identified a philosophical outlook informing the undeniable projection of massive force into the global arena. In *Paradise and Power* (2003) he acknowledges that while the Old World appears to subscribe to Immanuel Kant's notion of 'perpetual peace', the US sees itself operating in an anarchic, Hobbesian world where true security – and the defence and promotion of a liberal order – depend on the use of military might.

There is substance to this analysis, although it may be biased by the experience of George W. Bush's Manichaean worldview. When he took presidential office for the second time in January 2005, the main theme of his inaugural speech was liberty overcoming tyranny; he quoted Abraham Lincoln – 'Those who deny freedom to others deserve it not for themselves; and under the rule of a just God cannot retain it.' Nevertheless, this theme has emerged frequently in foreign policy since the Civil War. Theodore Roosevelt, for instance, espoused 'Big Stick Diplomacy' through his 'Corollary' to the Monroe Doctrine, declaring a willingness to intervene in countries that failed to show 'reasonable efficiency and decency in social and political matters'.

A spate of military deployments in the Caribbean and Central America followed Roosevelt's corollary. From 1909 to 1933, the US was rarely out of Nicaragua and it played a policeman's role in protecting lives and property in Santa Domingo, Cuba, Haiti and the Dominican Republic. In these cases, the dough of self-interest was leavened with the yeast of missionary zeal – to protect the freedoms or ordinary people denied the benefits of democratic institutions and/or to compel foreigners to accept the indisputable benefits of the American way of democracy. If this meant the exercise of violence for a good cause, then so be it. Nowhere is this attitude better expressed than in an exchange in 1913 between Walter Hines Page, US ambassador to the Court of St James, and Sir Edward Grey, British foreign secretary. At the time, Mexico was proving a thorn in the American flank and the US was sizing up for a fight:

> Grey: 'Suppose you have to intervene, what then?'
> Page: 'Make 'em vote and live by their decision.'
> Grey: 'Suppose they will not so live?'
> Page: 'We'll go in again and make 'em vote again.'
> Grey: 'And keep this up for two hundred years?'
> Page: 'Yes. The US will be here two hundred years and it can continue to shoot men for that little space of time till they learn to vote and rule themselves.'

Woodrow Wilson used more mellow tones when sending his troops to Europe to fight in the First World War and his words were pointedly anti-imperialistic:

> The world must be safe for democracy. Its peace must be planted on the tested foundations of political liberty. We have no selfish ends to serve. We desire no conquest, no dominion ... We are but one of the champions of the rights of mankind.

Much confusion about the question of American imperialism stems from this combination of right and might. Belief in the rectitude of the American Way, backed with superior military force, demonstrates for some the fact that the US is imperialistic while others see this tradition as evidence to the contrary. The argument can easily distil into a sterile debate about semantics: is the US 'hegemonic' (enjoying a paramount influence over other countries, but not the will to compel obedience), 'imperial' (displaying its power to overawe others) or 'imperialist' (territorially expansionist and/or bent on controlling the policies of weaker states)?

The answer is probably all of the above, some of the time, differently, in different situations. However, for the anthropologist intent on surveying the American Way, the answer is less important than the nation's preoccupation with the question. This would appear to indicate a pressing need to make sense of America's place in the world. To be an American, it is said, is to be a champion of all those who yearn for liberation. A substantial armed force has been established, therefore, not only to defend the republic but also to bring freedom to the oppressed around the globe. This mission is articulated in different ways, in keeping with the tenor of the times. It may be in the uncompromising language of Walter Hines Page or in the more naive and benign tones of Arthur Schlesinger, who has said of the early years of the Kennedy administration, 'We thought for a moment that the world was plastic and the future unlimited.' This is how the National Security Strategy puts it today:

> The presence of American forces overseas is one of the most profound symbols of [our] commitments to allies and friends. Through our willingness to use force in our own defense and in defense of others, the US demonstrates its resolve to maintain a balance of power that favors freedom.

There is, of course, a significant minority in the country who argue against this projection of power overseas. On 7 March

2002, an open letter was published by the 'Not In Our Name' project:

> The US has commenced a series of wars, beginning with Afghanistan where they killed thousands of innocent civilians ... The government has targeted Arab and Muslim immigrants, rounding up over 1,000 and still holding hundreds in indefinite detention, refusing even to release their names. They have gutted longstanding civil liberties and unleashed police spying. The executive branch of government has seized vast new powers, unchecked by either the legislature or the judiciary. They have attempted to intimidate all dissenting voices, and tried to make critical thought itself suspect.

Seven months later, a young Illinois state senator called Barack Obama addressed an anti-war rally in Chicago's Federal Plaza, where he told them that he was not opposed to all wars, but that he could not support the use of military force against Saddam Hussein because this would be 'a dumb war, a rash war, a war based not on reason but on passion, not on principle but on politics'. For Obama, now Forty-Fourth President, the US's challenge is to move the world in the direction of greater equity, justice and prosperity without assuming that the country can single-handedly liberate other people from tyranny. He joins his predecessor in believing that there is a universal desire to be free but he has acknowledged the problems that occur when freedom is delivered through outside intervention.

This has not stopped Obama from deploying an additional 17,000 troops to Afghanistan, assessing that the Taliban pose a threat not only to that country's fragile democracy but also to US national security. In doing so, on 27 March 2009, he reminded the world that 'the United States of America stands for peace and security, justice and opportunity: that is who we are, and that is what history calls on us to do once more'. Four weeks later, in Arlington Cemetery on Memorial Day, he asked his fellow citizens to 'advance around the world' the enduring ideals of justice, equality and opportunity, for which so many American soldiers have died.

But the ideal of the honoured and honourable warrior fighting to make the world a better place – an ideal dramatized in films like *Saving Private Ryan* (1998) and in the TV mini-series *Band of Brothers* (2001) – has been challenged by accounts of the Global War on Terrorism. US troops are seen by some observers to be operating abroad with ignorance, indifference, and even soulless cruelty. For instance:

- Evan Wright's experience as a *Rolling Stone* journalist with a Marine battalion in Iraq, led him to describe the young soldiers as *Generation Kill*; they have been raised on computer games where they shoot first and ask questions later: they are, he believes, incapable of applying any ethical judgment about the targets in their scopes;
- Charles Clover was a journalist embedded with the 1st Battalion, 505th Parachute Infantry during operations in Falluja; this resort town of 300,000 on the banks of the Euphrates, west of Baghdad, became a centre of resistance after American troops fired indiscriminately on a largely peaceful demonstration against their presence on 29 April 2003; Clover has described the alienating impact of these 'Kevlar-plated stewards of a modern-day manifest destiny' as they conduct raids on Iraqi homes.

Here's the paradox. The champion of liberty is compelled to develop an engine of war to safeguard cherished freedoms at home. In response to complex events in an unstable and globalized world, arguments can be made – some principled, some tendentious and self-serving – for taking the fight overseas to crush the oppressive enemies of freedom. But even with the best of intentions, the deployment of 'boots on the ground' and 'kinetic force' can be seen to repudiate the values that inspired the mission. This moral confusion has been reinforced, for Americans in the opening decade of the new millennium, by images of Iraqis tortured in Abu Ghraib; stories of atrocities against prisoners-of-war in Bagram; revelations about extra-judicial renditions and the extra-territorial concentration camp at Guantánamo; and the corpses of innocents counted as collateral damage in air-strikes against the Taliban in Afghanistan.

These are not new dilemmas, although America's impassioned advocacy of freedom adds an edge to the issue. The moral philosopher Immanuel Kant wrestled with this riddle when, in the eighteenth century, he envisaged a global government charged with instituting a 'state of universal peace': this could only be achieved, he concluded, by a level of despotism that would destroy human freedom. And Shakespeare expressed the dilemma mordantly when – in *Julius Caesar* – Brutus commands Caesar's assassins to go out into the streets of Rome, having washed their hands in the dead dictator's blood: 'and waving our red weapons o'er our heads, Let's all cry *Peace, freedom and liberty!*'

We have found that a substantial investment of physical and emotional capital is dedicated to America's martial institutions. The war-fighter is highly regarded as a guardian and protector of the American Way. The reaction to the 'Fort Hood Massacre' (in November 2009) bears testament to this: the nation was shocked when Major Nidal Malik Hasan – an army psychiatrist and Arab-American – turned on his fellow-soldiers, killing thirteen and wounding many more in a shooting spree at the largest military base in the world, in Texas.

One has to conclude that America's commitment to liberty is greater than its commitment to peace. Everett Carl Dolman encapsulates this when he opens *The Warrior State* (2004) with the sentence, 'Political freedom begins with military service'. Self-belief in the righteousness of the American narrative, coupled with the conviction that American values are universal, has led the richest nation in the world to maintain a military force of unprecedented power. Its mission is explicitly and simplistically benign: to protect the Land of the Free and to liberate those suffering oppression (although realism frequently prevails, cautioning that this should apply only where there is good reason and justification for doing so).

America has become, determinedly, a unipolar power in the world in response to the chimes and knells of Liberty's cracked bell. It has pushed out its virtual frontier through long-range radar, armed encampments abroad, the threat of intercontinental ballistic missiles and the reality of Tomahawk strikes in distant lands (with the 'Red' Indian's weapon of choice now transformed into the American weapon against today's 'Injuns').

But the message of 9/11 is not reassuring. Military might projected overseas to preserve national security can be powerless against acts of 'asymmetric warfare' that strike America within its borders. The innocuous, inconspicuous, besuited passenger sitting on an internal flight to Los Angeles is capable of destroying the nation's sense of self-confidence, optimism and invulnerability with a box-cutter and an unfinished flying course. The frontier 'out there' is breached 'in here', evoking a sense of instability similar to that generated by those Escher images – the Impossible Torus or the Klein Bottle – whose surfaces should not exist in three-dimensional space.

Citizens of the Republic are frequently reminded of the blood shed in historical conflicts within their own borders. Some fear that the United States could turn on itself yet again: in a society prone to conspiracy theories, they look with trepidation at internal security measures such as the Homeland Security Department, the Patriot Act, and the creation of a new military command (NORTHCOM) responsible for the North American continent. These measures themselves add to the levels of insecurity, emblemized not only in movements that protest against the erosion of civil liberties but also in national scares about hostile alien fauna – Africanized killer bees, South American fire ants, Burmese pythons and Korean snakehead fish – that invade and overwhelm peace-loving American species.

In the face of instability and threats abroad, and with fear of terrorist attacks and civic strife at home, Americans may well look anxiously towards 2021. When the Periodic Cicada next invades, there can be no certainty that its wing will bring any respite by bearing an imprinted 'P' with its portent of peace.

CHAPTER SEVEN

Liberty Under the Law – On Freedom and Conformity

On the second anniversary of 9/11, US television channels ran a series of advertisements promoting a commodity close to the heart of every American.

Viewers saw victims of totalitarian regimes (Cambodia, Ukraine, Soviet Armenia) talk about their redemption through escape to the US. As they spoke, symbols of imprisonment were intercut with images of Abraham Lincoln and the Statue of Liberty. The soundtrack suggested metal shutters rolling back, perhaps, or a sword drawn from its sheath. Finally, words flashed by at speed: 'Freedom'; 'Appreciate it'; 'Cherish it'; 'Protect it'.

This was the second stage in a 'Campaign for Freedom' by the Advertising Council to inform, involve and inspire all Americans to celebrate their freedoms. Ads in 2002 had pictured an imagined American dystopia, where a citizen could be arrested for requesting the wrong book in a public library. Now the 'Inspire' phase, with its focus on refugees from political imprisonment, wanted the viewer to reflect upon the underlying freedoms that define the American way of life.

Liberty is, indeed, the defining motif in American society. Barack Obama was the latest in a long line of leaders to extol the importance of this value for his people, when – in his inaugural address in January 2009 – he described freedom as the permanent hope of mankind, the hunger in dark places, the longing of the soul. In obeisance to the Divine, he said, 'History has a visible direction, set by liberty and the Author of Liberty.' He went on to refer to the Liberty Bell sounding out when the Declaration of Independence was declaimed. It meant something then, he said, and it still means something today: 'America, in this young century, proclaims liberty throughout all the world, and to all the inhabitants thereof.'

However, there is an errant side to this spirit of liberty. The germ of 'freedom' has been glimpsed behind each paradox encountered in our survey of twenty-first-century America: the image of the citizen wrestling to be free of an ethnic heritage that will not always let go; the intoxicating drive to consume, whatever the cost in unintended consequences; the clash and confusion of unshackled creeds; the tradition of innovation tangling with unreconstructed interest-groups; the myth of the liberating wilderness in a land whose frontiers closed long ago; and the warrior state marshalling its arsenal to defend and extend the American Way of peaceful opportunity.

This chapter will now survey the domain of 'freedom' but will also explore liberty's hinterland – the American spheres of crime, punishment and intolerance. We will keep company with lawyers as they patrol the porous, irregular, elusive boundary between the two – always remembering the poet Robert Frost's words: 'Something there is that does not love a wall.' This, then, is the heart of the matter: the ultimate American paradox of Liberty under the Law.

According to poll data, 'personal freedom' – defined as the opportunity to make one's own choices and priorities in life – features second only to religion as the overriding personal value in the United States – ahead of family, job security and financial success. 'Freedom' is identified with archetypal American heroes like George Washington, Abraham Lincoln, Martin Luther King and Thomas Jefferson. Freedom is expressed in the most commonplace of objects: in the nineteenth century, coins showed a seated female figure representing Liberty, and today the one-cent coin bears the word in large letters. The licence plate FR33DOM is highly prized by car-drivers and the 'eternal' first-class postage stamp shows the Liberty Bell and the word 'Forever'. The greatest national icons are, of course, the Statue of Liberty and that Bell with its inscription from Leviticus.

In a tradition dating back to 1988, the Declaration of Independence is read aloud every 4th of July by presenters (notably the mellifluous Carl Kasell) on National Public Radio's *Morning Edition*. In the nation at large, the most quoted clause from this document represents a mission statement for many Americans: 'We hold these truths to be self-evident, that all men are created equal, that they are endowed by their Creator with certain inalienable Rights, that among these are Life, Liberty and the pursuit of Happiness.' The declaration goes on to list the 'oppressions' imposed on these American colonies by the King before asserting that the 'United Colonies' are now free and independent states. Jefferson, the author of these words, had been inspired by an ethnographic fantasy of pre-feudal, pre-Norman, Saxon tribes who had lived in the dark forests of Germany without the encumbrance of rulers. The Constitution itself is more nuanced in its references to freedom, with the Preamble looking to 'secure the Blessings of Liberty to ourselves and our Posterity'. The only other reference to freedom is in the sub-section on taxation, where a distinction is drawn between 'free Persons', Indians and 'all other Persons' (i.e. slaves, who, for fiscal and other purposes, counted as three-fifths of a free man). It was only in the amendments to the Constitution that the Declaration's commitment to liberty came to life.

The 'Charters of Freedom' described above are enshrined in the Rotunda of the National Archives and have gained an emblematic or totemic status. The Declaration of Independence, Constitution and Bill of Rights are barely legible, but the faded script on fragile parchment has the symbolic allure of holy relics. Visitors walk reverentially past dim-lit cabinets containing the documents, pressing their noses to the armour-plated glass to pay their respects before buying reproductions of the texts for their walls at home. It seems fitting that when, in May 2009, President Obama spoke about the values that underpin his foreign and national security policies, he did so in front of these charters saying, 'I stand here today as someone whose own life was made possible by these documents.'

Those interested in a more idiosyncratic expression of this national faith in liberty should travel to the Lilly Library at Wabash College, Crawfordsville, Indiana. Here, in 1957, businessman Pierre F. Goodrich designed and built a chamber to help students understand the evolution of individual liberty. Limestone slabs mark milestones in the history of freedom with the names of key people and events; the west wall, facing the entrance, carries a vacant space corresponding to the Dark Ages. The sequence opens with the cuneiform inscription from a clay document dating from 2300 BC in the Sumerian city-state of Lagash – it represents the word *amagi* ('liberty'); the journey ends with the Declaration of Independence as if this represented the culmination of some evolutionary process leaving the US at its apogee. The shelves beneath contain books of relevance to each step along the path to freedom, with works extending through to the twentieth century.

The evolution of the ideas underpinning the US's dominant focus on freedom has been charted by Michael Kammen (in the Curti Lectures, given to the University of Wisconsin in October 1985) and by Yehoshua Arieli in a 1964 work published, appropriately, by Harvard's Center for the Study of the History of Liberty in America. They demonstrate the link to a vibrant tradition sustained for centuries in the British Isles, described in a speech by Virginia's Governor, Patrick Henry, in the aftermath of the Revolution:

> We are descended from a people whose government was founded on liberty; our glorious forefathers of Great Britain made liberty the foundation of everything . . . We drew the spirit of liberty from our British ancestors; by that spirit we have triumphed over every difficulty.

Arieli – who died in 2002 – plotted the subsequent development in America of a distinctive attitude towards the individual and the community, generating deeply engrained beliefs that persist to this day. Notions about mankind's innate morality and sociability, advanced by British eighteenth-century philosophers like Lord Shaftesbury, Francis Hutcheson and Adam Smith, formed the ingredients of a Utopian confection that would – it was believed – sweeten any bitterness between the rights of the individual and the needs of society. Hutcheson coined the aphorism 'the greatest happiness of the greatest number' in 1725 and his *System of Moral Philosophy* (1755) was the principal text-book of America's colleges on the eve of the Revolution. These enlightened ideas inspired the Founding Fathers to create a nation that would demonstrate the perfectibility of man and the progressive nature of voluntary social cooperation.

There was also a belief from the early days of the republic in the merits of *laissez-faire* ('Let do!') – a slogan of economic liberalism that upholds the value of private initiative and production over state interventionism and taxation. The phrase was introduced into the English language by Benjamin Franklin and George Whatley in *Principles of Trade* (1774), and *laissez-faire* sentiment shines out from the writings of J. Hector St John de Crèvecoeur, who argued that the US had become the most perfect society in the world in his letter entitled 'What Is an American?' (1782): 'We are all animated with the spirit of industry which is unfettered and unrestrained, because each person works for himself . . . Here man is free as he ought to be.'

The view took root that *laissez-faire* would dissolve economic, social and political privileges, leading to the liberation of all forms of labour and enterprise in a free society where there was equal opportunity for all. This theory was doubtless reinforced by unbounded horizons to the west and ready access to sea-passages offering sea-captains and merchants of the eastern ports the chance to make their fortune. Over time, the benevolent vision of the Scottish Enlightenment hardened into an American model, where the capitalist and the entrepreneur became standard-bearers of the revolution and the Utopian dream.

The social philosopher, Senator John Taylor of Caroline, was an early advocate for change, replacing the pursuit of happiness in Jefferson's list of basic rights with property. Then, in the nineteenth century, Edwin L. Godkin started arguing for the primacy of the individual as a free agent, unencumbered by the compulsion of status or privilege, conducting his affairs exclusively on the basis of contract. Less emphasis was given to social justice and improvement, although balm was applied with the assurance that justice was a natural adjunct to these freedoms. By the start of the twentieth century, a philosophy of rugged individualism had become embedded in the national narrative, reinforced by notions of a Chosen People in a Chosen Land.

The English philosopher Herbert Spencer – often described as a Social Darwinist, with his passionate advocacy of the rights of the individual – fuelled the debate: his influence is apparent in the controversial Supreme Court judgment *Lochner v New York* (1905) which found that New York's regulation of the working hours of bakers (to protect their health) was not a justifiable restriction of the right to contract freely under the Fourteenth Amendment. Over the next three decades, the court – led by a quartet of conservative justices nicknamed 'The Four Horsemen of the Apocalypse' would strike down, in the name of liberty, numerous attempts by state governments to improve working conditions or protect consumers.

Today, the cause of freedom is most frequently espoused by reference to a small number of political tracts – Lincoln's 'Gettysburg Address', for instance, and Martin Luther King's memorable 'I Have a Dream' speech with its coda 'Free at Last!' The arts also play their part: before Jack Kerouac took to the road, one fictional outcast seemed to represent the spirit of freedom – Mark Twain described Huckleberry Finn as someone dreaded by all the mothers of the town because he came and went of his own free will: 'Everything that goes to make life precious that boy had.'

The spirit of Huckleberry Finn is be found in another American icon – the free-wheeling, free-thinking, boundary-breaking artist who has appeared in different incarnations over the years. Walt Whitman, the great American poet of the nineteenth century, was an outspoken advocate of freedom: 'I have allowed the stress of my poems from beginning to end to bear upon American individuality and assist it,' he wrote in 'A Backward Glance' (1888). Moondog is a more recent example: this blind composer, renowned for his minimalist music and innovative instruments (such as the 'Oo' and 'Trimba'), spent twenty years living on the streets of Manhattan and became known as 'The Viking of 6th Avenue'.

America's libertarian credentials gain lustre from the sanctuary offered to artists evading dogma and totalitarianism. Composers such as Béla Bartók, Paul Hindemith, Kurt Weill and Igor Stravinsky; artists like Josef Albers, Max Ernst, Roberto Matta, Yves Tanguy, and André Masson, fled Europe to push the boundaries of artistic expression in the Land of the Free. Albers taught at Black Mountain College in North Carolina – a beacon of experimentation in the visual, literary and performing arts. Other teachers there included Walter Gropius (the German architect and founder of the Bauhaus movement that aroused the ire of the Nazi Party), Merce Cunningham (dancer and choreographer), Buckminster Fuller (architect and designer) and John Cage (composer), connecting the college to the revolutionary compositional structures of Abstract Expressionism and the radical music of the New York School.

The American cult of freedom is seen in the spontaneity and energy of Jackson Pollock's 'action' paintings, and heard in the licks and phrases of improvised riffs that represent America's greatest contribution to world culture – jazz. Meanwhile, Cage's pupil, Christian Wolff, applied the concept of indeterminacy to his music: in Wolff's oeuvre, the performer makes choices about pitch, duration, timbre and rhythm. His works are impossible to reproduce, since each performance creates a unique constellation of sound. The score of *Edges* (1968) exemplifies this: it looks like a map dotted with symbols denoting aural limits (loudness, clarity, softness, etc.), with each instrumentalist picking his own path.

In the same year that Wolff composed *Edges*, his namesake – Tom Wolfe – published *The Electric Kool-Aid Acid Test*. This chronicled the adventures of Californian Ken Kesey and the Merry Pranksters as they crossed the US in a school bus called 'Further' (painted in the colours of the rainbow), distributing marijuana and LSD to people as they went. A cultural revolution was sweeping the country, exemplified by the Free Speech Movement on the campus at Berkeley, California, and Ken Kesey's hippies. Eldridge Cleaver (the radical writer and Black Panther acitivist) saluted these rebels from his cell in Folsom Prison:

> What do they care if their old baldheaded and crew-cut elders don't dig their caveman mops? They couldn't care less about the old, stiffassed honkies who don't like their new dances: Frug, Monkey, Jerk, Swim, Watusi. All they know is that it feels good to swing to way-out bodyrhythms instead of dragassing across the dance floor like zombies to the dead beat of mind-smothered Mickey Mouse music.

On the East Coast, Timothy Leary was dismissed from Harvard for promoting the use of psychedelic drugs and moved to Millbrook Big House to pick the locks of the subconscious and tweak the nose of the establishment. In 1966 he founded a new religion – the League for Spiritual Development – that incorporated the consumption of LSD into the Catholic mass. The hippie movement sought to uncover the Huck in a generation of Americans who wanted to dismantle the barriers of 'square' order and authority. Leary wanted his followers to break free from the bonds of human nature, to achieve the status of a deity – as described in an article he wrote in 1966 for an East Village underground newspaper, introducing his 'Do-It-Yourself-God-Kit Program'. Although he died in 1996, Leary remains an iconic figure in American society; on 19 April 2007, *Time* magazine asked the question 'Was Timothy Leary Right?', as it reported that

Harvard was conducting its first research into therapeutic uses of psychedelic drugs since firing Leary for the practice in 1963.

Travellers through the US still encounter the stay-behinds from that era. The Age of Aquarius is now superannuated and sheltering in redoubts like Boulder, Taos and Haight-Ashbury, where spaced-out, grey-haired hippies read the Sixth Canto of the *Srimad Bhagavatam* and Carlos Castaneda's *The Teachings of Don Juan* (1968). Some commentators uphold these texts as far more than joss-stick-scented novelties: it has been argued that the revolution in cyberspace, the spread of the PC and the liberating power of the world wide web stems from the hippie counter-culture rather than the goal-oriented demands of the military-industrial complex.

There is also a connection between the spaced-out dopeheads and grasshoppers of the hippie era and the political activists who battled against racial segregation. The Freedom Riders were the precursors to the Merry Pranksters: in 1961 these black and white students travelled together on interstate buses into the South to test the impact of the Supreme Court's judgment (in *Boynton v Virginia*) to outlaw racial segregation. They suffered attacks from the Ku Klux Klan under the disregarding stewardship of Eugene 'Bull' Connor (commissioner of public safety in Birmingham, Alabama), but their passive resistance was an inspiration to others. In November 2001, the Freedom Riders Foundation celebrated their fortieth anniversary with a four-day event at Jackson, Mississippi: the gathering was overshadowed by the events of 9/11, but in their newsletter they resolved to carry on, announcing in block capitals: 'TERRORISM DID NOT STOP US THEN, WILL NOT STOP US NOW'.

Americans remind themselves, with narratives like these, that their allegiance to the cause of liberty is a defining feature of their society and something fundamentally noble, enlightened and courageous. This American creed of freedom would lead one to believe there is a national commitment to human liberty in all its varieties. In fact, many issues divide along party-political lines.

Census data show, for instance, that Republicans align themselves in particular with the right to bear arms. The first Congress sought to ensure that each state had a militia equipped to defend the republic, and this requirement, embodied in the Second Amendment, has been turned into a benchmark of personal freedom for one tranche of society. The National Rifle Association (NRA), founded in 1871, has a membership of almost 3 million who read *The American Hunter, The American Rifleman* and *America's 1st Freedom* and subscribe to the slogan 'I'll give up my gun when they pry it from my cold, dead hands.'

Democrats are more likely to support the efforts of the American Civil Liberties Union (ACLU) than the NRA. Its membership is a tenth that of the NRA, but its declared aims are not dissimilar – to Keep America Safe and Free. It has been championing liberty since 1920 and its list of issues include criminal justice, the death penalty, drug policy, free speech, immigrants' rights, lesbian and gay rights, prisoners' rights, racial justice, the rights of the poor and reproductive freedom.

Abortion is a divisive subject for Americans, as demonstrated in the 2008 presidential campaign by the 'pro-choice' position of the Democrats' Obama and the 'pro-life' position of the Republicans' McCain. Five years earlier, the country had commemorated the thirtieth anniversary of the Supreme Court ruling in *Roe v Wade* that overturned many laws against abortion since these breached the right to privacy under the liberty clause of the Fourteenth Amendment. The court considered the rights of the child, but concluded that those who framed the Constitution and its Amendments had never intended their rules to extend to the unborn. As a result, there were over 33 million legal abortions between 1973 and 2003; the trend is declining, but there were still 820,000 legal terminations in 2005.

The Supreme Court ruling sparked a sustained anti-abortion campaign led by right-wing Christians: this has included the picketing of abortion clinics, the intimidation of their clients and violent attacks. In 2003, the State of Florida executed Paul Hill, a former Presbyterian minister who murdered a doctor who ran an abortion clinic. Six years later, on 31 May 2009, Dr George Tiller – whose clinic specialized in late-term abortions – was shot dead outside the Reformation Lutheran Church in Wichita, Kansas, where he was serving as an usher at the Sunday service. Scott Roeder, a fifty-one-year-old man who was later arrested, drove off from the scene in a car embellished with the 'Jesus Fish'. Newspaper reports linked him to 'The Freemen' – a group of anti-government 'Christian Patriots' that kept the FBI at bay in an armed standoff at Jordan, Montana, for almost three months in 1995–96.

Debates over gun laws and abortion demonstrate the paradox facing any society that takes liberty as its dominant ideology. A 'pro-choice' doctor who terminates foetuses to enhance the quality-of-life – freedom? – of young, unmarried, white girls (over 50 per cent of abortions fall into this category) has his life taken by a 'pro-life' Christian using a hand-gun whose ready availability is taken as testament to America's commitment to liberty. There is enough syzygy here to win the World Scrabble Championship.

It is self-evident that no nation can grant its citizens unbounded freedom without creating conditions where some become less free than others. Sidney Hook put it this way in *The Paradoxes of Freedom* (1962):

> All too often the meaning and associations of the specific historical freedoms won by the American Revolution have become absorbed in the penumbral emotive overtones of the words, which then function as slogans and thus get in the way of clear thought. The term becomes a fetish, and is invoked by groups who want diametrically opposite things.

Those, then, who claim to govern a land where liberty prevails must introduce measures that operate to bind the free. In United States they call this 'justice'. The paradox is openly expressed in inscriptions engraved into the stonework of many public buildings. The walls of the National Archives carry the message that 'Eternal vigilance is the price of freedom'. The Supreme Court Building captures the theme in the allegorical sculptures over the front door, with a group entitled *Liberty Enthroned Guarded by Order and Authority*. The rear entrance reinforces the point, with an architrave bearing the legend 'Justice the guardian of liberty'.

There is an affinity between these inscriptions and the memorable speech – entitled 'Liberty under the Law' – proclaimed by Warren G. Harding in August 1920 when campaigning for the presidency. He warned against throttling liberty in response to the threat from communism. Freedom of speech, press and assembly, he said, were as sacred and inviolable as the freedom of religious belief, the rights of life and the pursuit of happiness. However, in almost the next breath he asserted that government had the right to defend liberty by crushing sedition and stamping out threats to the republic.

> Security and the majesty of the law are the first essentials of liberty ... Men have a right to question our system in fullest freedom, but they must always remember that the right to freedom impose [*sic*] the obligations which maintain it.

He who shows contempt for authority, Harding argued, ceases to be a loyal citizen and forfeits his rights to American freedoms.

This harsh articulation of the *realpolitik* values of American freedom contrasts with idealistic exponents of libertarian views, who are frequently portrayed as marginal figures – lunatics, cult-members, outcasts – as in this passage from Hugh Henry Brackenridge's quixotic *Modern Chivalry* (first published in 1792):

> In the next apartment was an insane person, who stiled himself the Lay Preacher, and who took his text as usual; and began to preach. Book of Judges, 21.25. 'In those days there was no king in Israel; and every man did what was right in his own eyes.' That was right, said a mad democrat,

who was confined in a cell across the passage. When we got quit of a king, the same thing was expected here, 'that every man should do that which was right in his own eyes' but behold we are made to do that which is right in the eyes of others. The law governs, and this law is made up of acts of assembly, and the decisions of the courts; and a kind of law they call the common law . . . We see honest men knocked down with the jaw bones of lawyers.

This reminds us of a tradition of anarchic libertarianism – far removed from the communist ideology that so troubled President Harding – that is vehemently opposed to the idea of government and judicial interference. In recent years, there have been armed groups like the Montana Freemen, while movements like the Free State Project (FSP) and Free State Wyoming (FSW) seek to achieve their goals democratically. FSP, founded in 2001 by Jason Sorens, aims to create a libertarian stronghold in the nation and targeted New Hampshire in October 2003. This led Kenneth W. Royce (a.k.a. 'Boston T. Party') to form FSW – opting for a west-coast site rather than an east-coast one: he wants to liberate the Cowboy State, establishing 'a haven for Americans who desire not to live as, or under, government supremacists'. The dream, according to their website, is 'truly to enjoy our rights of gun ownership, privacy, schooling, health and diet, unrestricted travel, and property' – although counter-intuitively these freedom-lovers require you to register before participating in their virtual Wyoming community.

We can sense, here, that same impulse that led the Pilgrims to cross the Atlantic, pioneers to cross the prairies, migrants to cocoon themselves in ethnic island-communities and individuals to seek an unencumbered wilderness. But if the bounty of seemingly endless tracts of virgin land helped to create the wealthiest nation in the world, and the illusion of independence, so it has engendered the dark matter of prejudice and bigotry that weighs on the condition of liberty in the US.

*   *   *

The Southern lynch-mob is the most abominable manifestation of intolerance in the Land of the Free. A recent estimate suggests up to 20,000 African-Americans were killed by the Ku Klux Klan between 1868 and 1871, and a further 3,417 were lynched between 1882 and 1944 (over one a week on average); in *The End of Blackness* (2004), Debra Dickerson has raised that total to approximately 4,742 between 1882 and 1968. This grim episode in America's history is captured in the Allen-Littlefield Collection of photographs and postcards held today by Emory University in Atlanta, Georgia. (Some of these were exhibited at the Martin Luther King Jr National Historic Site – under the title *Without Sanctuary* – from May to November 2002.) The images are harrowing. They show corpses – mostly of African-American males – hanging by the neck from tree branches, bridges, lamp-posts and other makeshift scaffolds; some are dismembered and burnt beyond recognition. A record of faculty discussions at Emory about the aptness of exhibiting these images includes the following observations:

> The perpetrators and spectators (including children) in the photos often appear proud, even gleeful. Their faces suggest a festive, carnivalesque atmosphere. Adding to the brutality are the messages scrawled on the cards: 'This is the Barbecue we had last night'; 'The answer of the Anglo-Saxon race to black brutes who would attack the Womanhood of the South'.

The nature of this gruesome ritual is illustrated in a contemporary account in *The Springfield Weekly Republican* of the justice meted out to Sam Holt of Newman, Georgia, in 1889, who was accused of raping a white woman. A crowd of 2,000 took him and tied him to a tree: he was stripped and a heavy chain wound round his body:

> Before the torch was applied to the pyre, the Negro was deprived of his ears, fingers and genital parts of his body. He pleaded pitifully for his life while the mutilation was

going on, but stood the ordeal of the fire with surprising fortitude. Before the body was cool, it was cut into pieces, the bones were crushed into small bits, and even the tree on which the wretch met his fate was torn up and disposed of as 'souvenirs'. The negro's heart was cut into several pieces, as was also his liver.

This macabre theatre goes beyond what Michel Foucault has described as the poetics of jurisprudence. There is a political and psychological dimension to the spectacle: the liberated ('uppity') black man is emasculated by white men who have themselves been culturally neutered in military defeat. The power of the impotent is ritually and brutally reasserted.

However, the illiberal culture has deep and extensive roots. Students of American literature are taught that the continent's first book of satire was *The Simple Cobbler of Aggawam* (1647). The witty work, full of word-play and extended conceits, is by Nathaniel Ward, who studied law at Emmanuel College, Cambridge, before becoming a Calvinist minister. In 1633, Ward was effectively gagged for non-conformity by Archbishop Laud and he sailed to join the Puritans of the Massachusetts Bay Colony. Here, he helped to compile the first code of laws for the colony – 'The Body of Liberties' – and Ward was living in Boston when he wrote *The Simple Cobbler*. Humour is used both as a shield and a weapon, and it is salted with passages of dyspeptic prejudice that give an ironic twist to the principles of freedom (and, indeed, to the idea of laws called 'Liberties'):

I dare take upon me, to be the Herauld of New-England so farre, as to proclaime to the world, in the name of our Colony, that all Familists, Antinomians, Anabaptists and other Enthusiasts, shall have free Liberty to keep away from us, and such as will come to be gone as fast as they can, the sooner the better.

You still find Americans who express twenty-first-century versions of the Cobbler's worldview. Dennis McCroskey is a case

In the same article, Sean Aaron, an IT consultant who moved from California to Stirling in Scotland with his wife Michelle, says one thing he likes about Britain is the way diverse views are tolerated. If anyone revealed communist leanings in the US, he says, people would call them insane:

> But here it is like, hey, you can have the Scottish Socialist party calling for Scotland to become a socialist republic and they have six seats in the Scottish parliament. Regardless of what you might think about the Scottish Socialist party I think that says a great deal about tolerance and diversity of viewpoint. I find it very reassuring.

The individual experiences of Tracy and Sean chime with the findings of Louis Hartz, the American political scientist. In a number of works published in the mid-twentieth century, he compared the fixed dogmatic liberalism of the US with the British variety, which exhibits 'a marvellous organic cohesion [that] has held together the feudal, liberal and socialist ideas':

> Freedom in the fullest sense implies both variety and equality; but history, for reasons of its own, chose to separate these two principles, leaving the one with the old society of Burke and giving the other to the new society of Paine . . . A society like England, in the very midst of its ramshackle class-ridden atmosphere, seems to contain an indefinable germ of liberty, a respect for the privacies of life, that America cannot duplicate. At the bottom of the American experience of freedom . . . there has always lain the inarticulate premise of conformity.

We are dealing with matters of degree, here, but the people occupying a crowded archipelago on the edge of Europe have – through centuries of interaction between competing cultures and ideologies – established the conditions to accommodate what the American philosopher, John Rawls, called an 'overlapping consensus'. Liberty has inevitably evolved under different conditions in the US, where the open skies of a seemingly boundless land encouraged the idea that the independent spirit is sovereign: if the community accepts your lifestyle, that's fine; if not, move on and create a community of your own.

The British brand of liberty has also had to cope with the iniquities of a deeply entrenched property class. Compared, at least, to the American blueprint, there is far less equality of opportunity in Britain; so the impulse to create a fairer, more just society has focused on redistributing wealth and opening up opportunities. This has developed a reflex in the British 'body politic' that has never taken root in the US. It is found in the tenets of Chartism, the Cooperative Movement, the Fabians and the Labour Movement. The American challenge has been to achieve equality of difference – hence the strong Civil Rights tradition and the EEO machine.

In seeking some philosophical reference point to anchor our understanding, we can turn to John Rawls' teacher, Isaiah Berlin. In 1958, he gave his inaugural lecture as professor of social and political theory at Oxford University. His paper, entitled 'Two Concepts of Liberty', drew a distinction between a 'negative' liberty that seeks to curb authority and provide the individual with freedom from the coercion of other men; and a 'positive' view that is self-directive, giving an individual the freedom to be his own master and to participate in a chosen way of life.

It is tempting to argue that the positive ideal is in the ascendancy in the US; whereas in Britain, the vision of negative liberty seems to predominate. Each society cherishes its form of freedom, but in each case liberty has its limitations: Britain may have incorporated equality of difference into its national narrative, but it sustains a social structure that struggles to offer opportunities to all. Americans may speak of equality of opportunity, but we have seen that the spirit of individualized liberty brings unfortunate, unintended consequences of its own. Each society, in its own way and according to its own unique circumstances, seeks to reconcile liberty, equality and justice. Each fails, but the consequences – the afflictions of liberty –

seem especially acute in a society like America which gives liberty such a dominant status in its national narrative.

It would be irrational to deny the existence of an Anglo-Saxon consciousness, shared between the United Kingdom and the United States. The lineaments are present in a common language and the common law; in long-cherished values of freedom and independence that bring an aversion to authority; and in folk traditions carried westwards by thousands of migrants in America's formative years and embedded into the practices of everyday life.

However, just as language is transformed over time under the influence of 'pull-chain' or 'push-chain' effects, 'drift' and 'analogy', so cultures also shift and change. The UK can appear to be in transition – an American 'mini-me' – with the statistical data showing it to mediate between the US and Continental Europe in such diverse metrics as prison population, fiscal measures, teenage pregnancies, shelf-space, charitable giving, Nobel Prizes and levels of innovation. Yet our analysis has shown there to be little commonality between the set of American paradoxes examined in this book and Britain's contemporary culture. It has become apparent that *The Cracked Bell* is not addressing an Anglo-Saxon syndrome: the features described here are further evidence for the exceptionalism of the American Way.

Countless effects, many imperceptible, cause a culture to adapt and adjust. Analysts can point, for instance, to the mix of racial, ethnic and cultural traits that have shaped the American Way; also to environmental features such as geography, climate and the availability of natural resources; and to the political economy. However, the suite of paradoxes examined in these pages has exposed a particular grain of grit in the American oyster: the inflated, extravagant, nationalistic ideal of the independent, liberated individual.

It is this ideal of the liberated individual within an atomistic social order – this hyper-individualism – that distinguishes the US from its Anglo-Saxon cousin across the Atlantic. This ideal may derive from the British Isles – a cultural seed blown across the Atlantic to lodge in American soil – but it has acquired distinctive characteristics of its own. This was, for Louis Hartz, 'the secret root from which have sprung many of the most puzzling of American cultural phenomena'.

It is certain that cultural exchanges across the Atlantic will continue, in both directions. It can also be assumed that voices will be heard, in both the Old World and the New, bemoaning the consequences. This is, nevertheless, a creative tension full of potential and promise, and it is even possible to imagine a reconfiguration of American and British ways, with two different traditions of liberty synthesized to create conditions – in each nation – for a more just and equitable society.

In this spirit, it seems fitting to follow the path taken by our Anglophile lawyer to that recital of *A Sea Symphony* in May 2004. This work matches the visionary verses of Walt Whitman with the music of Ralph Vaughan Williams – a great Anglo-American production, a transcendent, universal work, which ranges across such varied themes as exploration and innovation, the movement of ships across the surging sea, the meaning of progress and the Second Coming. The symphony also includes words, sung that night by the black baritone Gordon Hawkins, that express an equation – a unity of being – that extends far beyond the narrow confines of any Anglosphere:

On the beach at night alone,
As the old mother sways to and fro singing her husky song,
As I watch the bright stars shining, I think a thought of the
    clef of the universes and of the future.
A vast similitude interlocks all,
All distances of place however wide, all distances of time,
All souls, all living bodies though they be ever so different,
All nations, all identities that have existed or may exist,
All lives and deaths, all of the past, present, future,
This vast similitude spans them, and always has spanned,
And shall forever span them and compactly hold and
    enclose them.

Beyond Hobbes and Hobbits

The bell from Liberty Hall is cracked, and chimes with a hollow dissonance.

We have someone to blame for the fracture in the Liberty Bell. In 1911, Emmanuel Joseph Rauch admitted to the *New York Times* that he, as a boy, had been tugging at the rope attached to the clapper on that day in 1846 when the bell cracked.

It is not so simple, however, to ascribe blame for the afflictions of liberty described in this book. In all likelihood, the fault was there from the very beginning, when the germ of freedom crossed the Atlantic, embedded within the aspirations and dreams of countless millions fleeing the oppression of the Old World. The flaw, indeed, is probably a feature of our humanity, with the United States – that great experiment in political science – providing the conditions to amplify and expose it.

I find it instructive – even ironic – that a century before the Liberty Bell arrived in Pennsylvania, the English philosopher Thomas Hobbes had chosen America to emblemize the state of what he termed natural liberty. The title-page of his masterpiece – *De Cive* – contains an allegorical image of 'Libertas' depicted as an Indian squaw with longbow and arrow. (The picture was adapted from a 1580s drawing, by John White, of an Algonquian chieftain.) Behind this frowning Liberty – so different to the benign, solemn gaze of New York Harbor's beloved statue – three near-naked men chase two others, while a fourth predator stands in ambush, with club poised to strike. Nearby, two figures squat by a trestle-larder that looks to be stocked with a dismembered limb. This is a dystopian vision where every man upholds the right to everything: liberation is a synonym for lawlessness, and for Hobbes the only logical outcome was war – a condition of unending hostility in which, ultimately, 'nature itself is destroyed'.

In my darker moments, I envisage an America under the sway of Hobbes' Libertas. Hobbesville USA is a frontier town, or an urban jungle like Liberty City in *Grand Theft Auto*. The radical spirit of the liberated individual is in the vanguard, with the emphasis on licence rather than liberty. There is intolerance and violence: conflict between and within ethnic groups; tension between classes of have-mores and have-nots. Hobbesville is radioactive with the fallout from rampant consumerism: debt, obesity, instant gratification, egoism and mindless disregard for finite natural resources. There is 'culture war' between religious and secular seekers after personal salvation, with charges of sinfulness exchanged between those who argue over the competing merits of the Second Coming and the Second Helping. Political grafters and corrupt lawyers are in the ascendant, and a strong police arm is available to the highest payer.

This is, I realize, a bad dream. Hobbes himself advocated the need for a social contract where the worst excesses of Libertas were contained by justice and good government; and the Founding Fathers were convinced that a society could be established in the New World that achieved the perfect balance between freedom and order, liberation and regulation. There are, indeed, moments of optimism when America appears to me as the idealized community of Hobbiton rather than Hobbesville. This archetype derives from the fantastical vision of J.R.R. Tolkien, who wrote of the Hobbits of Middle Earth:

In that pleasant corner of the world they plied their well-ordered business of living and they heeded less and less the world outside where dark things moved, until they came to think that peace and plenty were the rule in Middle-Earth and the right of all sensible folk.

Tolkien's inspiration came from the same utopian portrayal of early Saxon tribes that had sparked Jefferson's imagination. His creatures maintain a voluntary, ordered society where the sense of fellowship is strong and where government is small. They have an elected mayor who presides over a postal service and a small police force whose principal function is to round up stray livestock. There are rules, but all Hobbits obey them because they are just, and the few lawyers in the land are there to ensure that wills and contracts are drawn up in good order. There is also an underlying sense of destiny about this community – a feeling that the fruits of the land are evidence of a God-given Providence.

There is a piece of Hobbiton meshed into all but the most dysfunctional communities of the US, not least in the suburbs that harbour the bulk of the nation's population. The inhabitants of Hobbiton USA wrap themselves in a reassuring quilt of custom and ritual, material possessions and voluntary associations. Comfort and contentment come from a sense of consensus in common observances: the give and take of commerce in the mall; the uplifting quality of church rites; shared moments before the flickering flames of the television; the spectacular theatricality of myths narrated in the cinema or played out in computer games; the ritualized battles of baseball stadium, football field and NASCAR track; the drama and humour of parochial news; the cycle of the years marked out with Labor Day and Memorial Day, Thanksgiving and Halloween. A sense of solidarity comes from family and congregation, college fraternity and labour union, and just from being in the PTA or on the company's team. The residents of Hobbiton USA have little doubt that they are a chosen people and presume that the rest of the world wants to become like them.

However, in the opening decade of the twenty-first century the social cohesiveness of Hobbiton is undercut by the hyper-individualism of Hobbesville, creating a deep sense of insecurity about personal and national identity. Myth must inevitably crash against reality; aspiration fails to conform to expectation. This is the cultural equivalent to geological compression and contraction, creating a social topography that is confusing, threatening, even dangerous, for those who live on the slopes of the volcano.

If the spirit of freedom inspires the American Dream, the ghost of freedom infects the American Crisis, threatening to turn the dream into a nightmare. It may be simplistic to describe this syndrome as pathological, but Louis Hartz spoke of a 'psychic inflation' in describing how a fragment of English liberalism became isolated and subjected to metamorphosis in the decades after the revolution. There is resonance, here, with the Jungian concept of the 'inflated' neurotic who believes that an idealized image is the real self. This condition may not be contagious, but its damaging consequences extend beyond the borders of the fifty American states.

A fixation with consumption threatens to upset the ecological wellbeing of the whole planet as well as creating social, physiological and psychological problems at home. Many of the difficulties that the world is facing could be addressed by the bountiful marvels of American innovation but the pernicious presence of power-blocs in the country must inevitably suppress that spirit of invention. American ideas of liberty and 'chosenness' – reinforced by mythical notions of salvation and the frontier – underpin a subliminal logic of imperialism: if Everyman can enjoy the bounty of American individualism, Anyman who obstructs this pursuit of happiness stands in the path of progress and deserves to be thrown down.

I learnt from one wise old American – still operating at the heart of government after taking up his appointment thirty-five years ago – that it is best to focus on diagnosis and leave the therapy to others. For his part, the Swiss psychiatrist Carl Jung recommended that psychic inflation could be overcome only through patience, humility and self-analysis, and the reality is that legions of American citizens worry about the state of their nation, practising the very qualities that Jung espoused.

President Barack Obama is uniquely placed to apply balm to

the afflictions of liberty. He came to power on a tidal surge of good will and high hopes. Turnout in the 2008 election – at just under 63 per cent – has been bettered in the last fifty years only by the figure of 64 per cent in 1960, when John F. Kennedy beat Richard Nixon. He received multiracial support, with 95 per cent of blacks, 66 per cent of Hispanics and 43 per cent of whites supporting his ticket; and 66 per cent of all voters aged under thirty opted for Obama. The atmosphere that Obama conjured up during his campaign is evoked by the following commentary from one of those voices encountered earlier in *The Cracked Bell*. In the chapter called 'The Many and the One', David Giles described his experience of segregation in 1940s Virginia; and in 'The Lattice Constant' he extolled the entrepreneurial opportunities of America today. Now aged over seventy, he attended an Obama rally at Prince William County Fairground in Virginia, two days before the 2008 election:

What a spectacle! A boundless sea of arc-lit faces, amplifiers blasting out Soul Choirs and Bruce Springsteen – something between a rock concert and a Pentecostal-revivalist meeting. A huge American flag and illuminated signs proclaiming VOTE FOR CHANGE; a barrage balloon floating overhead advertising 'Boilermakers for Change', large yellow signs saying 'Fire-fighters for Obama'; everywhere the name and logo of Obama – on babies' caps and Dads' caps, on every coat and hat and T-shirt. And what a crowd: patient, cheerful, expectant, young and multiracial. The average age was 25–30; 60% black, 20% Hispanic, and 20% white. Young people were lending coats to old – it was a clear chilly night – everyone was swapping stories and Obama anecdotes. There was a huge cheer as Barack arrived. I've never felt such a surge of emotion, enthusiasm and hope. He spoke with ringing, almost religious conviction and confidence. As his slim figure reached the podium and he saw the huge crowd, a youthful sonorous voice rang out over the field: 'Wow . . . and this is Virginia . . . where the Union truly started: here at the first battle of the Civil War, at Manassas.' And that was his main theme – that the people before him were not black, nor white, nor Hispanic; nor 'real-American' nor 'part-American', nor Muslim nor Christian nor Hindu nor Jewish, nor 'red', nor 'blue' – but *American*. His soaring eloquence is extraordinary – a voice that cannot be connected with any race or state or territory. It seems to represent the voice and hopes of thinking Americans.

As an anthropologist, I am sceptical about the ability of one individual to change culture. Memetic engineering (the process of controlling social and cultural beliefs) is no easier than the genetic variety. Obama's battle-cry in his 2008 campaign may have been 'Change We Need', but we have seen in 'The Lattice Constant' chapter how the language of innovation and transformation can carry a symbolic power in American society that does not accord with reality. There is a risk that his aspirations come to be seen as the Audacity of Hype: this word-play was deployed by Obama's opponents during the election, and *The Audacity of Hype* became the title of an album by the former punk-rocker Jello Biafra, who was already expressing unease by August 2009 that Obama would renege on his promises. Meanwhile, conservative authors like Mark R. Levin and Bernard Goldberg have gone to print attacking Obama's 'Statist' tendencies. The lesson that a pessimist would draw from history is that economic depression at home and political turmoil abroad tend to reinforce rather than resolve anti-social, protectionist and xenophobic traits within society.

Nevertheless, Obama is well suited to the role of one striving to 'perfect an imperfect union'. His mixed-race parentage gives substance to his faith in America's ability to forge a national identity from disparate tribes and races. He acquired a political philosophy from his mother that was grounded in notions of community and justice; and it was in search of a practical application of her values that he worked as a community organizer in Chicago, operating in deprived communities where unemployment, drugs and a sense of hopelessness prevailed. He combines years of teaching US constitutional law with the practical experience of seeking votes from low-income neighbourhoods. He recognizes a cynicism in the country about politics but his agenda is based on the idea that fellow citizens have a stake in one another, and that what binds them together is greater than what drives them apart.

This has led the Forty-Fourth President to understand the potentially unstable balance between freedom and the common good, between Hobbesville and Hobbiton. He has written:

> In every society (and in every individual) these twin strands – the individualistic and the communal, autonomy and solidarity – are in tension . . . At times these values collide because in the hands of men each one is subject to distortion and excess. Self-reliance and independence can transform into selfishness and license, ambition into greed and a frantic desire to succeed at any cost.

Finding the right balance between competing values is difficult in a free society like the United States, he argues, because we live inherently in a complex and contradictory world.

People once spoke of President John F. Kennedy as King Arthur in Camelot. If Obama succeeds in rebooting the American Dream, future generations could come to regard him as a latter-day Alfred the Great, forging a true commonwealth from the fragments. As with King Alfred, philosophy, art and literature can provide Obama with a touchstone to express the alchemy of re-evaluation and self-renewal. He could turn, for instance, to the work of the American whose words closed the last chapter: Walt Whitman voiced a humanistic synthesis of liberty and justice that is closer to the moral code of the Enlightenment than to the rugged individualism that has dominated the narrative for the past hundred years. Or he could celebrate the musical genres of jazz and blues that represent a fused, syncretized, American identity; or champion the work of a living poet like Maya Angelou, who recited 'Still I Rise' so beautifully on national television the day after the 2008 election.

President Obama could also profit from the profound insights of an American philosopher who died at the beginning of the new millennium. In works like *A Theory of Justice*, *Political Liberalism* and *The Law of Peoples*, John Rawls constructed the foundations of a 'realistic utopia', seeking a better balance between liberty and justice. For Rawls, 'Justice is the first virtue of social institutions, as truth is of systems of thought.'

There already exist then, in America, sources of illumination that can light the way to a world beyond that of Hobbes and Hobbits. The nation can overcome the American Crisis and reclaim the American Dream.

The cracked bell can be re-cast.

BIBLIOGRAPHY

Suggestions for Further Reading

Introduction: The American Crisis and the American Dream

Alsop, George (1666) *A Character of the Province of Maryland*, London

Crèvecoeur, J. Hector St John (1908) *Letters from an American Farmer*, London: Chatto & Windus; New York, NY: Duffield & Co.

Enriquez, Juan (2005) *The Untied States of America: Polarization Fracturing and Our Future*, New York, NY: Crown Publishers

Geuss, Raymond, and Hollis, Martin (1995) 'Freedom as an Ideal', in *Proceedings of the Aristotelian Society, Supplementary Volumes*, vol. 69, pp. 87–112

Gorer, Geoffrey (1948) *The Americans: A Study in National Character*, London: Cresset Press

Harriot, Thomas (1588) *A Brief and True Report of the New Found Land of Virginia*, London

Hartz, Louis (1955) *The Liberal Tradition in America: An Interpretation of American Political Thought since the Revolution*, New York, NY: Harcourt, Brace

Hartz, Louis (1964) *The Founding of New Societies*, New York, NY: Harcourt, Brace and World

Hook, Sidney (1962) *The Paradoxes of Freedom*, Berkeley, CA: University of California Press

Kammen, Michael (1972) *People of Paradox: An Inquiry Concerning the Origins of American Civilization*, New York, NY: Alfred A. Knopf

Leach, Edmund (1982) *Social Anthropology*, Oxford: Oxford University Press

Maritain, Jacques (1958) *Reflections on America*, New York, NY: Charles Scribner's Sons

National Commission on Terrorist Attacks upon the United States (2004) *The 9/11 Commission Report*, New York, NY, & London: W.W. Norton & Co.

Niebuhr, Reinhold (1952) *The Irony of American History*, New York, NY: Charles Scribner's Sons

Obama, Barack (2008) *The Audacity of Hope: Thoughts on Reclaiming the American Dream*, Edinburgh: Canongate Books

Paine, Thomas (1999) *The American Crisis, Number 1*, Philadelphia, PA: Independence Historical National Park

Patterson, James T. (1996) *Grand Expectations: The United States 1945–1974*, Oxford: Oxford University Press

Patterson, James T. (2005) *Restless Giant: The United States from Watergate to Bush v Gore*, Oxford: Oxford University Press

Pynchon, Thomas (1973) *Gravity's Rainbow*, New York, NY: Viking Press

Smith, John (1608) *True Relation of Occurrences and Accidents in Virginia*, London

Smith, John (1624) *The Generall Historie of Virginia, New England & The Summer Isles*, London

Tocqueville, Alexis de (1994) *Democracy in America*, London: David Campbell

Wills, Garry (1978) *Inventing America: Jefferson's Declaration of Independence*, Garden City, NY: Doubleday

Zinn, Howard (2003) *A People's History of the United States: 1492–Present*, London: HarperCollins

Chapter 1: The Many and the One – On Identity

Barth, Fredrik (1969) *Ethnic Groups and Boundaries: The Social Organization of Cultural Difference*, London: Allen & Unwin

Blair, Jayson (2004) *Burning Down My Masters' House*, New York, NY: New Millennium Press

Confederation of American Indians (1986) *Indian Reservations. A State and Federal Handbook*, Jefferson, NC: McFarland

Cruz, José E. (1998) *Identity and Power: Puerto Rican Politics and the Challenge of Ethnicity*, Philadelphia, PA: Temple University Press

Dawson, Michael (2001) *Black Visions: The Roots of Contemporary African-American Political Ideologies*, Chicago, IL: University of Chicago Press

De Beaumont, Gustave (1835) *Marie, ou l'Esclavage aux États-Unis*, Paris: Charles Gosselin

Dickerson, Debra (2004) *The End of Blackness: Returning the Souls of Black Folks to Their Rightful Owners*, New York, NY: Pantheon

Du Bois, W.E.B. (1905) *The Souls of Black Folk*, London: Archibald Constable & Co.

Frantz, Klaus (1993) *Indian Reservations in the US*, Chicago, IL: University of Chicago Press

Garcia, Alma M. (2002) *The Mexican Americans*, London: Greenwood Press

Goldberg, Myla (2001) *Bee Season*, New York, NY: Anchor Books

Gordon, Dexter B. (2003) *Black Identity: Rhetoric, Ideology and 19th Century Black Nationalism*, Carbondale, IL: Southern Illinois University Press

Huntington, Samuel (2004) *Who Are We?*, London: Simon & Schuster

Loury, Glenn C. (2002) *The Anatomy of Racial Inequality*, Cambridge, MA: Harvard University Press

Melville, Herman (1971) *The Confidence-Man: His Masquerade*, London & New York, NY: W.W. Norton

O'Brien, Sharon (1989) *American Indian Tribal Governments*, Norman, OK: University of Oklahoma Press

Porter, Harry (1979) *The Inconstant Savage: England and the North American Indian 1500–1660*, London: Duckworth

Roosevelt, Theodore (1889–96) *The Winning of the West*, vols 1–4, New York, NY: G.P. Putnam's Sons

Schlesinger, Arthur (1998) *The Disuniting of America: Reflections on a Multicultural Society*, London & New York, NY: W.W. Norton

Sen, Amartya (2006) *Identity and Violence: The Illusion of Destiny*, London: Allen Lane

Smith, Claire (2005) 'Decolonising the Museum: The National Museum of the American Indian in Washington DC', in *Antiquity*, vol. 79, no. 304, June, pp. 424–39

Somkin, Fred (1967) *Unquiet Eagle. Memory and Desire in the Idea of American Freedom. 1815–1860*, Ithaca, NY: Cornell University Press

Tolzmann, Don Heinrich (1975) *German-Americana: A Bibliography*, Metuchen, NJ: Scarecrow Press

Tolzmann, Don Heinrich (2000) *The German-American Experience*, Amherst, MA, & New York, NY: Prometheus Books

Turner, Frederick Jackson (1893) 'The Significance of the Frontier in American History', in *Report of the American Historical Association for 1893*, Washington, DC: American Historical Association, pp. 199–227

Utter, Jack (2001) *American Indians. Answers to Today's Questions* (2nd edition), Norman, OK: University of Oklahoma Press

Vigil, James Diego (2002) *A Rainbow of Gangs: Street Cultures in the Mega-City*, Austin, TX: University of Texas Press

Zangwill, Israel (1915) *The Melting Pot*, New York, NY: Macmillan

Chapter 2: The Temple of Trade – On Consumerism

Bryson, Bill (1996) *Made in America: An Informal History of the English Language in the United States*, New York, NY: HarperCollins

Butterfield, Steve (1985) *Amway: The Cult of Free Enterprise*, Boston, MA: South End Press

Castronova, Edward (2004) 'The Price of Bodies: A Hedonic Pricing Model of Avatar Attributes in a Synthetic World', in *Kyklos*, vol. 57, no. 2, pp. 173–96

Cross, Gary S. (2000) *An All-Consuming Century: Why Commercialism Won in Modern America*, New York, NY: Columbia University Press

De Grazia, Victoria (2005) *Irresistible Empire: America's Advance through 20th Century Europe*, Cambridge, MA: Belknap Press of Harvard University Press

Douglas, Mary and Isherwood, Baron (1979) *The World of Goods. Towards an Anthropology of Consumption*, London: Allen Lane

Farrell, James J. (2003) *One Nation Under Goods: Malls and the Seductions of American Shopping*, Washington, DC, & London: Smithsonian Books

Friedman, Walter A. (2005) *Birth of a Salesman: The Transformation of Selling in America*, Cambridge, MA: Harvard University Press

Galbraith, J.K. (1958) *The Affluent Society*, London: Hamish Hamilton

Greider, William (2004) *The Soul of Capitalism: Opening Paths to a Moral Economy*, New York, NY: Schuster

Heinze, Andrew R. (1990) *Adapting to Abundance; Jewish Immigrants, Mass Consumption, and the Search for American Identity*, New York, NY: Columbia University Press

Hertslet, Evelyn (1886) *Ranch Life in California: Extracted from the Home Correspondence of E.M.H.*, London: W.H. Allen

Houthakker, H.S. and Taylor, Lester D. (1970) *Consumer Demand in the United States: Analyses & Projections* (2nd edition), Cambridge, MA: Harvard University Press

Kenny, Michael G. (1994) *The Perfect Law of Liberty: Elias Smith and the Providential History of America*, Washington, DC: Smithsonian Institution Press

Klein, Naomi (2001) *No Logo: No Space, No Choice, No Jobs*, London: Flamingo

Moseley, James G. (1992) *John Winthrop's World*, Madison, WI: University of Wisconsin Press

Noll, Mark A. (ed.) (2002) *God and Mammon: Protestants, Money and the Market 1790–1860*, New York, NY: Oxford University Press

Norton, Edgar (1987) 'Is Capitalism Christian?', in *Liberty Report*, Oct.

Piper, John Stephen (1986) *Desiring God: Meditations of a Christian Hedonist*, Sisters, OR: Multnomah Publishers, Inc.

Potter, David M. (1954) *People of Plenty: Economic Abundance and the American Character*, Chicago, IL: University of Chicago Press

Sellers, Charles (1991) *The Market Revolution: Jacksonian America 1815–1846*, New York, NY: Oxford University Press

Weber, Max (1976) *The Protestant Ethic and the Spirit of Capitalism*, London: Allen & Unwin

Woods, Thomas E. (2005) *The Church and the Market: A Catholic Defense of the Free Economy*, Lanham, MD: Lexington Books

Chapter 3: Trick or Treat – On Belief

Ahlstrom, Sydney (1974) *A Religious History of the American People*, New Haven, CT: Yale University Press

Berger, Peter L. (1967) *Sacred Canopy: Elements of a Sociological Theory of Religion*, New York, NY: Anchor

Berger, Peter L. (1970) *A Rumour of Angels: Modern Society and the Rediscovery of the Supernatural*, Harmondsworth: Penguin

Berger, Peter L. (1977) *Facing Up to Modernity*, New York, NY: Basic Books

Berger, Peter L. (ed.) (1999) *The Desecularization of the World: Resurgent Religion and World Politics*, Washington, DC: Ethics and Public Policy Center

Brewer, Priscilla J. (1986) *Shaker Communities, Shaker Lives*, Lebanon, NH: University Press of New England

Chapman, Matthew (2000) *Trials of the Monkey*, London: Duckworth

Cleaver, Eldridge (1979) *Soul on Fire*, London: Hodder & Stoughton

Conrad, Mark T. (2003) 'Pulp Fiction: The Sign of the Empty Symbol: The Death of God and the Royale with Cheese', www.metaphilm.com (posted 29 August 2003)

Cooke, George Willis (1903) *Unitarianism in America*, Boston, MA: American Unitarian Association

Dallimore, Arnold (1970) *George Whitefield*, Edinburgh: Banner of Truth Trust

Demos, John Putnam (ed.) (1972) *Remarkable Providences: 1600–1760*, New York, NY: George Braziller

Demos, John Putnam (1982) *Entertaining Satan. Witchcraft and the Culture of Early New England*, Oxford: Oxford University Press

France, David (2004) *Our Father: The Secret Life of the Catholic Church in an Age of Scandal*, New York, NY: Broadway Books

Gaustad, Edwin S. and Schmidt, Leigh E. (1996) *The Religious History of America*, San Francisco, CA: Harpers

Gilbert, James (1997) *Redeeming Culture: American Religion in an Age of Science*, Chicago, IL: University of Chicago Press

Hudson, Winthrop S. (1965) *Religion in America*, New York, NY: Charles Scribner's Sons

Israel, Charles A. (2004) *Before Scopes. Evangelicalism, Education and Evolution in Tennessee 1870–1925*, Athens, GA: University of Georgia Press

Jenkins, Jerry B. and LaHaye, Tim (1996–2007) *Left Behind Series* (13 vols), Carol Stream, IL: Tyndale House Publishers

Jorstad, Erling (1993) *Popular Religion in America: The Evangelical Voice*, Westport, CT: Greenwood Press

Kahn, Herman and Wiener, Anthony (1967) *The Year 2000 – A Framework for Speculation on the Next Thirty-Three Years*, New York, NY: Macmillan

Kennedy, D. James and Black, Jim Nelson (1994) *Character and Destiny: A Nation in Search of Its Soul*, Grand Rapids, MI: Zondervan

Lindsey, Hal (1973) *The Late Great Planet Earth*, New York, NY: Bantam Books

Marsden, George M. (1991) *Understanding Fundamentalism and Evangelicalism*, Grand Rapids, MI: W.B. Eerdmans

Marsden, George M. (2006) *Fundamentalism and American Culture*, Oxford: Oxford University Press

Mather, Cotton (1693) *Wonders of the Invisible World: Observations as well Historical as Theological, upon the Nature, the Number and the Operations of the Devils*, Boston, MA: Benjamin Harris

McCarthy, Cormac (2006) *The Road*, New York, NY: Alfred A. Knopf

McDannell, Colleen (ed.) (2001) *Religions of the United States in Practice*, Princeton, NJ: Princeton University Press

Miller, Perry (1953) *The New England Mind: From Colony to Province*, Cambridge, MA: Harvard University Press

Peretti, Frank (1989) *This Present Darkness*, Eastbourne: Minstrel

Pew Research Centre Pollwatch (2005) 'Reading the Polls on Evolution and Creationism', Pew Research Centre Press Release, 28 September

Pollock, John Charles (1966) *Billy Graham. The Authorised Biography*, London: Hodder & Stoughton

Schaeffer, Francis A. (1982) *A Christian Manifesto*, Basingstoke: Pickering & Inglis

Stowell, Daniel W. (1988) *Rebuilding Zion: The Religious Reconstruction of the South 1863–1877*, Oxford: Oxford University Press

Tipton, Steven M. (1982) *Getting Saved from the Sixties: Moral Meaning in Conversion and Cultural Change*, Berkeley, CA: University of California Press

Van Allen, Rodger (ed.) (1978) *American Religious Values and the Future of America*, Philadelphia, PA: Fortress Press

Warren, Rick (1995) *The Purpose Driven Church*, Grand Rapids, MI: Zondervan

Warren, Rick (2002) *The Purpose Driven Life*, Grand Rapids, MI: Zondervan

Williams, Sally (2007) 'The God Curriculum', in *Daily Telegraph* magazine, 7 April

Wilson, Charles Reagan (1980) *Baptized in Blood: The Religion of the Lost Cause*, Athens, GA: University of Georgia Press

Wuthnow, Robert (1988) 'Divided We Fall: America's Two Civil Religions', in *Christian Century*, 20 April

Yurica, Katherine (2004) 'The Despoiling of America: How George W. Bush Became the Head of the New American Dominionist Church/State', published on www.yuricareport.com on 11 Feb. 2004

Chapter 4: The Lattice Constant – On Innovation and Enervation

Allison, Kevin (2007) 'Man in the News: Mark Zuckerberg', in *Financial Times*, 29 September

Angel, David P. (1994) *Restructuring for Innovation: The Remaking of the U.S. Semiconductor Industry*, New York, NY: Guilford Press

Arendt, Hannah (1969) *On Violence*, New York, NY: Harcourt, Brace and World

Barnett, H.G. (1953) *Innovation: The Basis of Cultural Change*, New York, NY: McGraw-Hill

Boorstin, Daniel (1974) *The Americans: The Democratic Experience* (Part Nine 'Search for Novelty'), New York, NY: Vintage

Brzezinski, Zbigniew, and Huntington, Samuel (1963) *Political Power: USA/USSR*, New York, NY: Viking

Chubb, John E. and Peterson, Paul E. (eds) (1989) *Can the Government Govern?*, Washington, DC: Brookings

De Graaf, John, Wann, David and Naylor, Thomas H. (2002) *Affluenza: The All-Consuming Epidemic*, San Francisco, CA: Berrett-Koehler Publishers

DeSantis, Alan D. (2007) *Inside Greek U.: Fraternities, Sororities and the Pursuit of Pleasure, Power and Prestige*, Lexington, KY: University Press of Kentucky

Erikson, Erik (1963) *Childhood and Society*, New York, NY: W.W. Norton

Evangelista, Matthew (1988) *Innovation and the Arms Race: How the United States and the Soviet Union Develop New Military Technology*, Ithaca, NY: Cornell University Press

Evans, Harold (2004) *They Made America. From the Steam Engine to the Search Engine: Two Centuries of Innovators*, New York, NY: Little, Brown

Ewing Marion Kauffman Foundation (2006) *Kauffman Index of Entrepreneurial Activity 1996–2005*, Kansas City, MO: Ewing Marion Kauffman Foundation

Gardner, John W. (1963) *Self-Renewal*, New York, NY: W.W. Norton

Gilfillan, S. Colum (1952) 'The Prediction of Change', in *The Review of Economics and Statistics*, Nov., pp. 368–85

Guerrera, Francesco, Reed, John, and Simon, Bernard (2007) 'Drama in Dearborn', in *Financial Times*, 29 October

Hawthorne, Nathaniel (1981) *The House of the Seven Gables*, New York, NY: Bantam

Hughes, Thomas P. (2004) *Human-Built World: How to Think about Technology and Culture*, Chicago, IL: University of Chicago Press

James, Oliver (2008) *Affluenza*, London: Vermilion

Kelley, Tom (2006) *The Ten Faces of Innovation: Strategies for Heightening Creativity*, London: Profile

La Fontaine, Jean S. (1986) *Initiation*, Manchester: Manchester University Press

Lukes, Steven (1974) *Power: A Radical View*, London & New York, NY: Macmillan

Makinson, Larry and Goldstein, Joshua (1994) *Open Secrets: The Encyclopedia of Congressional Money and Politics*, Washington, DC: Washington Congressional Quarterly Press

Mills, C. Wright (1956) *The Power Elite*, New York, NY: Oxford University Press

Mintzberg, Henry (2004) *Managers Not MBAs: A Hard Look at the Soft Practice of Managing and Management Development*, San Francisco, CA: Berrett-Koehler Publishers Inc.

Moe, Terry (1989) 'The Politics of Bureaucratic Structure', in Chubb and Peterson (q.v.)

Mueller, Robert Kirk (1971) *The Innovation Ethic*, Herndon, VA: American Management Association

Nuwer, Hank (1999) *Wrongs of Passage: Fraternities, Sororities, Hazing and Binge Drinking*, Bloomington, IN: Indiana University Press

Phillips, Kevin (2006) *American Theocracy*, New York, NY: Viking

Rockwell, Llewellyn H. (2005) 'Working Around Leviathan', Ludwig von Mises Institute website www.mises.org (posted 23 June 2005)

Rogers, Everett M. (1983) *Diffusions of Innovations*, New York, NY: Free Press

Schumpeter, Joseph Alois (1989) *Essays on Entrepreneurs, Innovations, Business Cycles, and the Evolution of Capitalism* (ed. Richard V. Clemence), New Brunswick, NJ: Transaction Publishers

Stelzer, Irwin (2002) *From Grave to Cradle: Building a Meritocracy*, London, Social Market Foundation

endorsements

Art Thomas' book, *The Word of Knowledge in Action*, speaks of a lifestyle that is both practical and powerful—and ultimately available to every believer. He shares wonderful personal stories and insights that help to create great hunger in readers. These stories connect readers with their own ability to hear and activate them to walk in this gift in everyday experiences. *The Word of Knowledge in Action* is a timely book, as God is releasing His Church in a fresh and powerful way of bringing people into an experience with God.

Bill Johnson
Senior Pastor of Bethel Church in Redding, California
Author of *When Heaven Invades Earth* and
Face to Face with God

The Word of Knowledge in Action is a great book. Would that all pastors and their flocks would study it and live its message. Art Thomas is right when he says that if more Christians would seek the Lord for the gift of words of knowledge, and learn to apply them appropriately, that would vivify the Church and make words of knowledge powerful everyday tools for evangelism, for healing, and for the enhancement of nearly every other gift of the Holy Spirit.

Thomas imparts much needed wisdom and caution to a Church grown leery by wild and irresponsible applications of many spiritual gifts. Most appealing is that he centers on reception, use, and results of words of knowledge in the love and courtesy of our Lord Jesus Christ. I urge readers to purchase the book and let its words concerning words of knowledge seep into every other aspect of Christian living and ministry.

John Loren Sandford
Founder, Elijah House Ministries, Inc.
Author, *The Elijah Task, Elijah Among Us,* and
Healing the Wounded Spirit

We live in an age when more and more Christians have not only abandoned the essentials of the faith for doctrines of demons, but a time when supposedly spiritual practices and assumptions are increasingly based on experience rather than on the solid revelation of the Word of God. The result is a subtle—or not so subtle—drift that results in shipwreck of the faith, foolishness in ministry, and an erosion of creditability for those of us who do not share the foolishness.

Art Thomas' book is a solid, sane, and biblical exposition of the nature of the word of knowledge—a gift much misunderstood and most often interpreted through the filter of experience. The reader can trust what he writes. More significantly, Art has connected with the heart of the Father. I highly recommend this book!"

R. Loren Sandford
Senior Pastor of New Song Fellowship
Author, *Purifying the Prophetic, Understanding Prophetic People,*
and *The Prophetic Church*

There are many books to be found on spiritual gifts—and I've read my share—whose emphases tend to gravitate toward the individual distinctions of the gifts and how they are respectively applied. Art Thomas presents an insightful examination of the Word of Knowledge found throughout the Word of God. He responsibly demonstrates the unmistakable interrelationship between this and other spiritual gifts, as well as its companion support of various aspects of ministry including healing, deliverance, intercession, and evangelism.

Art brings a fresh contribution to the conversation on spiritual gifts and their integral function in everyday life. Many captivating stories underscore how the Word of Knowledge is active, even as they complement the Biblical examples found throughout the book. Assimilating its content will compel the reader to pursue the gifts of the Spirit with invigorated enthusiasm.

Quinn Schipper
Founder and President of OIKOS Network Ministries, Inc.
Author, *The Language of Forgiveness* and *Trading Faces*

Subjective interpretation of the prophetic has become problematic in the Charismatic church. God's Word is never subjective, but supernaturally objective toward setting captives free. Being the voice of revelation to a world in need of Him is an honor and a responsibility for ambassadors called by His name.

Art Thomas takes us on a journey toward plumb-line truth in the relevant and timely releasing of Father's "Words of Knowledge." There is no greater teacher than experience; and through biblically aligned experience, Art delivers a tremendous work that both teaches and empowers.

Robert Ricciardelli
Founder of Converging Zone Network and
Visionary Advancement Strategies

Christ only did what He saw the Father doing, and confessed that when He stepped outside of what the Father was doing, He was able to do nothing (see John 5:19). This is quite a statement coming from God Himself, walking the earth as a man. How did Christ know what the Father was doing, that He may be able to drastically change every situation working contrary to God's will? He supernaturally functioned in the Word of Knowledge via an intimate relationship with the Father. Without this majestic gift from above, we can be assured that Jesus would have worked far fewer miracles than He did. Surely it is of utmost importance for us to learn how to walk in this reality if Christ, God Himself, could do nothing outside of it.

Art does a wonderful job at explaining this imperative in *The Word of Knowledge in Action*. Mystical realities that have confused and confounded some in the past are communicated with a simplicity that causes the reader to think, "Wait a second, I can do this!" If you want some fresh revelation that empowers you to live a supernatural lifestyle and walk as Christ walked, consume the words on the pages of this book like a starved man eats bread.

Tyler Johnson
Founder of the Dead-Raising Teams
Author, *Stories of the Supernatural*

Art Thomas is not first of all a writer looking for his niche in the Christian book world. He is the "real deal" with a genuine heart to reach unconvinced people and help the convinced reach them as well. What better way to catch the attention of someone than to "read a piece of their mail" that only Jesus could have known about and cared to reveal!

Art's book is filled with real-life accounts and counsel that he has practiced and helped many people step into. Art is a personal friend and co-worker, but his best friend is Jesus, who he wants everybody to know. Read the book, step into it, and you can do "even greater things" just as Jesus promised.

Dan Vander Velde
Senior Pastor of Fowlerville Freedom Center, A/G
Fowlerville, Michigan

This book, *The Word of Knowledge in Action*, should cause us as true believers to rekindle our need for the operation of the Spirit. The Spirit of God has many gifts he longs to pour through our personal lives. I feel that Art encourages and prompts us, in our walk with God, to crave the Spirit and action of the gifts—especially to function in the Word of Knowledge, which has not been given much attention in this generation.

As I read the book, I reminisced over the Old and New Testament passages. I was moved by how many times God has worked through the Word of Knowledge throughout history. God has not changed. God desires, more than we could ever imagine, to utilize His people in this day to reveal His knowledge so that He can accomplish His will.

Also, the extraordinary personal testimonies that Art shares will stir your heart so that you long to experience God's Spirit working in your personal world. This Word of Knowledge, as I have individually experienced, is much needed for a world that is lost and disillusioned. People need to recognize that God knows them and He values them. I trust you will read this book and allow the Spirit to make use of your life.

Brooks T. McElhenny
Senior Pastor of Northville Christian
Northville, Michigan

Greek to say "Message of Knowledge." It's just that—a message. It's like getting mail. Opening a letter from someone doesn't cause you to instantly understand that person's entire life story. On the contrary, it gives you a glimpse into the specific subject the person wrote about. The Word of Knowledge is just as specific.

The Gift of Knowledge and Understanding

By and large, the ability to accumulate knowledge is merely one of those natural abilities God grants to all people, in varying capacities. The gifts of the Spirit, on the other hand, are distributed throughout the Church. Some of us have one gift, and some of us have another.

There are different kinds of gifts, but the same Spirit. There are different kinds of service, but the same Lord. There are different kinds of working, but the same God works all of them in all men.... All these are the work of one and the same Spirit, and he gives them to each one, just as he determines (1 Corinthians 12:4-6, 11).

If natural knowledge were a spiritual gift, that would mean many people in the Church (and even fewer outside the Church) could not learn anything at all.

However, there is another spiritual gift that does affect natural knowledge and is easily confused with the Word of Knowledge. In the book of Daniel, we learn that there is a special gift from God called "Knowledge and Understanding."

King Nebuchadnezzar took over Jerusalem and carried into exile some of the Israelites from the nobility and the royal families. Among them were Daniel and his three friends, best known by their Babylonian names of Shadrach, Meshach, and Abednego.

It's at this early point in the story that we first hear about this spiritual gift:

> To these four young men God gave knowledge and understanding of all kinds of literature and learning... (Daniel 1:17a).

This passage is clear that the knowledge and understanding the four young Hebrews had was "given" to them by God. That makes it a gift. And in their case, this gift had to do with "all kinds of literature and learning."

So the question naturally arises as to whether or not this was the same thing as the Word of Knowledge Paul talked about. I believe I can say with certainty that it's a different gift.

When Jesus walked this earth, he occasionally demonstrated the gift of a Word of Knowledge as the Holy Spirit supernaturally revealed something to Him that only His Father could have known—we'll see several examples of this later. But He also demonstrated a gift of Knowledge and Understanding, just like Daniel and his three friends.

It feels weird for some of us to think this way, but Jesus—though He was the Son of God—also had to learn. He didn't pop out of the womb preaching sermons in eloquent

Aramaic! Rather, He went through the process of development just like the rest of us. (See Luke 2:46-47; Luke 2:51-52; and Hebrews 5:8-9.)

In Luke's Gospel, we can see the gift of Knowledge and Understanding at work in Jesus. His family went to Jerusalem for the annual Passover feast. On their return trip, after a full day of travel, Joseph and Mary suddenly realized that Jesus wasn't with the caravan! They raced back to Jerusalem to find Him.

After three days they found him in the temple courts, sitting among the teachers, listening to them and asking them questions. Everyone who heard him was amazed at his understanding and his answers (Luke 2:46-47).

Jesus amazed the crowds with his understanding. That means He wasn't merely learning like any other twelve-year-old boy. Rather, He was demonstrating a capacity for knowledge and understanding that seemed, perhaps, supernatural in nature. This was a gift of Knowledge and Understanding just like the four Hebrew captives demonstrated in the book of Daniel.

Today, Jesus is no longer a humble servant walking the earth. Father God has exalted Him to the highest place of authority in Heaven and on earth. His name is exalted above every name! He is King of kings and Lord of lords! This means that He no longer needs to learn. Colossians 2:3 says that *"in Christ are hidden all the treasures of wisdom and knowledge."* In other words, Jesus now knows everything there is to know.

Nothing in all creation is hidden from Him. He knows the contents of every book that has ever been written. He even knows the hearts and intentions of the authors. For this reason, I have to believe that this spiritual gift should somehow have an even more dynamic manifestation today!

For Daniel and his three friends to have been given "knowledge and understanding of all kinds of literature and learning," it only makes sense that the Holy Spirit took from Christ's capacity for knowledge and understanding and made it known to them.[2] They partook in a supernatural ability to learn like Jesus.

The Word of Knowledge is a momentary revelation of certain facts in the mind of Christ. In contrast, the gift of Knowledge and Understanding is more of an ability or life-skill belonging to Jesus. It's not momentary, and it's not just one little chunk of information. On the contrary, it's what happens when the Holy Spirit enables a believer to learn and understand just like Jesus did.

The Original Language

In America, we hear the word "knowledge" and think of mere facts. The contestant who wins several weeks in a row on *Jeopardy* is clearly the one with the most knowledge, right? That may be how our culture understands the word, but that's not what was intended when Paul wrote First Corinthians 12.

For the Greeks, to have knowledge of something was to have certainty based on experience or personal interaction.

For instance, to have knowledge of Christ didn't mean merely knowing facts about Him; rather it meant that you enjoy a relationship with Him. In fact, Paul hailed from the Hebrew culture, where the word "know" implied deep intimacy. Consider Genesis 4:1, which says in the King James Version, "… *Adam knew Eve his wife; and she conceived…*" Clearly, "knowing" was a matter of being intimately acquainted.

So Paul—a self-proclaimed "Hebrew of Hebrews"— wrote to the Greeks with a very healthy understanding of the word "knowledge." He wasn't talking about the Holy Spirit revealing trivia. Rather, we're dealing with Christ's intimate involvement in the world. As the old song goes, "Jesus knows all about our troubles." He "knows" because He himself suffered in every way we ever will.

He was despised and rejected by men, a man of sorrows, and familiar with suffering. Like one from whom men hide their faces he was despised, and we esteemed him not (Isaiah 53:3).

For we do not have a high priest who is unable to sympathize with our weaknesses, but we have one who has been tempted in every way, just as we are—yet was without sin (Hebrews 4:15).

So when someone says Jesus knows what's going on in your life, it's not simply that He's aware. He truly knows. He's been there, and He struggles right alongside you.

This affects our definition of the Word of Knowledge because it means we're not just getting "information" from Jesus, but we're also getting the heart to go with it.

Getting the Heart

I once taught a class to a group of men and women who were about to serve as staff at a camp for foster children. The session was about letting God heal the hurts in our own lives so that we're more effective at soothing the hurts in the lives of others.

I really only spoke for about twenty minutes—describing the biblical work of sanctification and inner transformation. Then I opened the floor for questions before stepping into a time of practical application and ministry.

One woman raised her hand right away. I quickly found out she didn't really have a question. Rather, she must have been so stirred by the teaching that she couldn't wait any longer for the ministry time.

"I was hurt at a church. The pastor said some harsh things about me, and the whole congregation turned on me. I just don't know if I can really forgive them and trust another church!" she said.

Up until this point, I had never really experienced a Word of Knowledge. God had used me to prophesy, speak in tongues, and interpret tongues; but the Word of Knowledge was something about which I had only read. Nevertheless, while this woman spoke, a strange thing happened.

As she briefly mentioned that church, I suddenly had absolute certainty that she was in the right. She truly didn't deserve the treatment she had received at that church.

To be honest, my logical brain was saying, "She probably deserved it—there's no way a pastor and an entire church would do this without justification." But there persisted a strong conviction in my heart that she just wasn't at fault and didn't need to carry the guilt of what had happened to her.

So when she finished, I replied, "It wasn't your fault."

That was it. I didn't go into some great detail; I simply said it wasn't her fault. But this wasn't enough.

"Others have said that before, but how can I know it's true?" she asked, genuinely seeking an inspired reply.

Suddenly, I was certain of something else. I responded, "Because this didn't just happen to you at that one church. I have the feeling it happened to you at three different churches. Is that true?"

Tears welled up in the woman's eyes as she slowly nodded yes.

I then said, "Jesus was there at all three churches, and He knows it wasn't your fault."

The woman sobbed. I placed my hand on her shoulder and prayed for her. Those sitting around her prayed too. In one instant, God dramatically set that woman free from years of hurt, and the tool He used was the Word of Knowledge.

It wasn't that I simply had facts—the information came with conviction and a gut feeling that "this just isn't right!" My emotions were stirred as if I had watched the entire scene myself. Jesus knew all about her situation, and the Holy Spirit took that knowledge and made it known to me.

Simply Knowing

It didn't take a voice from Heaven, a vision, a dream, an angelic visitation, or anything else. I just somehow knew. I had never met this woman before that day—nor had I ever heard anything about her—but I simply knew what had transpired in her life. This happened not because I'm anything special. It's simply because Jesus had been there in her circumstance, and the Holy Spirit let me experience what Jesus knew. As a result, I simply knew.

This is the most foundational form of this gift. It's not the result of reading the Bible or seeking revelation in a time of prayer. It's simply the sudden realization that you truly know something that you couldn't possibly know apart from spiritual intervention.

Jesus practiced this as well. In Luke 11, Jesus cast a demon out of a man. The man had been unable to talk; but when Jesus commanded the evil spirit to leave, the man spoke! This shocked the crowd, and they began to wonder if Jesus was using the power of the devil to drive out demons.

Then comes verse 17, in which we see one quick statement: *"Jesus knew their thoughts...."* That's right! Jesus knew the thoughts of the crowd! I think that's pretty cool since we're not speaking about knowing one individual's thoughts but rather the thoughts of an entire crowd! This came by revelation of the Holy Spirit.

For who among men knows the thoughts of a man except the man's spirit within him?... (1 Corinthians 2:11a).

When Jesus walked this planet, He did so as a man rather than as God. Paul said that He gave up everything about Himself that could be considered "God" and humbled Himself all the way to the point of death on a cross.[3] In other words, Jesus "the man" didn't have the capacity to know men's thoughts on His own. "For who among men knows the thoughts of a man...?"

Jesus needed to rely on His Father in Heaven who *"knows the secrets of the heart"* (Ps. 44:21). He had Words of Knowledge by which the Holy Spirit made known what the Father knows.

Some might say that this affects our definition, but remember the passage from John 16 in which Jesus talked about the Holy Spirit. Pay attention to verse 15, in which Jesus said, *"All that belongs to the Father is mine. That is why I said the Spirit will take from what is mine and make it known to you."* In other words, all knowledge—both natural and supernatural—and all spiritual gifts originate with the Father. (See James 1:17.)

When Jesus walked this earth, He received Words of Knowledge when the Holy Spirit took what the Father knew and made it known to Him. But today, the Father has glorified His Son and delights to let Jesus be the source of everything for the Church. So He joyfully lets Jesus receive the credit for the Church's success.

Simplifying the Definition

In short, the gift of a Word of Knowledge takes place when the Holy Spirit takes from Christ's knowledge and makes it known to you. It is not the natural knowledge that we all accumulate throughout life, and it is not the supernatural ability to learn like Jesus. It is also not a strange ability to know all things. It is very simply a glimpse into the mind of Christ by which we share in His "knowing" about a specific incident, thought, or intention.

The following chapters will help unfold this biblical understanding with examples from Scripture, testimonies, and personal experiences to help you understand, embrace, and hopefully, to activate this spiritual gift. Like we saw in the ancient church of Corinth to whom Paul wrote, I believe it's time to re-kindle the normalcy of the Word of Knowledge in today's Church!

Summary Questions

1. Based on Jesus' words that the Holy Spirit will "take from what is Mine and make it known to you," how could we define Spiritual Gifts in general?

_____

_____

2. In what ways do the Greek and Hebrew definitions of "know" differ from our current English understanding of that word?

_____

_____

3. List some categories of things that Jesus knows that would otherwise be unknowable by you.

_____

_____

4. In the next chapter, we will talk about how the Word of Knowledge interacts with the gift of Prophecy. Before you read it, can you think of any ways the two gifts might relate?

_____

_____

Endnotes

1. Smith Wigglesworth (1998). *Smith Wigglesworth on spiritual gifts.* New Kensington, PA: Whitaker House.

2. Yes, I am referring to Old Testament figures receiving from Christ. Many struggle with the idea that Jesus was present in the Old Testament. Entire

books could be written to describe His presence throughout the Hebrew text, so I can only scrape the surface here. For the sake of quick reference, have a look at John 1:1-14; John 17:24; Colossians 1:15; 2 Timothy 1:9; 1 Peter 1:20; 1 John 2:13; Revelation 13:8; and Revelation 22:13.

3.   See Philippians 2:5-8. Also notice that in John 5:19, Jesus said, "...*the Son can do nothing by Himself...*"

Chapter 2

the word of knowledge and prophecy ↗

To prophesy is to speak on God's behalf. It's one of the ways God communicates with human beings. The Gift of Prophecy takes place when the Holy Spirit takes the words of Jesus and makes them known by placing them in the heart and mind of a person on earth who speaks them out. Sometimes this is a spontaneous message whereby the speaker doesn't know what he is going to say next until he says it; and at other times it's a prompting in the heart in which the speaker waits for the appropriate time to present the message. Those who practice the Gift of Prophecy are basically the heralds of God—speaking His words audibly when others may not be listening.

This is different from the Word of Knowledge in that prophecy has to do with conveying a message from the voice of Christ whereas the Word of Knowledge has to do with expressing part of the mind of Christ. The Word of Knowledge isn't always easy to put into words at first, whereas the Gift of Prophecy typically comes as words. Additionally, the Word of Knowledge often comes with a sense of ownership, as though you had personally witnessed the event. Prophecy, on the other hand, though it comes with conviction, still has a sense that you're speaking on behalf of another.

Paul said that the purpose of prophecy is to strengthen, encourage, and comfort people. (See 1 Corinthians 14:3.) This may be a message for the moment in which God expresses His love and care for a person, or it may be a message about the future. Either way, God speaks through a man or woman, and the listeners are built up and encouraged.

The Word of Knowledge, however, tends to deal more with information regarding the past and present. Rather than expressing a message, it tends to have more to do with facts surrounding events, thoughts, intentions, actions, ideas, and other such things.

It's important to know how these two gifts differ because it helps us understand how they can be used together. Both gifts are methods by which the Holy Spirit reveals Jesus through the Church, but they're different aspects of Jesus. One has to do with His message, and the other has to do with His knowledge.

Paving the Way for Prophecy

I once had a woman approach me after a church service who said, "Can I ask you to pray for my husband?" Though I had never really known this woman, suddenly the thought "alcohol" popped into my mind. So I simply said that one word.

The woman began to cry and asked, "How did you know?"

At this point, it was clear to me that what she needed most wasn't a teaching on the Word of Knowledge but rather encouragement from God. So I asked the Holy Spirit what Jesus would like to say to her. I then responded with a message from Him, "I feel like God's saying that He has seen your faithfulness in the midst of this trial, and your prayers have not gone unnoticed. He will deliver your husband soon."

I then prayed with her. She also invited a group of us over to her house to pray together. Three months later, the husband quit drinking, moved back to their bedroom from the basement, and started working on patching up their marriage. God opened the woman's heart with a Word of Knowledge, and this made her more receptive to the Gift of Prophecy that followed.

Looking back, I don't believe the prophecy would have been nearly as effective without the Word of Knowledge to break the ice. It was a pretty generic message on its own, and the woman could have easily written it off as the mere words of another well-intentioned Christian. But by my starting with a Word of Knowledge, her attention was captured! She knew that God was speaking, and it stirred her faith.

It's important to note that neither the Word of Knowledge nor the Gift of Prophecy changed this woman's husband. These only served to ignite her faith. Instead, it was that faith and her newfound hope that drove her to passionate prayer with other believers in full trust that God would do what He promised.

Comprehending Prophecy

Prophecy doesn't always have to start with a Word of Knowledge. I've also seen instances where a Word of Knowledge was beneficial afterward.

During the singing one Sunday morning, the Holy Spirit turned my attention toward an older lady in our church and said, "I have given her big spiritual feet. Go tell her."

To be honest, I was a little upset! If God was going to use me to speak His words to someone, why couldn't the message be a normal one? Why couldn't it be something cool? But no—just, "big spiritual feet."

So I walked over to her and said sheepishly, "Hi. I don't know if this means anything to you, but as we were singing, I really felt like the Lord was saying that He has given you big spiritual feet." Then, trying to ignore her attempt at choking back laughter, I asked, "Does that mean anything to you?"

"No, I'm sorry," she answered with a chuckle, "but I'll pray about it!"

Of course—"I'll pray about it"—the default phrase Christians use when they don't want to hurt your feelings with a solid "no."

I walked away saying, "Well, God, I did it. Maybe it wasn't You, but I'm glad I gave it my best shot. If it was You, though, I want to know what You meant so it can be more meaningful to her."

For three days, I prayed about it. To be honest, my primary motivation was mostly that I felt embarrassed! The woman's understanding and spiritual growth were only a secondary reason.

Sure enough, three days later, I left my college between classes to pray at my church, and the Lord finally brought a sudden clear understanding. In an instant, the prophecy made sense as though the message had originally come from my own mind. I understood and knew exactly what God meant.

I sped to the woman's office, and she welcomed me (which I thought was a good sign that she hadn't completely written me off as crazy).

I started by asking, "Hey, I'm just curious if that message I shared with you Sunday ended up meaning anything to you."

"Actually," she replied, "I didn't want to say anything at the time, but I've always felt very self-conscious about how small my feet are. I thought it was interesting that God was saying that, and it was sort of like He was telling me that any of my physical shortcomings would be countered by what He has given me in the spiritual realm. Why? Do you think there's more to it?"

After hearing her reply, I really didn't want to share what I had sensed from the Lord because it was yet another silly thought. But my Word of Knowledge seemed to mesh so well with the interpretation she shared that I couldn't resist.

"Well," I replied, "I was praying about it, and I felt like someone in your company is going to be leaving soon. And when they do, there are many aspects of his portfolio that you're going to need to pick up. When that time comes, you're going to feel like those shoes are too big to fill, but God has given you big spiritual feet to fill this man's shoes."

She laughed again, but I knew this time that she wasn't laughing at me. "Well," she replied, "I guess we'll just see what happens when that time comes! Thanks for coming by!"

I shook her hand and drove off to my next class.

Just a few weeks later, one of her co-workers left the company, and she had to pick up a lot of his portfolio. As it turns out, she later told me that she didn't even think once about the prophecy or the explanation. It wasn't until she left a staff meeting about a month later and prayed, "God, I don't know how I'm going to run this project! That guy's shoes are too big to fill!"

Within an instant, she remembered the message: "Big spiritual feet." Peace from the Holy Spirit overwhelmed her, and she moved forward with full confidence that her physical shortcomings would be matched with spiritual strength from the Lord.

One might wonder why I would call this a Word of Knowledge when it had to do with foretelling the future. But let's take another quick look at what transpired. The prophecy was that God had given the woman big spiritual feet. I simply conveyed a message the best way I knew how. The later explanation, however, was not a separate word of prophecy. I was no longer conveying a message, but rather expressing knowledge and understanding about the original message. I knew what Jesus meant as though I had meant it myself. The Holy Spirit took from Christ's knowledge and made it known to me. It was a Word of Knowledge.

Recognizing the Present Fulfillment of Prophecy

So far we've seen how the Word of Knowledge can pave the way for more effective prophecies. We've also seen how a Word of Knowledge can help us comprehend prophecy and make it more meaningful. Now I want to show you how the Word of Knowledge can help a person recognize the present fulfillment of prophecy.

In most cases, prophecies are proven and recognized as true only after the events foretold come to pass. Sometimes, though, it takes a Word of Knowledge to recognize when a prophecy is presently being fulfilled.

While still in Babylonian captivity, the prophet Daniel understood Jeremiah's prophecy. He recognized that the seventy years of captivity that were prophesied were about to end! Through a word of knowledge, Daniel understood when prophecy was about to be fulfilled rather than only noticing it after the fact. (See Daniel 9:2.)

Just before His final Passover feast, Jesus took the time to wash His disciples' feet. When He had finished washing the feet of His last disciple, Jesus joined them at the table and started to explain what had just taken place. Suddenly, though, His message took a dark turn.

"I am not referring to all of you; I know those I have chosen. But this is to fulfill the scripture: 'He who shares my bread has lifted up his heel against me.'

"I am telling you now before it happens, so that when it does happen you will believe that I am He..."

After he had said this, Jesus was troubled in spirit and testified, "I tell you the truth, one of you is going to betray me."

His disciples stared at one another, at a loss to know which of them he meant. One of them, [John], was reclining next to him. Simon Peter motioned to [him] and said, "Ask him which one he means."

Leaning back against Jesus, he asked him, "Lord, who is it?"

Jesus answered, "It is the one to whom I will give this piece of bread when I have dipped it in the dish." Then, dipping the piece of bread, he gave it to Judas Iscariot, son of Simon. As soon as Judas took the bread, satan entered into him.

"What you are about to do, do quickly," Jesus told him, but no one at the meal understood why Jesus said this to him (John 13:18-28).

Jesus started with prophecy—He quoted Psalm 41:9 as a means of foretelling the future. The purpose of the message was to strengthen, encourage, and comfort His disciples because He said that when it happens, they'll believe that He truly is the Messiah. As we learned earlier, a revelation from God that is spoken to strengthen, encourage, and comfort believers is a prophecy. And the fact that Jesus was foretelling the future was also a form of prophecy.

There was really no emotional connection to the message at this time—He was simply conveying a message that the Father had revealed to Him. But then it says that "after He said this, He was troubled in spirit and testified." That's when the

Word of Knowledge hit Him. He was no longer prophesying a message but suddenly had a download of what God the Father knew and felt for His Son. The events that His prophecy foretold were ready to transpire within mere moments.

Notice that when Jesus said, "One of you is going to betray Me," it wasn't any longer a matter of prophecy. Jesus wasn't just conveying a message that God had revealed. Rather, it says that He was deeply troubled in spirit and He "testified." In other words, He was explaining what He had suddenly witnessed. In an instant, Jesus knew without doubt that it was time for the Scriptures to be fulfilled.

As an eyewitness, John remembered vividly the shift in Jesus' emotions and demeanor. He noticed something changed after Jesus prophesied a message for the group's comfort. He saw the moment when Jesus was suddenly troubled in spirit. The Word of Knowledge itself would have been impressive enough on its own. But the prophecy preceding it gave the moment that much more weight. Not everyone understood exactly what was taking place, but the young apostle named John was certainly impacted by it.

The "More Certain" Word of Prophecy

As we've seen, the Gift of Prophecy is expressed in various ways. It's always for the benefit of a group or individual, and it's always a message from God. Sometimes it has to do with what God says about the past, sometimes what He says about the present, and sometimes it's a promise or prediction about the future.

It's easy to get wrapped up in the present-day expressions of this gift and overlook the ancient ones that still have meaning to us. I'm talking, of course, about the Bible. Peter called the Scriptures "*the word of the prophets made more certain*" (2 Peter 1:19). The words of Scripture have been proven true throughout time and are still meaningful to us in today's world and culture. So if we take the perspective that the Bible is a form of prophecy, then we see how our examples of the Word of Knowledge apply.

For instance, have you ever been reading the Bible and had something click for you? When it happens, it feels like something suddenly makes sense that had never really come together for you before. One little verse reveals the big picture, and it's like fireworks go off in your heart. Has that ever happened?

This is what we call a "revelation," and it's part of the Word of Knowledge. In the previous chapter, I shared a story about suddenly knowing information as though I had been there to witness it. That too was a revelation. It didn't become a Word of Knowledge, though, until I spoke it out.

Paul said that the purpose of spiritual gifts is "*for the common good.*" (See 1 Corinthians 12:7.) So as long as I keep something bottled up inside, it's only a gift to me. But if we want it to be a spiritual gift to the Church, then it needs to be articulated.

The same thing goes for a revelation born out of Scripture. When it's spoken in order to strengthen others, the message goes from being mere internal revelation and becomes a Word of Knowledge.

Perhaps the most practical example I can offer you is this book itself. As you may recall, I was reading Jesus' words about the Holy Spirit when the gifts of the Spirit suddenly made sense to me. In one instant, the Holy Spirit unfolded a Scripturally-based definition for every spiritual gift in the Bible. Something Jesus has known and understood from the beginning of time was somehow made known to me as I read the Scripture. That's a revelation.

I could have sat on that information, and it would have been very satisfying for me personally. My frustrations in seeking for a sensible, biblically sound definition for the Word of Knowledge would have been alleviated! But alas, God's revelations rarely work like that. Instead, I found myself like Jeremiah:

> *But if I say, "I will not mention him or speak any more in his name," his word is in my heart like a fire, a fire shut up in my bones. I am weary of holding it in; indeed, I cannot* (Jeremiah 20:9).

It's a joy to share revelation (and many times, a relief)! The Church can be edified when we articulate what the Holy Spirit has revealed.

Why is the Church edified? There are practical reasons: we understand God's Word better, we understand God better, and we're encouraged in our faith. But there's also a supernatural reason: if the Holy Spirit reveals something to you that came from Jesus, you don't just understand information—you have experienced Jesus! And when you convey that revelation to the Church, we all get a glimpse of Jesus! I didn't write this book so you can just learn information; I did it because I want you to encounter an aspect of our Lord that has previously seldom been discussed.

Jesus is the Head of the Church; and the better we all know and understand Him, the easier it is for those of us in His Body to function in unity! To receive a spiritual revelation from the Scripture is to receive a spiritual revelation of Christ Himself! You cannot separate the Scripture from the Word of God; and Jesus is the Word of God!

Jesus is the Word of God

If you've read the Gospel of John, you know that Jesus is the Word of God. John starts his book by saying, *"In the beginning was the Word, and the Word was with God, and the Word was God..."* (John 1:1). In other words, Jesus was present at creation. In fact, not only was He present, but He was the means by which everything was created!

> *For by him all things were created: things in heaven and on earth, visible and invisible, whether thrones or powers or rulers or authorities; all things were created by him and for him* (Colossians 1:16).

And when we read Genesis, we find that the entire universe was spoken into existence by God. God's Word created everything, and Jesus is the Word of God.

Not only this, but we see yet another example in the book of Genesis. After Adam and Eve committed their first carnal sin, they realized they were naked and hid in the bushes.

And they heard the voice of Jehovah God walking in the garden in the cool of the day... (Genesis 3:8 ASV).

Other versions say "sound" instead of "voice," but this is a very valid translation from the original Hebrew text. The voice of God was walking! That means God's voice had form! Jesus—the Word of God—is found all throughout the Scripture! Then we find that Peter wrote this:

Above all, you must understand that no prophecy of Scripture came about by the prophet's own interpretation. For prophecy never had its origin in the will of man, but men spoke from God as they were carried along by the Holy Spirit (2 Peter 1:20-21).

Scripture is prophecy, which is another gift of the Spirit. "Men spoke from God" through the Holy Spirit! In other words, the Holy Spirit took from the Father and made it known to human beings. And what was the message? The Word of God! Who is the Word of God in the flesh? Jesus! All of Scripture is a prophecy, and so all of Scripture reveals Jesus!

...the testimony of Jesus is the spirit of prophecy (Revelation 19:10b).

All prophecy—and therefore all Scripture—reveals Jesus Christ. He is the Word of God. This is how all the gifts of the Spirit work—the Holy Spirit reveals some part of Jesus to someone in the Church, and that person becomes a vessel through whom the rest of the Church then encounters Him. The gifts of the Spirit are "for the common good."

The Word of Knowledge, Prophecy, and Scripture Working Together

Perhaps the most well-known prophetic message throughout Scripture is the hundreds of Old Testament prophecies pointing to one Person: Jesus Christ. The Old Testament is chock-full of prophecies about the Messiah—how He would come, how He would live, how He would die, and how He would win ultimate victory in the end!

So when the angel appeared to the virgin Mary to say that she would bear this child, it wasn't just a random occurrence. Rather, there were thousands of years of prophecies to back up everything that would take place! And these weren't just prophecies that were spoken out and forgotten; they were prophetic declarations that were written in songs, letters, history books, poetry, and more—all of which became sacred Scripture over time.

Soon after Mary's miraculous conception of Jesus, she went to visit her cousin Elizabeth. Here we see two clear examples of a Word of Knowledge expressing an understanding of Scripture and the present fulfillment of prophecy.

When Elizabeth heard Mary's greeting, the baby leaped in her womb, and Elizabeth was filled with the Holy Spirit. In a loud voice she exclaimed: "Blessed are you among women, and blessed is the child you will bear! But why am I so favored, that the mother of my Lord should come to me? As soon as the sound of your greeting reached my ears, the baby in my womb leaped for joy. Blessed is she who has believed that what the Lord has said to her will be accomplished!" (Luke 1:40-45).

First, little baby John the Baptist—who was himself a fulfillment of prophecy—recognized the presence of the Messiah for whom he would become a forerunner, even while they were both still inside their mothers' wombs! Before he even had the words and logic to articulate what was happening, John expressed the excitement in his heart about what he knew to be true as a result of spiritual revelation. The Word of Knowledge requires clear communication of the point but doesn't necessarily have to be spoken in words. John the Baptist communicated to his mother that something was special about this cousin and her baby!

Then comes the even clearer example of a Word of Knowledge. Elizabeth is filled with the Holy Spirit and proclaims about Mary what she now knows to be true! When everyone else probably thought Mary was lying about her "virgin conception," this cousin of hers had a Word of Knowledge that brought vindication from the Lord! Not only that, but it showed a realization that the prophecies of Scripture were coming to clear fulfillment!

Prophecy is the Word of God, the Bible is the Word of God, and Jesus is the Word of God. Therefore, a Word of Knowledge regarding prophecy or Scripture is actually a direct look into the thoughts and intentions of God in Jesus. To have a Word of Knowledge about the Word of God is not just to understand Scripture, but to commune with the divine Author of that Scripture. It is to experience Jesus Christ! Through revelation from the Holy Spirit, Jesus shares Himself with us!

The Word of Knowledge is a spiritual gift that powerfully unveils the person of Christ.

Summary Questions

1. What are the basic differences between the gift of Prophecy and the gift of a Word of Knowledge?

_____

_____

2. What are some ways that the Word of Knowledge interacts with the gift of Prophecy?

_____

_____

3. What did Peter call "the word of the prophets made more certain"?

_____

_____

4. Who is the Word of God?

_____

_____

be uncovered. In other words, God, in His wisdom, allowed a certain illness as a way of hinting at a person's spiritual condition.

For instance, I once knew a woman who was diagnosed with cancer in her womb. The doctors scheduled her for a hysterectomy within a matter of a few weeks. Our church prayed for her at length, but there were no results. However, a lack of results is not necessarily evidence of a lack of faith or a lack of God's will, so I kept seeking God for an answer.

I saw a vision in my mind of a black silhouette of a person (sort of a cartoon) with a white, fibrous mass in the location of the womb. The picture zoomed in, and I saw tentacles reaching out from the cancer and a word written on the main body of it: "bitterness."

I took the woman aside and shared the vision. As I did this, I received further insight through the Word of Knowledge and said, "I specifically feel like the bitterness is directed toward a prominent female in your life—like your mom or your sister. Does that make sense?"

"Not that I can think of," she replied; so I shrugged it off and excused it away as though it was probably just my imagination.

Three days later, however, she called me to say that she had prayed about what I said. "I realized I had bitterness toward both my mom and my sister, so I asked God's forgiveness. I feel a lot better now, so I'm hoping the tests come back negative tomorrow." Sure enough, the doctors couldn't find the slightest trace of cancer.

I didn't realize it at the time, but in hindsight, I can see the correlation between the woman's spiritual condition and her physical one. As she sowed seeds of bitterness against significant women in her life, she reaped the ramifications as an attack against her own womanhood. Not only that, but just as she was cursing the womb from which she was born, she was receiving a curse in her own womb.

> *Do not be deceived: God cannot be mocked. A man reaps what he sows. The one who sows to please his sinful nature, from that nature will reap destruction...* (Galatians 6:7-8a).

"Sowing and reaping" is a spiritual law. Just as orange seeds grow orange trees and apple seeds grow apple trees, so a spiritual harvest will be directly related to the seeds sown. You can see, then, why this woman's physical condition was so closely related to her spiritual condition.

Does this mean that all women with cancer like this have bitterness toward their mothers and sisters? Not at all. And if you pray for such a woman and she is not healed, this also does not necessarily mean that there is a similar spiritual root.

Not all physical ailments have spiritual roots. That's why the Word of Knowledge is so vital. We must receive revelation from God. We need to have the humility to admit that we don't know why healing doesn't always happen. Since the Bible doesn't tell us why, we can't say for sure. And, of course, there's really no value in speculating. But if the Holy Spirit reveals what's happening in a specific case, then we can deal with the issue and have confidence that God will carry through on His end.

The Word of Knowledge Building Faith

One of the men who has mentored me in my life, Pastor Dan, occasionally demonstrates a special form of this gift. I've seen him stop in the middle of his sermon and say something like, "Pardon me for a moment, but I just had a quick pain in the lower left area of my back. Is there anyone here struggling with that same pain? I think the Lord wants to heal you." Sure enough, someone would raise their hand, he would pray, and God would bring the healing.

In this case, God used the Word of Knowledge to build faith. Speaking as someone who has been healed in this way myself, I know what a shift takes place in your mindset when someone calls out your exact condition without any prior knowledge. It builds a person's faith. After all, if God can supernaturally reveal my condition to someone, then He can heal it too!

This particular operation of the Word of Knowledge has become popular among the so-called "faith-healers" and tel-evangelists of today. In one sense, I love the fact that many people do indeed get healed as they watch these programs or visit these meetings. But I am also aware that many of those people are really only being healed by their own faith. It's unfortunate that the minister often gets the glory that should be going to Jesus.

I certainly won't judge every minister on television with a blanket accusation. But there are very likely certain cases where the person is merely listing diseases without actually having a Word of Knowledge. Even this, however, can activate people's faith and affect their healing, which brings credibility to the minister. And the bigger the audience, the more likely it is that someone is watching who has the condition being named.[1]

For this reason, I don't know how to classify this kind of a Word of Knowledge. In one sense, it could be called weak because it is so easily counterfeited and has led many people astray after false teachers. In another sense, however, it can be called strong because it does often result in genuine physical healings with little effort on the part of the minister.

Perhaps the best approach is to simply guard it. When we're practicing a Word of Knowledge meant to build someone's faith for healing, we need to be careful not to get caught up in the moment. We need to watch ourselves lest pride set in.

Many times, Jesus said, "Your faith has healed you." But never once did He say, "My Word of Knowledge healed you." I've actually heard ministers declare this from the pulpit— that their Word of Knowledge came from God, and when he or she spoke it out, it brought healing to the person. This mindset gets people looking at a man rather than God. It lacks humility and is contrary to the nature and example of Christ.

Instead, why not praise God for the healing and encourage the person that his or her faith was effective? We don't even need to point out that our Word of Knowledge was the catalyst to ignite that faith. What are we trying to gain? Let's walk in humility.

How This Form of the Word of Knowledge Works

As mentioned before, knowledge—in the biblical sense—is not about information but rather experience. So it's not so much that a person has suddenly received information that someone is sick. Instead, it comes more in the form of truly knowing.

In some cases, like with Pastor Dan, it may be that you share the same sensation. This can enhance your compassion and ignite your own faith to pray for someone's healing. When this happens, you "know" because you are experiencing the same pain or illness. As we saw in Chapter One, "Jesus knows all about our troubles."

In other cases, I know of people who experience a tingling sensation or intense internal heat through which God is making them aware of a particular part of their body. They then know that God wants to heal that part of someone else.

In still other cases, it may come in the form of a vision or dream. Sometimes, like the story of our waitress, Andrea, it's a picture of the condition itself. In other instances, you might see the healing taking place.

I know of ministers who will see a vision of a vague figure getting out of a wheelchair. Then they'll ask the Lord for more detail and start to see identifiable features—like a shirt color, hair style, etc. After asking for further detail, they'll receive a clear picture in their mind of what the person looks like—sometimes even the person's name. Upon arrival at a meeting or other destination, they'll look for that person and have the opportunity to be the vessel God uses to bring healing.

Responsibility and the Word of Knowledge

Be careful what you wish for, though. When you ask God for a Word of Knowledge regarding healing, realize that you're then responsible to carry out your part to administer that healing. If you don't, God won't condemn you, but you'll feel bad for not seizing the opportunity.

When I was first discovering this gift, I had not yet prayed for anyone regarding physical healing. But in my passion for the things of God, I really wanted it to happen and regularly asked the Lord for a gift of healing.

One day, our youth group had planned a trip to a Bavarian-themed city in Michigan called Frankenmuth. While I was praying over the trip—which would really only consist of shopping and eating—the Lord gave me a Word of Knowledge. I suddenly knew that I would come across a middle-aged woman in a wheelchair with short, black, curly hair.

In my naivety, I begged God, "OK, but please don't let her be a total paralytic who can only move her chair by blowing in a straw. I don't think I have the faith for that."

Sure enough, there I was sitting on the porch of a little candy shop when who should emerge from behind the next building but a middle-aged woman with short, black, curly hair—blowing in a straw to move her chair! Fear seized me. I argued with God. On one hand, I was convinced I didn't have enough faith. On the other hand, He had told me about this beforehand. I even considered the fact that I probably only thought about the "blowing in a straw" thing because God may have revealed that too.

I stood up. I sat down. I squirmed awkwardly. The woman and her family even stopped in front of the porch while her husband counted his money. My heart was pounding, and every excuse in the book was racing through my head. *I'm not ready for this. What makes me think I have a gift of healing? What if she doesn't get healed? Then what?*

As I battled inwardly with my fears and basic lack of compassion, the family moved on and I never saw the woman again. I felt worse having missed the opportunity than I would have felt if I had prayed without results. After the fact, I realized something: What was the worst that could have happened? Only that she might not get healed but would still learn that there are Christians who believe it can happen!

It's not that I still live with the regret—at least in the sense that I do not feel condemned or like a failure. But I do hold onto the feeling of heartache and remorse so I never forget the pain of missing an opportunity. Now, when the Lord speaks, it stirs me to act. If you receive a Word of Knowledge about someone's healing, step out and expect the results.

Summary Questions

1. How should we respond when people are not healed?

2. Describe how the spiritual law of sowing and reaping often affects people's physical condition, including their health.

3. Why is it that people can be healed even when someone fakes a Word of Knowledge?

4. Put yourself in my shoes during the last story I shared. How would you have responded when the woman in the wheelchair came around the corner? How should we respond to situations like these?

Endnote

1. Even in Jesus' ministry, people were often healed as a result of their own faith. So many times, Jesus would say, "Your faith has healed you." In the same way, people are often healed because their faith in God was activated through the Word of Knowledge or even a faked "Word of Knowledge." For examples of people being healed as a result of their own faith, see Matthew 9:22, Matthew 9:29, Mark 5:34, Luke 7:50, Luke 8:48, Luke 17:19, and Luke 18:42.

Chapter 5

the word of knowledge and intercession ↗

I hated my biology class. It was a cold winter morning in Michigan, and I was not in any way prepared for my final exam. Nevertheless, I drove to college to face my doom.

My heart was racing. I had struggled all semester to memorize all the information like our professor wanted. Not only that, but I got a few low scores on some projects, so I was already off to a rough start. And here I was on the day of the final exam with a blank mind. I couldn't remember anything. I was panicking. No matter how hard I tried, I couldn't meet my professor's high standards.

I pulled into my parking space ten minutes before class, which was great since it meant I had ten minutes to scramble through my textbook and hope to grab something of value.

God had different plans, though. As I got out of my car, a young lady got into the car in front of me and drove away. As soon as I saw her, the Holy Spirit gave me a Word of Knowledge. I suddenly knew that this young lady was about to face one of the most painful trials of her life, and I needed to pray for her.

It was sort of like when Jesus said to Simon Peter, "... *satan has asked to sift you as wheat. But I have prayed for you, Simon, that your faith may not fail...*" (Luke 22:31-32). How else would Jesus know this, apart from revelation from the Holy Spirit?

So there I was with a choice to make. I could use my ten minutes before class to cram for the most important exam of the semester, or I could pray for this young woman whom I had never met before, simply because I had an inkling in my spirit that she would need it soon.

I walked into class, sat down in my seat, and pushed my textbook aside. For the next ten minutes, I prayed silently for a total stranger. Through a Word of Knowledge, the Lord showed me someone who needed prayer and even prompted me how to pray.

I know what you're probably thinking: How do I know that I actually heard from God—especially since I never knew the young lady or ever saw her again? In one sense, I suppose I don't. However, the rest of the story seems to imply to me that God honored my actions—whether they were genuine obedience or merely an attempt.

I agonized through the test—guessing answers, writing paragraphs from my imagination, and doing everything I could to at least try to pass the test. Our professor gave everyone the option to wait in the hallway when we finished.

Then, one by one, he would call students back into the room to grade their test and give them their final score.

I was one of the last people to finish, so I sat in the hallway for some time. One by one, my classmates emerged from the room with looks of horror on their faces. Girls were crying. Guys were clenching their jaws and avoiding eye contact. One woman stepped out and sharply complained to her friend, "I can't believe I got a 'C!' I studied for days! That man doesn't know how to teach!"

Then came the moment of truth. My teacher poked his head out the door and flagged me in. I felt like I was walking to my execution. He lifted my test from the pile and dropped it unceremoniously onto the desk. His red pen flew down the first page and wrote a "20" at the bottom of the page—the same with the next two pages. Then came the essay questions. One question after the next, he wrote "5/5" without even reading the answers.

When I finally shook off the shock of what was happening, my conscience kicked into gear. "Umm...I actually didn't know the answer to that one..."

"Shh!" ordered my professor with a smirk.

He worked his way through the entire test, closed it, and wrote "4.0" at the top—for those who may not be familiar with this form of grading, a 4.0 is the highest score one can receive. Then he entered the score into his grade book and punched some numbers into his calculator.

"Looks like you're finishing the class with a 3.8. Is that what you were hoping for?"

"Wow…well…" I stammered, "This is more than I expected; but I, uh…I guess if you're asking what I was 'hoping' for, it would be a 4.0."

"Done."

My teacher wrote "4.0" in his grade book, shook my hand, and said, "Have a great break!"

I honestly didn't do anything to deserve this. I had not been a teacher's pet. The closest thing we had in common was our belief in a Creator; but he was Muslim, so it's not like we were chummy with our faith. To this day, I cannot figure out any earthly explanation for what took place that morning. The only thing that makes sense is that God was blessing me as a means of confirming that I had made the right decision to pray in response to the Holy Spirit.

Through a Word of Knowledge, the Holy Spirit can prompt you how to pray and what to pray. Jesus knows what is happening everywhere in the world, and at any given moment He may ask you to pray about something only He knows.

Revealing Strategic Details

Several years ago, I helped plant a church with Pastor Dan (whom I introduced in the previous chapter). One day, he and I drove out to a rural auto parts store to get what he needed to fix his daughter's truck. The place was huge and included a garage, a storage warehouse, and a salvage yard.

As soon as he and I walked into the front office, I felt like I had stepped into a spiritual steam room. The air felt thick and heavy—not physically, but spiritually. The atmosphere just felt uncomfortable in my spirit. It was as if something was sitting on my chest.

What I was experiencing in that moment would be best defined as "discerning spirits" because I was perceiving the spiritual environment. Not only that, but I could also discern that the spiritual environment I was sensing had something to do with sensuality and lust. These being two primary sins from which Christ has set me free, I tend to be particularly sensitive to them.

The guy took us into the warehouse to get the part needed. The deeper inside we got, the darker it felt.

On the way out, I asked the Holy Spirit what I had sensed. Through a Word of Knowledge, I suddenly knew that a pornography business was being run out of that building. In fact, I had the sense that it wasn't just being sold there but was actually being produced.

Getting into the car, I asked Pastor Dan, "Did you feel that in there?"

"Sure did. What do you think it was?"

"Well," I answered, "at first I was just sensing spiritual darkness, but then, I think I sensed something more specific…"

"Pornography. I know. I sensed it too," he responded, "And I think there was more going on there than just selling it…"

filled with a cloud of dust, the circle of daylight overhead grew bigger and bigger.

Jesus waited patiently. There was no sense trying to continue preaching.

Suddenly, like an eclipse, the room grew dark again. Something had been moved to cover up the hole. And then, that "something" started to come through the hole! Light burst into the room once again as a package was lowered with ropes right down to the feet of Jesus.

When the cloth parcel hit the floor, the four corners lowered to reveal none other than Frank the paralytic. The whole crowd stood in stunned silence, waiting to see what Jesus would do.

At this point, I am convinced that Jesus had a Word of Knowledge. Think about it. Jesus was known all over the countryside for healing people, and now a paralyzed man was staring up at Him from the floor. The logical reaction would have been for Jesus to take the man by the hand and heal him. That's what everyone expected Him to do.

Jesus didn't heal him. He knew the more important first problem. Even though Jesus had never met Frank before, the Holy Spirit revealed his most pressing felt need.

Jesus broke the silence by saying, "Son, your sins are forgiven."

Now some teachers of the law were sitting there, thinking to themselves, "Why does this fellow talk like that? He's blaspheming! Who can forgive sins but God alone?"

Immediately Jesus knew in his spirit that this was what they were thinking in their hearts, and he said to them, "Why are you thinking these things?" (Mark 2:6-8).

Jesus was receiving Words of Knowledge left and right! I love the fact that no one else said a word. Only one voice filled the dusty air. Only one voice escaped through the hole in the roof. First, Jesus looked at the man and said, "Your sins are forgiven." Then He looked at the crowd and asked, "Why are you thinking these things?"

The silence continued—broken only by the uncomfortable shifting of weight in the crowd.

Jesus continued, "Wouldn't you say it's easier for me to tell this man, 'Your sins are forgiven,' than it would be for me to say, 'Get up and walk!'?"

The crowd still stared in shock over everything that was taking place, but in their minds, they knew Jesus' logic was correct. It was indeed an easier thing to say.

"Well then, how about I say the more difficult thing so that you will know that the son of man has authority on earth to forgive sin."

Jesus looked Frank in the eye and smiled. "Get up," He said, "take your mat, and go home."

The four friends' heads loomed over the sides of the hole above, and they watched as Frank slowly stood to his feet, rolled up his mat, and took his first steps. The formerly impenetrable crowd now parted like the Red Sea, and Frank went home.

The four friends let out a sigh, relieved that they didn't have to hoist Frank back up through the roof. Then they high-fived each other and ran away before the owner of the house had a chance to bill them for the damages. (OK, I made that last part up.)

The Word of Knowledge can help us know exactly how to minister to people even when their physical circumstances are jockeying for our attention. In ministry, you will regularly come across total strangers who have a very visible need. Many times, however, if their deeper need isn't dealt with first, they will have a hard time sensing God's love through even the most amazing miracle. The Word of Knowledge can help make that need known.

The Word of Knowledge and Pastoring People

Let's go back to the couple with the "ghost" problem in chapter three. To refresh your memory, they received Christ and decided to sleep in separate bedrooms, turning completely to lives of celibacy until they could get married. We baptized them in bathtubs and rejoiced with them as we watched their lives transform before our eyes. The young man proposed within a month, and I was asked to officiate the wedding.

At first I was excited! We had seen God do such a work in this couple's relationship and individual lives. On the surface, it looked like a fairy-tale testimony. Nevertheless, a Word of Knowledge shook things up about two months later.

The Holy Spirit revealed something to me that only Jesus could know: these two shouldn't get married. I felt that their relationship was utterly wrong, even though everything looked so right.

For some reason, the Lord didn't reveal every detail— perhaps because He wanted me to walk out the process in a healthy way. I approached the groom-to-be and said, "If I'm going to officiate your wedding, I need to have peace about something. Forgive me if I'm totally off on this, but I get the sense that you two shouldn't be getting married."

The man took a deep breath and nodded his head. "Well, actually," he began, "I know we told you guys that I'm divorced, but I'm technically still married to my wife right now. We've been estranged for two years, and now we're just waiting for the paperwork to go through. What should I do?"

"Well," I answered, "You should call off the wedding and go patch things up with your wife."

"I haven't been on speaking terms with my wife in two years! How am I supposed to do that?"

I thought for a moment and replied, "Let's just ask the Lord to make it easy." Then we prayed together.

The next day, the bride-to-be got upset and stormed out of the house, saying she was leaving for good. There was step one. My wife, Robin, spent some time with her to walk her through the sudden chaos.

God likes to bring order out of chaos, though. Two days later, the man's actual wife called him—without knowing what was going on—and said, "I think we should patch things up."

Within a week, she had moved back in with him, and their marriage was restored. I was invited to come meet her for the first time, and that night she received salvation and was baptized in her bathtub! Then I prayed for both the husband and the wife to be filled with the Holy Spirit, and they received! Within another month, they renewed their vows and restarted their lives together, raising their two sons as a family.

At first glance, someone in the world might say that the Word of Knowledge I received was destructive—separating a lovely relationship between two Christians. But God is more powerful than that. God loves to find the darkest death and breathe resurrection life into it! In this case, the Word of Knowledge provided a turning point that set in motion a course of events that brought God far more glory than any of us could have imagined.

The Word of Knowledge is a powerful tool in ministry. Whether you're pastoring people, counseling them, or teaching them, the Word of Knowledge can accelerate the work of God and accomplish things that would otherwise be impossible. Every person in ministry should eagerly desire this gift.

Summary Questions

1. Why is it so important to wait to receive God's heart before acting on a Word of Knowledge?

    _____

    _____

2. List some reasons why the Word of Knowledge is such a necessary spiritual gift in the Church.

    _____

    _____

3. What ministry or ministries are you currently involved in? How could a Word of Knowledge be of help in that specific area?

    _____

    _____

4. Can you think of a ministry that would not benefit from someone receiving a Word of Knowledge? Why did you answer the way you did?

    _____

    _____

Endnote

1. This concept is mentioned in an audio teaching by John and Paula Sandford about "Small Groups" in *The Relationship Series,* which is available through Elijah House Ministries at www.ElijahHouse.org.

Chapter 8

pitfalls to avoid ↗

The enemy loves to attack those of us who have spiritual gifts because we are the most detrimental to his plans. Due to this, every spiritual gift has its potential pitfalls.

Before I start getting specific, I want to underscore the root of all the pitfalls, which is pride. If we do not deal with the self-life by crucifying ourselves with Christ, then we cannot receive the resurrection life of His Holy Spirit. (See Galatians 2:20 and Romans 6:5-10.) Receiving the power of the Holy Spirit without new life from the Holy Spirit tends to feed our egos rather than revealing Christ.

That's why the disciples struggled so much in Luke 9 with carrying the authority they were given. Until Jesus died, their sin couldn't die; and until God poured out His Holy Spirit, they were not able to receive His baptism. Instead, they continued to live out of their self-lives—arguing over who is the greatest, desiring to force people to accept them, and believing that they were the only ones who should be in ministry. (See Luke 9:6, 46, 49, and 54.)

Even Spirit-filled Christians struggle with pride. The Corinthian church was noted for the fact that they did not lack in any spiritual gift. (See 1 Corinthians 1:7.) However, only a couple of chapters later, Paul pointed out that they were still carnal because their pride was getting the best of them (in the form of envy, strife, and divisions). (See 1 Corinthians 3:3.)

We should not think that we are any more immune to pride than the Corinthians. Where spiritual gifts are present, the enemy plants magnetic landmines that have an unshakable attraction to pride. Those of us who do not live in unity with Christ in His death and resurrection fall victim to the attack.

I recognize that there is a danger in exposing specific pitfalls. That danger is that some readers may focus on the pitfall rather than the root issue of pride. If you're wearing an iron suit in a magnetic minefield, it won't do you any good to pull ticking mines off yourself and try to throw them away. Nor will it do any good to try avoiding them. Take off the iron suit!

On the other hand, by admitting a struggle with one of the pitfalls, our pride gets exposed and can be dealt with more effectively. It's like when you go through a metal detector at an airport. You might think you put every bit of metal on the conveyor belt, but you may have forgotten about your watch. Consider the pitfalls I share to be "pride detectors." If you see yourself slipping up in an area, the solution is not to focus on that area itself. The solution is to deal with your pride by returning to the cross and putting it there with Christ.

With that in mind, let's take a look at what I will call the first common pitfall for those who practice the Word of Knowledge.

Acting Like You Know Everything

As soon as I started practicing the Word of Knowledge, people started looking at me differently. One friend of mine said he didn't want to hang out with me anymore because he was afraid that God would tell me all his secrets and he would be too embarrassed. I've heard other Christians talk about someone with this gift as though he or she were some sort of guru who "sees all and knows all."

If we have pride, it's very easy to start playing along with the assumptions of others. It's not hard to walk with a different posture, offer mystical glances, and speak vaguely to imply that you know more than you really do. All this brings plenty of glory to us, but little glory to Jesus.

Another form of this pitfall is finding out information from someone and responding as though it's not news to you—like God had revealed it to you already. If something doesn't surprise you, that's one thing; but it is a lie to act like God revealed it to you when in reality you only had an ordinary human hunch.

If you're going to practice this gift with authority from God, then you need to remain submitted to Him. Constantly give Him the glory. Be real with people by explaining exactly how you know what you know—rather than letting them think that you have some psychic power to expose all their secrets.

Cheapening the Gift with Vague Intuition

Related to the first pitfall, this happens when we have a natural human hunch about something based on knowledge gleaned naturally.

For instance, you notice the way a man and woman talk to each other, and you get the feeling that they might be in a relationship. What do you do with that information? If one of those people is your friend, you might ask, "Is something going on between you two?" That's normal. However, it would not be right to say, "I think the Holy Spirit was showing me that you have feelings for each other." This is a lie because you didn't get that thought from the Holy Spirit; you got it from observation.

When we pick things up with natural human intuition, it is not right to pretend that we heard from the Holy Spirit. For one thing, it would be a lie, and for another thing, it cheapens the gift. Human intuition is often wrong in whole or in part, so to attach the name of God to it will cause people to mistrust your so-called revelations. Before long, they won't put much weight in what you have to say because they have not seen consistent accuracy.

Again, the root is pride—wanting to be seen as being more gifted than we actually are. But the result is that we're seen as less gifted. Only attribute things to God when you are certain that they are from God. You may fool people, but you won't fool Him; and His opinion is the only one that matters.

Saying More Than You Actually Know

Sharing a Word of Knowledge is like balancing on a tight rope—we have to step only where there's rope and constantly check our balance. If God only reveals one thing, just share that one thing—adding extra thoughts only muddies the water. The further we stray from the actual word, the more we lose our balance. Deviate from the word completely, and you're sure to fall.

A Word of Knowledge is not a person's life story. It is just a word (or single message). We only know in part. (See 1 Corinthians 13:9.) Don't feel obligated to have a huge revelation in order to be effective. If God only gave you one little thought, then that's because He knows that one little thought is all that you need.

This is especially true when the Word of Knowledge is related to dreams, visions, and their interpretations. It's very easy to add details to images that weren't really there, and it's also easy to look for meanings in symbols that God wasn't actually revealing. We have to walk the balancing act that keeps us focused on the actual revelation of God and not slip into the pitfall of sharing extra ideas.

In my experience, many times the Holy Spirit will only share a tiny bit of revelation with me and wait to see what I do with it. My pride wants to share a sermon-length message, but He only showed me one little thought. If I add to it, the person might walk away a little bit blessed. But if I'm faithful and only share the little bit, the Spirit will often share more within a few moments. Often times God wants to see what we will do with a few things before He entrusts to us many things. (See Matthew 25:21.)

Welcoming a Spirit of Divination

In Acts 16:16-19, we read about a slave girl who had a demon that enabled her to foretell the future. The slave owners were marketing her ability and earning money from her fortune-telling. When she saw Paul, Silas, and the rest of their entourage, she received what might have looked to many like a Word of Knowledge. The slave girl followed them for days and kept shouting, "These men are servants of the Most High God, who are telling you the way to be saved."(See Acts 16:17.)

As always, the root was pride. It is actually possible that this girl started out earlier in life with a genuine, God-given gift. But driven by the need to perform, she started to listen to any spirit that would give her information.

When we start to get performance-oriented and feel compelled to always have a "word," we open ourselves up to evil spirits. It doesn't matter if you're trying to please men or please God with your performance—the result is the same.

There's no need to perform to please God. When He opened the heavens over Jesus and said, "This is my most loved Son in whom I am well pleased," it was before Jesus had started His ministry or even worked one miracle. God is not looking for performers; He is looking for sons.

Likewise, there's no need to please man because that is of no eternal value. Who are you trying to impress? Why do you feel that you need to impress? It's pride, plain and simple, and it opens the door to a spirit of divination.

Furthermore, if someone comes to you asking for a Word of Knowledge, don't give them one unless you already have it. What they're really asking for is a sign to help them dispel their unbelief, but that's not how Jesus works.

The Pharisees came and began to question Jesus. To test him, they asked him for a sign from heaven. He sighed deeply and said, "Why does this generation ask for a miraculous sign? I tell you the truth, no sign will be given to it." Then he left them, got back into the boat and crossed to the other side (Mark 8:11-13).

When we try to please people and perform, we look for any stray voice that will help us out. Pride opens the door to evil spirits.

Marketing the Gift

Another thing that can give access to a spirit of divination is marketing the gift as if it were something to be peddled.

Marketing isn't necessarily a bad thing for the church. It's OK to invite people to events and services. It's even OK to say that you're going to expect the Holy Spirit to show up in power. But it's not wise to say definitively that the Holy Spirit will do this or that unless He specifically tells you to say it.

Why? Performance orientation! Just because you have a tendency to exercise a certain spiritual gift doesn't mean it will happen at every single meeting. What happens when everybody shows up expecting a Word of Knowledge and you have nothing to offer from the Lord?

Spiritual gifts are designed to function within the context of community. People should come to church to encounter God—not to see a circus act. When a spiritual family of believers collectively relies on the Holy Spirit to move in and through them, anyone stepping into their midst is sure to encounter God. It's not because anyone is performing; rather, it is because Jesus Christ is free to receive glory through His Body. Marketing the church or the meeting is one thing; but marketing a particular gift takes the focus away from the person of Christ and focuses it on one little part of His Body.

What would you do if you had traveled several hours to see your favorite recording artist perform; but when the artist came out on stage, he hid behind a curtain and held his finger over the top? No singing, no music. Just a finger. Would you be happy? In the same way, you're not the attraction—you're just one little part of Jesus. People should be attracted to Christ in the Church, not to you. If you want people to see the fullness of Christ, then don't market your gift as though it is the be-all-end-all of Christian ministry.

When I do a meeting, I make it a point not to promise any particular gift. If people want to come hear me speak or lead worship, that's fine; but I don't promise them anything other than my presence. If I did, it would pressure me to perform and meet expectations, potentially opening me up to a spirit of error. On the other hand, if I haven't promised anything, then I'm not required to perform, and the Holy Spirit is free to use me in whatever way He sees fit—teaching, healing, prophecy, music, miracles, exhortation, or Word of Knowledge.

Focusing on the Response of People

It is very easy to slip into a mindset in which you feed on the reactions of others. All it takes is one string of compliments to make you look for a pat on the back the next time you use your gift.

This can trap you in two ways. The first way is, again, performance-orientation. You could start trying to perform—not to please people or God, but simply to please yourself and stroke your own ego, always looking for the next compliment. The second way this can trap you is with discouragement. When you have this mindset, all it takes is one meeting when no one sings your praises. Suddenly, you find yourself feeling like nothing worked—possibly even drifting into depression.

The enemy is subtle like that. It is easy to slip into such pitfalls. Nevertheless, if we keep our pride in check, then we have nothing available for the enemy to snare. It is not your responsibility to get compliments; it is your responsibility to be an ambassador of Christ. Focus on Christ and revealing Him.

Fear of Failure

On the other side of all this is the tendency to remain silent. It seems like the opposite of the other pitfalls because it involves being quiet rather than rambling or saying too much. Nevertheless, it is still rooted in pride because it typically stems from a fear of failure or a desire to protect one's reputation.

We don't want to look bad. We don't want to mess up. We don't want to look like some sort of lunatic. We may say we don't want to hurt God's reputation, but really we're just trying to preserve our own! God can stick up for Himself, so don't worry about defaming Him. The issue is you.

Don't be afraid of messing up. The same God who once transformed dirty water into the best wine is still capable of smoothing over our rough edges. The key is simply that we operate in humility and crucify all pride. If your heart is to bring glory to God, then He'll get glory. People tend to have a lot more patience with those who are genuinely humble, and God has promised to exalt the humble in due time. Keep your focus on Him, and step out in faith. If your heart is right, there's no such thing as failure. If your heart is full of pride, then even your success is a failure. God opposes the proud and gives grace to the humble. (See James 4:6.)

Sharing the Word but Missing the Heart

As mentioned in the previous chapter, having a Word of Knowledge is great, but we must also receive the heart in which God intends it to be conveyed. If all you have is information, then you don't really "know" in the biblical sense of the word. Demons can convey information without any trouble, but only God can convey heart.

If you receive a Word of Knowledge, don't act on it until you have clarity about how God wants you to act. Ask Him for His heart on the matter and wait until you can see the person and the situation through the lenses of His perspective. You'll know you've got it when you feel overwhelmed with love for the person. Never act on a Word of Knowledge without love.

First Corinthians 13 goes into great detail about the love of God and how it relates to spiritual gifts. You could have the most detailed Word of Knowledge that God has ever given, but if you don't have love, it means absolutely nothing.

Those who share spiritual gifts without the supernatural love of God backing them up are loose cannons. Rather than targeting the enemy, such a person also risks wounding other believers. Those who shoot guns know that you have to take your time and focus your breathing in order to make a good shot. People tease me when I shoot skeet because I often wait until the clay pigeon is almost too far away to hit before I pull the trigger. They tease me, but I often shoot more skeet than them! In the same way, when we restrain ourselves and choose not to speak or act until we can do so in love, we more often find the ability to have pinpoint accuracy.

Apathy

The final pitfall I want to discuss is apathy. Many ministers find themselves no longer caring like they used to. There are probably thousands of superficial reasons for it to set in, but again the root is pride.

Apathy sets in when we stop putting others ahead of ourselves. Oftentimes it comes with a mindset that says, "I deserve a break." As soon as you start thinking about what you deserve, pride has already set in.

Apathy can also come from a lack of satisfaction with ministry. Satisfaction will wane if you start to believe that your spiritual gift is about you and your ability. Likewise, if you believe your gift is about others and how they receive it, you will quickly find yourself discouraged. It's not about you, and it's not even about others. If you want your gift to be perpetually fueled with passion, you must see it as a matter of obedience to the God you love. It's all about Him and no one else.

The only way to steer clear of apathy is to keep your focus humbly on God. Cultivate your relationship with Him. Spend time with Him in prayer, meditation, worship, study, journaling, and reading the Word. Engage in meaningful fellowship with other believers so that you can encounter Christ through the lives of others. It's all about Him.

CHAPTER ONE

On a cold Monday in November, Detective Inspector Ian Carmichael Hamilton entered the High Street police station with a feeling of foreboding. His superior officer, Detective Chief Inspector Crawford, had not been himself lately, and no one seemed to know what the matter was. Not a particularly cheerful man under the best of circumstances, DCI Crawford had been even moodier of late, muttering under his breath, looking peeved and distracted. Worse, he had become absent-minded, forgetting orders he had given and countermanding others. Morale was shaky, the men under him jumpy. Officers were coming in late, if they showed up at all, and a sense of chaos pervaded the squad room.

After hanging his cloak on the rack, Ian sat at his desk in the corner, turning his attention to the growing mound of paperwork. But he found it difficult to concentrate, sensing expectant looks from the other officers around him. Conversation had ceased when he entered, and there were low murmurs he couldn't make out, the words lost in the room's lofty ceilings. It was clear something had to be done.

DCI Crawford was not the sort of man to take anyone into his confidence, but DI Hamilton was the closest thing he had to a friend on the force. Though it was more of a father-son relationship—and a fraught one at that—Ian knew if anyone could break through the chief's intimidating personality, he could.

He didn't relish the idea of confronting Crawford—his commanding officer's tirades were legendary and, over the years, had reduced more than a few recruits to tears. Ian looked up to see Constable Bowers hovering nervously nearby. His blond eyebrows were knit with concern, terror in his deep-set blue eyes.

"What is it, Constable?"

"Well, sir, he won't talk to anybody—just sits there in a black mood, starin' out the window, y'see." Like Ian, Bowers came from Invernesshire, but DCI Crawford had the ability to intimidate even the Highlanders on the force.

"And you're waiting for me to do something about it, I suppose?" said Ian.

Constable Bowers fiddled with his truncheon and bit his lip. "Well, are you going to, sir?"

Several other policemen stared at him from their desks. The tension in the room was as thick as the evening fogs that rolled in from the Firth of Forth.

"All right," Ian declared, standing up and squaring his shoulders. "I'm going in."

He felt all eyes on him as he strode toward Crawford's office, projecting a confidence he did not feel. The chief inspector's office was at the front of the building, separated from the main room by a wood-and-glass partition, the door facing the larger central chamber. Ian knocked on it crisply and waited. No reply. He looked back at Bowers, whose face had gone a shade paler.

"He's in there, sir," the constable said.

Ian knocked again more sharply—still no response. He took a deep breath and opened the door. He braced himself for reprimand, but the figure slumped behind the desk barely moved to acknowledge his presence. The seat was turned toward the window, so all he saw was the back of the chief inspector's bald head over the top of the chair.

"Sir?" he said.

"Do you know what I hate, Hamilton?" Crawford said without turning around.

"What's that, sir?"

"I hate this whole blasted existence. We eat, we sleep, we trudge off to work, return home again only to eat and sleep some more. What's the bloody use? That's what I'd like to know."

"We also catch criminals, sir. We make the city a safer place to live."

"Do we, Hamilton? Is it really safer?"

"I should venture to say so, sir."

"How can you tell? Because it feels like a cesspool to me right now."

"Then imagine what it would be without us."

Ian's remark was met with a thin sigh. "I can't really imagine anything at the moment—that's the trouble."

"Would you care to talk about it, sir?"

Another sigh, then what sounded like a muffled sob, and DCI Crawford slowly swiveled around toward Hamilton.

Ian was shocked by the sight of his superior officer's face. It had a pasty greenish cast, as though all the blood had drained from it. His cheeks sagged, his eyes were dull and lifeless—even his bushy red muttonchops seemed to droop. Normally a robust, portly man, he looked shrunken and pale.

Ian took the liberty of sitting in the chair in front of Crawford's desk. Usually a stickler for rules, the chief inspector didn't take any notice of this violation of protocol. Crawford gazed at Ian listlessly, twisting a piece of string restlessly between his fingers.

"Sir," Ian began, "the men have noticed something is wrong, and—"

Crawford interrupted him with a laugh—a short, bitter burst of air. "Oh, they have? Bully for them! Perhaps we should promote them

5

all to the rank of detective, eh?" He gave another laugh, but it caught in his throat, becoming a deep, shuddering sob. His body shook as he let his head fall forward to rest on his folded arms.

Ian watched Crawford give in to his grief, his large, ungainly body racked with weeping. Ian felt for the man, but he knew the policemen on the other side of the glass partition could hear them, and when DCI Crawford returned to his senses he would be horrified at the public nature of his breakdown.

But for now there was nothing to be done except sit and wait. Crawford's sobs were punctuated by sounds from outside—the clop of horses' hooves, shouts of street vendors, and the cries of gulls. The birds were a constant reminder of how close Edinburgh was to the sea, the Port of Leith on the Firth of Forth lying only a couple of miles from the center of Old Town.

Finally, Crawford's grief wore itself out. Wiping his face with a blue kerchief, he blew his nose loudly and cleared his throat.

"Well," he said, "that was damned embarrassing."

"'Everyone can master a grief but he that has it,'" Ian said gently.

Crawford's eyes narrowed. "Another one of your Shakespeare quotes?"

"Much Ado About Nothing."

Crawford grunted. "Well, at least this one's appropriate."

Ian was relieved to hear the inspector sounding more like himself, some of the old vinegar creeping into his voice.

The chief stood and stretched his bulky form. Well over six feet tall, Detective Chief Inspector Crawford was an imposing presence. Curly red whiskers grew in reckless abundance upon his chin, as if to make up for the hair that had long since abandoned his head. A pair of magnificent bushy eyebrows, black as a chimney sweep's broom, presided over his face. Everything about him was writ large—his long, oval face; bulbous nose; and thick lips, all set atop a big-boned, fleshy body.

"Are you quite all right, sir?" Ian asked.

"We'll speak no more of this, Hamilton," he said, straightening his cuffs and brushing lint from the sleeves of his uniform. "Now then, what did you want to see me about?"

Ian hesitated. "Well, sir—"

Crawford's small eyes narrowed. "Did I give you permission to sit?"

"No, sir, I—"

"Just thought you'd take advantage of my inattention, eh?" Crawford said, giving his nose another mighty blow into the kerchief.

"No, sir, it was just—"

He was interrupted by a knock on the door.

"Who is it?" Crawford barked, settling back in his chair.

"Sergeant Dickerson, sir," came the voice from the other side.

"Come in, Sergeant."

The door opened to admit a short, unprepossessing young man with ginger hair and pink skin. Hamilton gazed at him gratefully—not only because he had interrupted an uncomfortable moment, but also because Dickerson was Ian's most trustworthy and loyal colleague. In spite of his unimpressive appearance, he had proven to be resourceful and brave, if a bit plodding at times.

"What is it, Sergeant?" said Crawford.

Dickerson cleared his throat and glanced apprehensively at Ian.

"Out with it, man!" Crawford barked. "We haven't got all day."

"I was wonderin' if I could work an extra shift today, sir, in exchange for next Friday off."

"Why did you not take this up with the shift sergeant?"

"I did, sir, and he said I was t'see you."

"Well?"

"I have a—er, commitment."

Crawford frowned. "What sort of 'commitment' could possibly take precedence over your work as a police officer?"

Ian noted with some relief that the sergeant's presence seemed to have invigorated DCI Crawford. Perhaps scolding his subordinates was just the thing to conquer his melancholy. Poor Dickerson was squirming uncomfortably, sweat gathering on his ruddy face.

"Well, sir, y'see . . . I'm in a play."

"A *play*?" Crawford bellowed. "You're in a *play*?"

"Not just any play, sir—*Hamlet*. I've been given the role of the Second Gravedigger."

"Well done, Sergeant," Ian remarked, but Crawford glared at him.

"And who has made the colossal error of casting you in this—*play*?" he inquired.

"It's a charity event, sir—the Greyfriars Dramatic Society. All the proceeds go to feed the needy."

"And were you required to demonstrate your fitness for the role of—what is it?"

"Second Gravedigger. Yes, sir—I had t'audition for the part."

"'Alas, poor Yorick,'" the chief inspector remarked with a smug smile at Hamilton.

"That's Hamlet's line, sir," Ian corrected him.

"What difference does it make whose bloody line it is?"

"The Second Gravedigger gets to ask, 'Who builds stronger than a mason, a shipwright, or a carpenter?'" said Dickerson.

The chief inspector thought for a moment. "I give up—what's the answer?"

The sergeant blushed. "Er, I dunno, sir."

Crawford scowled. "Why not?"

"'Cause that's when Hamlet enters, and Shakespeare never answers the riddle."

"That's bloody rude of him," Crawford muttered. "All right, go ahead—and tell the shift sergeant next time not to bother me with such bosh and bunkum."

"Yes, sir—thank you, sir," Dickerson said, backing out of the office. As he did, he bumped into Constable Bowers.

"What is it, Bowers?" asked Crawford.

"There's a lady here, sir. Says she won't leave until you see her."

"What sort of lady?"

A strident voice behind Bowers led Ian to think that perhaps the term "lady" had been misapplied. "It's murder, I tell you, plain and simple!" The accent was English, a bit plummy—probably central London, Ian guessed.

"Good heavens," Crawford said, his thick eyebrows rising halfway up his shiny forehead like climbing caterpillars.

The personage herself barged past Constable Bowers, shouldering both him and Sergeant Dickerson out of the way. She strode across the small office to stand in front of Crawford's desk, hands on her broad hips, breathing heavily. Clad in a plain black bodice over an ample gray skirt, she was nearly as tall as Ian, her dark hair parted in the middle and pulled back into a severe bun at the back of a muscular neck. Her eyes were dark and rather deep-set, over a small, determined mouth and firm chin. Though she was no beauty, Ian observed that her brusque manner and style of dress conspired to make her less attractive than she otherwise might have been.

She crossed her arms over her impressive bosom. "I demand an investigation!"

"Into what, madame, if I may be so bold?" Crawford inquired.

"The death of Mr. Thomas Caruthers."

"And how did he die?"

"He was poisoned."

"And you know this because—?"

"I recognize the signs of arsenic poisoning."

"Who are you, if I may ask?"

"Dr. Sophia Jex-Blake."

Crawford's mouth fell open. Jex-Blake was one of the most famous—and notorious—women in Edinburgh. She and six other women had attempted to upset centuries of tradition by petitioning the university to let them study medicine. Known as the Edinburgh Seven, they were derided and savagely attacked; there was even rioting in the streets. Crawford shot a look at Dickerson and Bowers, who had been watching from just outside the office.

"Close the door, Constable, and go about your duties. I'm sure you must have plenty to do."

"Yes, sir," Bowers gulped, swinging the door shut reluctantly, leaving Ian and the chief inspector alone with their visitor.

"Assuming you are who you claim to be," Crawford began, "why—"

"Why on earth would anyone pretend to be me?" she interrupted impatiently.

Knowing her reputation, Ian was convinced she was exactly who she claimed to be.

Evidently the chief inspector agreed. "Very well," he said. "Pray be seated."

"That's more like it," she said, settling her sturdy form into the nearest chair.

"Now then," said Crawford, "exactly why do you believe a murder has been committed?"

Jex-Blake returned his gaze. "Are you familiar with the symptoms of arsenic poisoning?"

"Some of them, yes."

"Then you are perhaps aware that it can easily be attributed to other causes, such as stomach viruses, dropsy, or even cholera."

"What in particular leads you to believe Mr. Caruthers is the victim of arsenic poisoning?"

"His fingernails display pronounced horizontal striation."

Crawford's broad face puckered. "Horizontal stri—?"

"White lines along the width of the nails," she explained, as though addressing an exceptionally slow child. "It is a telltale sign of arsenic poisoning."

"I see," Crawford replied, stroking his ginger whiskers.

"What relationship have you to the victim?" Ian inquired.

Dr. Jex-Blake squinted at him as though he were an unusual laboratory specimen.

"Why is that of any consequence?"

"In any investigation, it is crucial to identify the persons surrounding the victim," he replied, uncomfortable under her scrutiny. "You are the one to report this crime—if indeed such it is—so I am starting with you."

"Mr. Caruthers' wife has been under my care since her pregnancy."

"Under your care?" said Crawford.

"You are evidently unaware that I run a clinic for women on Grove Street," she said drily, as though their ignorance was an offense against her honor.

"Ah, yes—quite commendable," Crawford said with a little cough. "So Mrs. Caruthers informed you of her husband's death?"

"Actually, no. I was the one who found Mr. Caruthers after his demise."

"How did that come about?" Ian inquired, exchanging a look with Crawford. It was a given in crime investigation that the person who "discovers" the body must be considered as a potential suspect.

"I did not poison Mr. Caruthers, if that's what you're thinking," Dr. Jex-Blake snapped. "I happened to be checking in on Mrs. Caruthers, and not finding her at home, I thought to wait for her."

"How did that lead to the discovery of the body?" said Ian.

"Mrs. Caruthers had given me a key to her home. When I let myself in, I felt something was not quite right, so I went into the bedroom, where I found Mr. Caruthers."

"I see," said Crawford. "Upon which you diagnosed arsenic poisoning."

"Precisely."

"And where is Mr. Caruthers at this moment?"

"His poor wife was quite beside herself with grief, so we had him taken to the city morgue."

Listening to Dr. Jex-Blake, Ian Hamilton thought this seemed a very interesting case. He had no way of knowing it would prove to be far more than that.

CHAPTER ELEVEN

Vickie Caruthers was a slight, sallow woman with sad eyes and a wan, worn-out face. Her loose-fitting bodice, shawl, and hand-knit skirt made no attempt to conceal her advanced pregnancy. There was something disturbing about the sight of a protruding belly on such a diminutive person; looking at her, Ian had the disquieting thought that she was about to give birth to a demon or other monster. He attributed this unpleasant association to his recent reading of *Frankenstein; or, The Modern Prometheus*, by Mary Shelley. The book was much in vogue in Edinburgh, and Aunt Lillian had recently given him a copy.

Mrs. Caruthers led the men into a dingy but tidy room that appeared to serve as combination parlor and dining room. Beckoning them each to a chair, she attempted to perch upon a milking stool, but Ian would have none of it.

"Please, madame," he implored, indicating a tattered blue armchair. "In your condition, you should take the weight off your feet."

She did not argue, and sank wearily into the chair. In her cloth cap and shawl, she looked anything but a murderess and sat demurely with her hands folded, waiting patiently for Ian to speak.

"I am so very sorry about your husband's tragic and untimely death," he began.

She gave a shallow sigh, her thin shoulders barely moving, as if that was all the energy her small body could muster.

"He was a good man, my Tom," she said in a low voice. "Don' know what we'll do weaout 'im."

"'We'?" said Ian.

"Me an' the baby," she said, patting her distended abdomen.

"Do you have anyone to look after you?"

She shook her head and stared into the distance. "Lost me mum an' da in the cholera. Tom's folks live in Aberdeen—s'pose I could go live with them, if they'll have me. Unless they think I did 'im in. You don' think I killed my Tom, do you?" she said, a flush creeping into her pale cheeks.

"Of course not," Ian blurted out, startled by her directness. Sergeant Dickerson caught his eye and frowned, but Ian pretended not to notice. The truth was, he didn't think she was guilty. Her innocence and lack of guile, stooped shoulders and quiet grief—surely these were not the traits of a cold-blooded poisoner. Of course, she could be putting on a show, but if so, she was an actress of preternatural talent. Ian's instinct told him she was as much a victim as her unfortunate husband. "We'd like to question you," he said, "to help us find the person who did this."

"Oh, aye," she said earnestly. "I'll do whatever I can t'ketch poor Tom's killer."

"Can you think of anyone who would want to hurt him?"

"I've thought of naught else, but nae one comes to mind."

"Did he have any friends we can talk to?"

"Ye might talk to 'is mates at the rail yards."

There was a light, quick knock at the door, and she struggled to rise from her chair.

"Please, allow me," said Ian.

He opened the front door to see a bright-eyed young woman with an abundant crown of blond hair holding a basket in the crook of her arm. She frowned upon seeing Ian but, spying Vickie, waved cheerfully.

CHAPTER FIFTEEN

The landscape of Scotland, ripped apart by volcanoes, torn and scraped by centuries of glaciers, pockmarked by lakes and crags, was like its inhabitants—besieged by internal warfare, blown and scattered by invading armies, and dotted with remnants of tribes hardy enough to eke out a living from its rocky soil and rugged climate. The descendants of those tribes loved the land with a fierceness born of centuries of deprivation and hardship. Scotland's harsh beauty inspired dogged devotion from a people given to excess, in love with the romance and nobility of suffering.

Nowhere in Edinburgh was this suffering more apparent than in Holy Land, the ironically named swamp in the neighborhood known as the Canongate. Just as the Irish ghetto on the west end of town lay in the shadow of Edinburgh Castle, the Canongate's tenements slumped directly below the posh residences of Royal Terrace and Holyrood Palace. Stark poverty was bracketed on every side by extreme affluence—no doubt contributing to the city's violent and bloody past.

These cruel disparities were not lost on Sergeant Dickerson as he alighted from the hansom cab carrying himself, DI Hamilton, and Derek McNair at the entrance to Holy Land. A couple of grubby

Carole Lawrence

children peered through soot-covered windows at the unfamiliar sight
of a hackney carriage invading their dim and dusky corridors.

Detective Hamilton's knock upon the front door was met with
silence—Dickerson glanced up to see the children's mother pull them
away from their window perch. Hamilton tried knocking again, but
to no avail.

"Why don' they answer?" the sergeant asked.

"Folks 'round here don' much like coppers," Derek observed.

"How do they know we're policemen?" Dickerson said.

"They can smell us," replied Ian.

"C'mon," said Derek, darting around the side of the building.
"Follow me."

He led them to the back, then up some rickety stairs that hugged
the stone walls, a rusted handrail the only thing between them and
the cobblestones below. Hamilton pounded loudly on the second-floor
landing door; what was left of its green paint peeled off in flakes beneath
the blows of his fist.

"I know you're in there," he called. "Open the door or we'll break
it down!"

The door swung open abruptly to reveal a large, fleshy woman of
indeterminate years, dressed in a low-cut yellow frock. Her skin had the
pale hue of one who rarely saw the sun; her hair, an unlikely shade of
copper, was tightly curled around her flushed, round face.

"Why would ye want to do that, now, lovey?" she asked Ian. "You
know Kate's always glad to see your handsome face. Who's this fresh
young thing?" she asked, giving Dickerson a look that made his cheeks
burn.

"This is Sergeant Dickerson," said Ian, "and this is—"

"Oh, no need to introduce young Master McNair," she responded
with a laugh that was meant to be lewd and worldly, but the sound
of it filled the sergeant's heart with sadness. She turned to Dickerson.
"Pleased t'meet you. 'Round here they call me Fair Kate."

86

Unsure of the proper response, Dickerson nodded and tipped his hat. She grinned, revealing crooked front teeth, and crossed her plump white arms over her bulging bosom. She was the picture of degraded femininity, yet he could not ignore his body's response—her presence excited him. Kate smelled of camphor and oil soap and freshly laundered linen; she was motherly and sensual and wholly, utterly different from his lady friend, the proper and exquisite Caroline Tierney. He adored Caroline with all his heart, yet there was something wild and thrilling about Fair Kate that shook Dickerson to his core. Confused and perplexed, he wiped the sweat from his upper lip and shoved his hands into his pockets.

"Well?" said Ian. "Are you going to invite us in?"

"'Will you walk into my parlor,' said the spider to the fly,'" she replied, holding the door open for the three of them.

Dickerson was startled to see Derek McNair run his hand over Kate's buxom behind. She swatted it away but seemed neither surprised nor annoyed by his rude familiarity.

"Cheeky little scamp," she muttered.

The boy winked at the sergeant before sauntering into the building.

This confused Dickerson even more. He was utterly flustered by the fallen woman, with her outrageous curls and insinuating smile. Not for the first time, William Chester Dickerson felt himself an outsider, a clumsy interloper in a society whose rules he did not understand. He stumbled after Hamilton, hoping the detective did not notice his discomfort.

The room they entered was evidently a kitchen, judging by the bubbling coming from the far corner where a gas stove sagged beneath the weight of a gigantic cast-iron pot.

"I'd offer ye some," Kate said, observing Dickerson eyeing the pot, from which steam poured with such abandon a thin film of mist covered his entire face. "Trouble is, I don't think ye'd want any." She walked over and dipped a wooden spoon into the boiling cauldron, lifting forth a sopping garment he recognized as a pair of women's bloomers. He felt himself blush helplessly as she threw back her head and guffawed, full-throated and hearty as a sailor. "Round here, there's as likely to be laundry cooking as dinner, lovey," she said, wiping the sweat from her own brow.

Detective Hamilton seemed less than enchanted by her quips. His ascetic face was stern, his gray eyes glimmering with impatience. "Would you be so kind as to take us to the scene of the crime?" he said.

"Don't get yer knickers in a twist—we're on the way," she said, wiping her hands on a dirty dish towel.

Dickerson couldn't help marveling at how at ease she was in the company of two policemen and a lewd street urchin. The presence of the police put most people on edge, but Kate was as relaxed as if she was entertaining old friends. They followed her through a beaded curtain and down a narrow hallway with peeling flowered wallpaper. She stopped in front of a door at the end of the corridor.

"This is the room where he—well, we left him just as we found him, like the lad told us," she added with a glance at Derek.

Ian turned his gaze on the boy. "Just exactly what *were* you doing at an establishment like this?"

"Told ye, I were visitin' a friend. Anyway, wha' diff'rence do it make? I found ye another victim, innit?"

"That remains to be seen," Ian remarked. "We may find the poor blighter died of natural causes."

"Well, have a wee look-see fer yourself," said their hostess, swinging the door open to reveal a midsized bedroom.

The interior was dim; the only source of illumination was the feeble sunlight struggling to penetrate the layers of soot and grime covering the windows. The room was sparsely furnished, with a simple pine dresser between the two windows and a brass bed against the wall at the other end. The atmosphere was musty and damp, the stale air suggesting the windows had not been opened for some time. There was another odor Dickerson recognized immediately.

It was the smell of death.

CHAPTER SIXTEEN

The dead man on the bed was fully clothed, for which Dickerson gave silent thanks. William Dickerson had never enjoyed the sight of another man's body, finding it especially embarrassing to gaze upon a naked dead man. In addition to being personally distasteful, it always struck him as a violation of privacy, a final indignity, so to speak. Luckily, that was not the case with this gentleman, who had apparently been overcome by death before he could divest himself of his garments.

The dead man appeared to be in early middle age, with a solid physique, well-groomed and prosperous-looking. His beard was neatly trimmed, Van Dyke style, and his dark-blue wool suit was of the finest gabardine. The jacket hung from the bedpost behind his head; the matching waistcoat and trousers he wore appeared quite new and in excellent condition.

But the body itself was shocking. His limbs were twisted grotesquely, splayed at unnatural angles, and oddly stiff, more than the usual effects of rigor mortis, as if he had died in the midst of violent convulsions. His face was contorted into a mockery of a smile, the teeth bared, and the sergeant could make out a faint rim of dried foam around his mouth.

The other students stared at him as though he had just proposed decapitating the patient. Bell, however, looked at him thoughtfully. "Intriguing idea, Hamilton."

"In addition to glucose or saline solution, one might inject controlled doses of alcohol to prevent potentially fatal withdrawal symptoms."

"You may have something," said Dr. Bell. "Bring your patient to Operating Theater Three—I'll join you in fifteen minutes, when I finish my rounds." He strode off down the hall, the medical students scampering after him like ducklings.

"Follow me," Donald said to the orderlies who had been standing by patiently. The men complied, wheeling the gurney after him as Donald strode confidently down the polished corridors. "You know, it occurs to me that we might ask Dr. Bell if he'd be willing to have a look at your boss's wife. I hear he's quite the diagnostician."

"If you're willing to approach him, I'm sure DCI Crawford would be most grateful," said Ian. He had completely forgotten about his promise to Crawford, and his head felt fuzzy as he followed his brother through the halls of the infirmary.

Ian had not been in a hospital since his treatment for burns sustained in the fire that killed his parents, and as he trailed after his brother, his left shoulder began to throb and pulse. It all flooded back—the sharp odor of antiseptic, the hollow ring of footsteps in hallways, the murmur of voices as they passed various wards. He felt dizzy and light-headed as they turned the corner toward the surgery ward. He blinked in an attempt to dispel the dark spots darting through his field of vision.

As they neared the entrance to the operating theater Ian's legs felt rubbery and weak. Clutching the air, he stumbled and pitched forward as the black spots swelled and became a thick curtain of darkness. He was vaguely aware of his brother's hand on his shoulder as he plummeted into a long black tunnel.

Voices, when they returned, were thin and faint, as if coming from great distance.

"Wait—he's coming 'round. Ian, can you hear me?"

He knew the voice belonged to his brother, but at first Ian didn't know where he was. He imagined he was lying on the sofa in the sitting room of his own flat. Then he caught the scent of rubbing alcohol and oil soap and remembered. He fought to open his eyes, but it felt as though someone had draped a cloth over his face. His vision was blurred, even as he squinted to bring the room into focus. The light hurt his eyes, yet everything was so dim. He heard footsteps, followed by more voices, farther away this time.

"What happened?" It was a man's voice—authoritative, sharp, commanding.

"He fainted." Ian recognized Donald's voice.

"So now we have two patients instead of one."

Two patients . . . A cold blade of panic sliced Ian's stomach as he remembered what he had done. He struggled to sit up, to will himself into full consciousness, but felt hands upon his shoulders. It was then he realized he was dressed in a hospital gown instead of his own clothes.

"Easy, now." The voice belonged to the other man . . . Dr. Blue . . . Bull? Bell, that was it. "You've had a nasty fall."

"Dr. Bell, I think this man is coming 'round." The voice belonged to a young woman—a nurse, Ian supposed—but it came from the other side of the room.

"Your patient seems to have recovered before we could try your treatment, Hamilton," the doctor said. "Too bad—it would have been interesting."

"His recovery is the most important thing, sir," Donald replied.

"Of course, of course," said Bell. "Still, it's a pity we didn't get to test your theory."

Ian's brain fought to bring back the details of what had transpired. Something about alcohol and a coma . . . but the effort was too much, and he sank back onto the pillow, letting go of the need to figure anything out. He was so tired . . .

He awoke to a view of starlight. The tall windows looked out onto a clear night, and above the flicker of gas lamps, constellations shone bright and cold in the November sky. Feeling wide awake and rested, Ian sat up in bed. A sharp pain in his left shoulder distracted him momentarily—perhaps he had injured it in the fall—but he rested his weight on his other arm and surveyed the room.

His bed was in the middle of a Nightingale ward, a large room containing multiple patients, the beds lining the walls on either side of the chamber, creating a wide corridor in the middle. All the other patients appeared to be asleep; he heard snoring and the occasional murmur coming from the beds around him. Next to his bed, slumped in a chair, his brother, Donald, slept. Ian didn't know whether to wake him or not, so he pulled his covers off and climbed quietly out of bed.

"I say—you probably shouldn't be up."

Ian turned to see the tall, muscular medical student they had encountered in Dr. Bell's entourage.

"It's all right—I'm quite recovered now," he replied.

"You're Donald's brother, I believe?"

"Detective Ian Hamilton, Edinburgh City Police," he answered, not wishing to be known simply as "Donald's brother."

"Yes, he mentioned something about having a brother who was a policeman. Arthur Conan Doyle," he said, extending a hand. "Fourth-year medical student."

His grip was firm, the hand strong, matching his athletic build. Ian was taller, but Doyle was broader, with thick, strong legs and a powerful torso. It was, Ian thought, the body of a sailor rather than a physician. He was a fine-looking fellow, with an oval face and strong chin beneath the elaborately twirled mustache.

"You're one of Dr. Bell's students—the one who diagnosed chronic alcoholism," Ian said. "That was very clever."

"I was merely applying Dr. Bell's methods," Doyle replied. "He has taught us to observe patients closely and deduce from what we see."

"That's exactly what I do in my line of work."

"Indeed? My father always claimed you lot rounded up likely suspects and beat confessions out of them."

"Regrettably, he's not entirely mistaken," Ian said with a wry smile. "But I intend to reform the way police detectives approach their work."

"That's a rather tall order, I should think."

"I'm sorry medicine has already claimed you—we could use more chaps like you on the force."

His companion smiled, causing pouches to appear beneath his heavy-lidded, almond-shaped eyes. There was something exotic about his face—manly and leonine yet with a suggestion of the Orient in his wide-set eyes.

"It doesn't take much of a diagnostician to see you've a nasty contusion and possible concussion," he said, gazing at Ian's face.

Ian put a hand to his temple, swollen and hot to the touch.

"That's why I fainted?"

"I should imagine so. How do you feel now?"

"Not too bad. A little shaky."

"Go easy for a while, if you can."

"Where is the man we brought in?"

"Ah, you mean Gordon Kinsey. He's gone."

"He's been released already?"

"Not exactly. He regained consciousness and staggered out, against medical advice. Muttered something about finding a drink before the pubs closed."

"That sounds entirely in character to me."

"Do you mind if I ask a rather personal question?" said Doyle.

"As long as it relates to medicine or murder."

Doyle smiled. "How did you come by that scar on your shoulder? I noticed it when we removed your shirt."

Ian took a deep breath and considered lying. After all, he had just met Doyle, and owed him no personal information. But something about the man's open, honest demeanor made lying seem small and dirty. "In a fire," he said, hoping the medical student would probe no further. To his relief, Doyle seemed satisfied with his answer.

"Does it bother you much?"

"Sometimes."

Doyle shuddered. "Nasty thing, burns. I once helped treat a woman who was disfigured when a jealous lover threw carbolic acid at her."

"Did they catch him?"

"They did, may he rot in prison forever. You mustn't be too impressed with my diagnosis today," he added with a rueful smile. "I'm afraid I've had rather more experience of the effects of chronic alcoholism than I'd like."

Ian was at a loss for how to respond to this confession.

"My father suffers from the condition," Doyle explained. "Since childhood I have had ample opportunity to observe its devastating effects."

This personal revelation from a man he had just met made Ian uncomfortable. He had an impulse to mention Donald's struggles with alcohol but felt it inappropriate. He had no idea what his brother had revealed to his fellow students and colleagues.

As if aware of Ian's thoughts, Donald stirred in his sleep, then jerked up in his chair and opened his eyes.

"Ah, I see you're out of bed," he said to Ian. "What are you doing here, Doyle?"

"I came to check on your brother."

"Couldn't resist, eh? Came to compare notes?"

"I don't know what you mean," Doyle replied unconvincingly.

"Don't pretend with me, old man. I can see right through you." Donald stood up and stretched his massive frame. Taller than Ian and considerably heavier than Doyle, he loomed over them like a watchful

"They are all quite busy—I'd appreciate it if you direct any further questions to me."

"I should like to at least question the nurses responsible for his treatment."

"Very well," she conceded. "I'll arrange for it. And now if you'll excuse me, I have patients waiting."

"Thank you for coming in," Ian said, rising from his chair. "Shall I escort you out?"

"Very gallant of you, Detective, but my legs are quite as sturdy as they look."

Ian thought she winked at him.

When she had gone, Sergeant Dickerson shook his head. "That woman gives me the willies."

"I think she's rather impressive."

"I'm not sayin' otherwise, sir, but she's frightenin'."

"'Angels and ministers of grace defend us.'"

"Sir?"

"Surely you recognize that quote."

"It's, er, Hamlet speaking to 'is father's ghost, ain't it?"

"We'll make a thespian out of you yet, Sergeant."

"I shouldn't wonder, sir."

"Come along," Ian said, springing to his feet.

"Where are we off to, sir?"

"We're going to a funeral."

CHAPTER THIRTY

Ian liked to wander through the National Gallery in his spare time, a habit he'd acquired from Aunt Lillian, who was considered quite an artist in her youth. The gallery was open late on Friday, and was a short walk from his flat. His lack of success in the case was making him restless, and he needed to take his mind off it. He skirted the western edge of the Princes Street Gardens, the twittering of birds just audible over the rumbling from the underground train tunnel buried beneath its mounds of flowers and greenery.

His footsteps took him, as they did so often lately, to the room containing the work of seventeenth-century Spanish artist Diego Velázquez. He was especially fascinated by the painting *An Old Woman Cooking Eggs*, dazzled by its rich textures and remarkable realism. He was staring at the shine on the ceramic bowl containing the eggs, marveling at the painter's ability to render such stunning details, when he became aware of someone entering the room from the far side.

He saw with displeasure it was Fiona Stuart, the nurse on whose behalf he had intervened at the White Hart, and whose subsequent ingratitude so rankled him. He looked away immediately, but it was too late—she had seen him.

"Oh," she said, "it's you." She made no attempt to hide her disappointment.

Ian longed to blurt out that people should be grateful to strangers interceding on their behalf.

"Nice to see you again," she said.

"If you insist," he muttered.

"Remarkable painting," she said, gazing at the Velázquez.

"Yes, it is," he replied tightly.

They stood uncomfortably studying the painting for a while, then he turned to leave.

"I'm sorry if you thought I was rude, but I didn't ask for your help, you know," she said.

"I beg your pardon?"

"You needn't have troubled yourself on my account. I can look after myself."

"You've made that abundantly clear."

"I understand you meant well, but it's people like you who are responsible for—"

He wheeled around, dizzy with fury. "For what—the rising crime rate in Edinburgh? The orphans and widows who go hungry every night for lack of bread? For desperate young mothers who smother their children because they can't afford to look after them?"

Her face reddened as she looked away, and he realized everyone was staring at them. He was acutely aware of how silent the room had become. He heard the street sounds outside, the clatter of horses' hooves and the rattle of carriage wheels on cobblestones. He was desperate to be out there—or anywhere—rather than in this chamber with all these people gaping at him as though he were one of the paintings.

"I was *about* to say that it's attitudes like yours that keep women as second-class citizens," she said in a low voice.

"You don't have the slightest idea what my 'attitudes' are."

"You thought I was someone who needed rescuing."

The other patrons pretended to be looking at the paintings, but Ian could tell they were still listening.

Very well, he thought peevishly, *I'll give them a show.*

"What I *saw* was you being bullied by a man who outweighed you by at least eight stone. It had nothing to do with you being a woman."

Her nose wrinkled, and a little frown line appeared between her eyebrows. "He wasn't attacking me physically."

"Let me tell you something I know a bit about, Miss—" In his anger, her name suddenly escaped him.

"Stuart."

"Miss Stuart, I spend my days apprehending the worst offenders this town has to offer. I can assure you that fellow I rescued you from has done bodily harm to any number of people."

"Is that any reason to go and get yourself battered about? He could have killed you."

"Yet here I stand—sound of body, if not of mind."

"You acted like a fool because you thought it would impress me."

"Impress *you?*" Ian sputtered. "You give yourself far too much credit, I assure you!"

"Then who were you aiming to impress?"

"I was merely attempting to correct an injustice."

"If you really cared about injustice, you would be petitioning to improve conditions for the widows and orphans you mentioned earlier."

"How do you know I'm not?"

She narrowed her eyes, which were a warm green, the color of dark jade. "You don't strike me as the petitioning sort."

"What I am is a bloody good detective, and I've put away a fair number of criminals who prey upon your widows and orphans."

"I am not accustomed to being told what to do by a policeman," Bell interrupted, pronouncing "policeman" as if it were synonymous with a species of cockroach. "And now if you'll excuse me, I am late for my morning rounds." With that, he turned and walked briskly away.

"Well," Donald remarked, watching him go, "I guess you told him, didn't you?"

"I didn't intend to put him off. I just—"

"He'll get over it. Or he won't, and my medical career is over."

"Surely he wouldn't—"

Donald laid a hand on his shoulder. "I was joking—relax, Brother. Dear me, you are in a bad way, aren't you?"

Ian was about to respond when the double doors swung open and Conan Doyle emerged, carrying the tray of instruments covered with a towel.

"Where's Dr. Bell?" he said.

"He said something about rounds," Donald remarked. "Though, by my watch, they aren't due to start for another hour."

"That's what he says when he wants to escape from people," said Doyle.

Donald gave Ian a meaningful look. "That makes sense."

"Did you say something to annoy him?" Doyle asked.

Donald shook his head. "I didn't, but—"

Doyle looked at Ian. "It was you, then?"

"Now see here," Ian said, fed up with the whole situation. "I just—"

Doyle burst out laughing. "Join the club! We've all gotten on the wrong side of him sooner or later—haven't we, Hamilton?"

Donald smiled. "I must admit, he can be rather touchy."

"I merely suggested that—"

"You could have asked him for the time of day, and if he was in one of his moods, he would take it as an insult," said Doyle.

"Excuse me a moment," Donald said, heading in the direction of the lavatory. "I'll be right back."

"By the way, I have something for that shoulder of yours," Doyle told Ian. "An old Jesuit priest showed me how to make it. Can you spare a minute?"

"Well, I—"

"Capital!" Doyle said. "Let me dispose of these instruments, and I'll be right back."

Standing alone in the corridor, inhaling the smell of antiseptic and floor polish, Ian felt strangely calm. Perhaps it was his aggregate exhaustion, but he felt himself slipping into a contemplative frame of mind.

He was roused from his peaceful state by his brother's hand jostling his elbow.

"Looks like you've made a friend as well as an enemy today," Donald remarked.

Ian saw Conan Doyle hurrying toward them, a silver tube in his hand.

"Here it is," Doyle said. "Just happened to have left it on Dr. Bell's desk. What exactly did you say to him, by the way? I've never seen his nose so out of joint."

"Can't we just let it go?" Ian said, feeling too exhausted to explain.

"Sorry, old man—of course. Put this on twice a day," Doyle said, handing him the ointment. "Really takes the sting out."

"What sting? What's it for?" asked Donald.

"His shoulder," said Doyle.

Donald frowned at Ian. "You never told me—"

"It's nothing," said Ian, slipping the tube of salve into his pocket.

"How can it be nothing when Doyle noticed it, for Christ's sake?"

"Thanks very much for that vote of confidence," said Doyle.

"Look," Ian told his brother, "you have your own—situation, and I didn't want to compound that with complaining about my—"

"Well, isn't that just too noble of you?" Donald said angrily. "Just like our dear sainted mum, eh? So I can be the 'problem child,' and you can suffer in silence and feel superior. Well, I'm just about fed up with that attitude, let me tell you!"

With that, he spun on his heel and marched away with as much speed as he could muster.

"Well," said Doyle, "this just isn't your day, is it?"

"Damn!" said Ian. "Donald was going to let me use a microscope, and now I've driven him off."

"I can show you one."

"Would it be terribly inconvenient?"

"Not at all," Doyle said, leading him to a room off a side corridor. On the frosted glass door was stenciled the word "Pathology." Inside, a few men in white coats were hunched over microscopes along the walls or working at the lab table in the center of the room. A couple glanced up when he and Doyle entered, but went straight back to their tasks.

Doyle showed Ian how to place the hair on a glass slide. "There you go," he said, sliding it under the lens. "What do you see?"

There was no denying that the hair was red—a rich auburn color, like autumn leaves.

"May I?" Doyle asked.

"Certainly."

"I want to study a cross section of the sample." Taking a sharp pair of medical scissors, Doyle carefully cut a small piece from the hair and placed it on the slide.

"Ah! Curly red hair," he said, studying it.

Ian frowned. "How do you know it's curly?"

"You see the oval-shaped follicles?"

"Yes," Ian said, a sour ball of dread forming in his stomach.

"Straight hair has round ones. This hair belongs to a curly-headed person."

"I am in your debt," Ian said, folding the hair back up inside his handkerchief.

"Pish tosh, old man. Have you eaten?"

"No, but I should be getting back to work."

"Nonsense—it's Sunday! The Sheep Heid Inn serves a decent ale. I'll buy the first round."

Ian sighed. He was too muddled to concentrate properly, and it was many hours since breakfast. "Perhaps the walk will do me good."

"That's the spirit!" Doyle said, rubbing his hands heartily. His enthusiasm was infectious, and his presence was reassuring.

"What about Dr. Bell?"

"He can get along for a few hours without me. Anyway, best to leave him alone when he's in one of his moods."

"Very well," Ian said. "'Lay on, Macduff.'"

Surprise crossed Doyle's frank, friendly face. "I say, isn't it supposed to be bad luck to quote that play?"

Ian shrugged. "It's difficult to imagine my luck getting much worse than it already is." But even as he said it, he realized the folly in his words.

CHAPTER
THIRTY-FIVE

The Sheep Heid Inn was tucked away in the village of Duddingston, nestled along the southeastern edge of Holyrood Park. It was a short walk from Arthur's Seat, the volcanic ridge dominating the park's landscape. If seated near the pub's front windows, one could watch the shadows cast by the rocky outcropping move as the sun made its daily journey across the sky.

The inn laid claim to being the oldest pub in Scotland, reputedly opening in 1360. The ancient structure cradled the past within its low ceilings, crooked walls, and uneven floorboards. Perhaps it was this sense of bygone times that appealed to the clientele—it certainly wasn't the gruff service or mostly unremarkable menu. But the Scots were a sentimental race, and looking back on the past was a national pastime.

Ian and Conan Doyle arrived just in time to scoop up the last two servings of lamb shank with roast potatoes and carrots. They finished the meal with a round of Glenlivet, by which time Ian was feeling considerably cheerier.

"That's your problem, Hamilton—you don't *think*. You just pursue what's in front of your nose, and if it's to do with a case, well and good, but God help us if other people's lives get in the way."

"I truly am sorry, sir."

"It makes you a good detective, I suppose, but not much of a man sometimes."

Ian's ears burned with shame. The chief was right—it *was* bloody-minded of him to react to Bell like that. Maybe the renowned doctor deserved it, but that was no excuse.

"I'll apologize to him, sir."

"Just leave it. Don't cause any more trouble than you have already."

"Yes, sir."

"Get along with you," said Crawford without turning around. "You've someone waiting out there."

"Thank you, sir," Ian said. Leaving the office, he felt a coward and a fool. When he emerged into the main room, there was no sign of Sergeant Dickerson. Fiona Stuart stood in the middle of the room, hand on one hip, lips curled in an expression somewhere between a smile and a challenge. She was smartly dressed in a pale-green riding habit with black trim, which set off her dark-red hair exquisitely.

"I have a message for you," she said, removing her tall black hat, which he noted was carefully brushed.

"Yes?"

"Arthur Doyle said to tell you there was a large amount of laudanum in Margaret's blood."

"Indeed?" Ian said coolly, trying to conceal his excitement. "Did he say anything else?"

"Only that if you care to discuss it more, he would be happy to meet with you."

"And how did you come by this knowledge?"

"I occasionally serve as Dr. Bell's scrub nurse. Arthur and I are well acquainted."

"It would seem there's no end to your abilities."

She examined the buttons on her riding jacket, then fixed him with a steady gaze. "Well? Are you going to offer me tea?"

He stared back at her. "I cannot help wondering if you manage to irritate everyone you meet?"

She frowned. "I merely asked for some tea."

He tried not to look at the dimple on her chin, which appeared whenever she frowned—or smiled. "Lacking evidence to the contrary, I must conclude your ability to exasperate people is universal."

She rolled her eyes—which were very round, and rimmed with dark-red lashes. "Why is it that women are expected to be meek and retiring, and never ask for anything?"

"I believe there is a way of asking for things without implying the person you are addressing is an idiot."

"I certainly did not mean to imply—"

"Never mind, Miss—"

"Stuart. I should think a police officer would have a better memory for names."

Ian turned away, permitting himself a little smile. He had not forgotten her name this time; he simply wished to annoy her. He was not in the habit of insulting young ladies, but she had it coming.

"So this is where you work?" she asked dubiously, surveying the room.

"That would be a fair assumption."

"What do you do beside catch criminals and rescue people who don't need rescuing?"

"Believe it or not, there is quite a lot of paperwork."

"It is the same in medical care," she replied with the first hint of sympathy he had heard. "If only we could devote all our time to care of our patients, we would be able to do so much more for them. Meetings are even worse—someone should outlaw committee meetings."

"My aunt says the same thing about her Amateur Photography Society."

"She is a photographer?"

"And an artist," he said, feeling an urge to brag.

"Your aunt sounds like an extraordinary woman."

"She is, though I wish she would stop going to those wretched séances." He instantly regretted his remark, as Fiona Stuart pounced on it, like a cat on a mouse.

"She attends séances? Whatever for?"

"She believes the medium is in contact with her departed husband. Such silliness is unworthy of her."

"It probably gives her life a sense of purpose."

"It is mere delusion."

"Delusion or not, who does it harm? Can you not understand how she feels?"

It was indeed hard to imagine the absence of such a person as Uncle Alfred—his large, shiny face and ruddy cheeks ablaze with goodwill and liberal amounts of gin. Such a solid physical presence, so keen a mind and energetic a personality—how was it possible for such a man to all at once be there no more? Ian did indeed understand how his aunt felt.

But he was not about to confess this to Fiona Stuart. "Superstition will be the ruin of mankind," he remarked darkly.

She burst into peals of laughter. "Will it, now? And what of our thirst for blood—our willingness to slaughter one another cheerfully as one might fry eggs for breakfast?"

"Many a war has been fought over religious differences."

"Oh, is it all religion you're calling superstition now?"

He took a deep breath before responding. "Yes."

She laughed again. "Aren't you a deep one, then?" He was about to protest that she was shallow for saying so, but she shook her copper curls, distracting him from everything but the way the sunlight glanced off the shiny surface of her hair. "Besides, religion is just an excuse."

"For what?"

"For our desire to slash and hack at one another. It's in our bones, I say, and any excuse will do. Religion, land, women—"

"Women?"

She pursed her lips and cocked her head to one side. "If we're to believe our Greek history, a whole war was fought over one lass. Do you really believe Helen of Troy was so much more comely than any other woman of that time?"

"No, but—"

"So there you have it—another excuse to fight a great bloody war."

"You seem to have an opinion on everything."

"Only things worth having an opinion on."

"You know," he said, "if everyone conversed like you, there would be no wars, because your opponents would be too exhausted."

For an instant her face darkened, then she burst into the strange chortle he found both irritating and compelling.

"Do you really find me so disagreeable, Detective Hamilton?"

"In my experience, women only ask a question like that if they are sure of their own attractiveness."

She reddened, but her voice was steady as her gaze. "You cannot deny you have been cold to me from the start. Is it too much to ask why?"

"Perhaps I am not accustomed to being pursued so aggressively by young women."

"Oh, you are much mistaken," she replied hotly. "I am not pursuing you—I am merely interested in your profession."

He noted with satisfaction that she was a hopeless liar.

She placed the hat back on her head, fastening it with a long hatpin. "I must be off—I'm expected at the clinic. You needn't see me out," she added breezily, as if expecting him to protest.

"Very well," he said, enjoying her surprised look.